The Wage-Price Guideposts

JOHN SHEAHAN

The Wage-Price Guideposts

THE BROOKINGS INSTITUTION
Washington, D.C.

THE BROOKINGS INSTITUTION is an independent organization devoted to nonpartisan research, education, and publication in economics, government, foreign policy, and the social sciences generally. Its principal purposes are to aid in the development of sound public policies and to promote public understanding of issues of national importance.

The Institution was founded on December 8, 1927, to merge the activities of the Institute for Government Research, founded in 1916, the Institute of Economics, founded in 1922, and the Robert Brookings Graduate School of Economics and Government, founded in 1924.

The general administration of the Institution is the responsibility of a self-perpetuating Board of Trustees. The trustees are likewise charged with maintaining the independence of the staff and fostering the most favorable conditions for creative research and education. The immediate direction of the policies, program, and staff of the Institution is vested in the President, assisted by an advisory council chosen from the staff of the Institution.

In publishing a study, the Institution presents it as a competent treatment of a subject worthy of public consideration. The interpretations and conclusions in such publications are those of the author or authors and do not purport to represent the views of the other staff members, officers, or trustees of the Brookings Institution.

Foreword

DURING THE YEARS of high prosperity and rapid growth that have characterized the Western world since the end of World War II, the problem of rising prices has become one of the most vexing concerns of economic policy makers. Unwilling to throttle down their economies sufficiently to stabilize the price level by that means, and equally unwilling to accept a sharply rising price level as the necessary price of prosperity, a number of governments of the Western industrial countries have tried to check the rate of price increase by seeking to influence the process of wage- and price-setting.

"Incomes policy" is the rubric generally applied to these efforts. In the United States, the most ambitious and systematic effort to evolve an incomes policy was the enunciation early in 1962 of the wage-price guideposts. The purpose of this monograph is to analyze the issues in wage-price policy and to evaluate the United States experience with the guideposts.

The author, John Sheahan, is Professor of Economics at Williams College. He has had assistance and advice from many people in the preparation of the manuscript. He wishes to record his gratitude to Sara Clark for assistance in computations; to John Corina, Fred Jones, E. H. Phelps-Brown, and Andrew Shonfield for explanations of British experience with incomes policies; to H. C. Bos and Pieter de Wolff for developments in the Netherlands; to Anne Romanis for information about experience of both countries; to Otto Eckstein for help in interpreting the incomplete published information about events in the United States; to

Nathaniel Goldfinger of the AFL-CIO for insights into labor attitudes toward the guideposts; to Roger Bolton for innumerable clarifying debates; and to William M. Capron and Joseph A. Pechman for encouragement, multiple forms of direct assistance, and continuously polite pressure to complete the task. The reading committee, consisting of Myron L. Joseph, George P. Shultz, and Robert M. Solow, made numerous and extremely helpful criticisms of the original manuscript. Evelyn Breck edited the manuscript and Florence Robinson prepared the index.

The controversy which surrounds the issue of the guideposts will not be stilled by the publication of this study; indeed, some of the students of the subject whose assistance is acknowledged above will object to some of the interpretations and results. Empirical tests of the effects of the guideposts yield findings that are too suggestive to be ignored, but they involve too many possible distortions to be conclusive. Arguments about theoretical implications are caught in the misty terrain between aggregative and microeconomic analysis. Some critics will object that the guidepost approach is feeble in fire-power, while others will contend that the guideposts are likely to lead to governmental intervention so extensive as to undermine the price system.

The author has tried to put these matters in perspective. Just as the guideposts were initially put forward to raise the level of public understanding of the interrelations among prices, wages, and productivity, so the present study is intended to illuminate public discussion and debate on the issues raised by five years of experience with the guideposts. This study was financed by a special grant from the Alfred P. Sloan Foundation for research in the economics of market organization.

The views expressed in this volume are those of the author and are not presented as the views of the trustees, officers, or staff members of the Brookings Institution or the Alfred P. Sloan Foundation.

KERMIT GORDON
President

July 1967
Washington, D.C.

Contents

PART ONE

OBJECTIVES OF THE GUIDEPOSTS

I

The Problem

THE WAGE-PRICE GUIDEPOSTS were intended to provide more freedom for the use of expansionary fiscal policy by preventing arbitrary increases in unit labor costs and prices in conditions of adequate supply. They were not proposed as a set of theoretical principles but as a response to the unpleasantly real problem that prices tend to rise despite unemployment and underutilized productive capacity, and to go up even faster when productive resources are put more fully to work.

The guideposts raise many issues. These concern such matters as the use of incentives, the efficiency of the economic system and its capacity for growth, equity in the distribution of income, the functions of labor unions and of the antitrust laws, and the fundamental role of the government in relation to the private sector in making economic decisions. Much of the debate about them refers to technical issues, but a great deal of concern goes to another level. It is perhaps best conveyed by a quotation from John Dewey: "Let us admit the case of the conservative: if we once start thinking no one can guarantee where we shall come out, except that many objects, ends and institutions are doomed. Every thinker puts some portion of an apparently stable world in peril and no one can wholly predict what will emerge in its place."[1]

The guideposts will continue to be modified, perhaps even dropped completely for a time or at least formally disowned, but the search for

[1] Joseph Ratner, ed., *Intelligence in the Modern World* (Modern Library, 1939), Foreword.

3

effective principles of action closely related to this concept will go on for a long time. It will go on because the problem that they sought to answer is serious and will not go away by itself.

Changes in the Behavior and Significance of Prices

A general upward movement of prices is by now such a familiar phenomenon that it is sometimes taken for granted as practically inevitable. Whether or not it is inevitable now, it may be worth noting that it has not been typical in American economic history. Wholesale prices were no higher in 1940 than they had been in 1801. The experience in this long period was not characterized by a persistent upward drift reversed only in depressions. Rather, the usual trend of prices was downward, except for violent upward bursts of all-out inflation associated with wars.[2]

Considering consumer prices rather than wholesale, it is interesting to compare the pattern of change in the 1920's to that in the 1950's. In 1920-21, with food output rising and a brief recession slowing down demand, the index of consumer prices fell 10 percent. From 1922 to 1926, the index increased almost imperceptibly. In the next three years, even before the depression, the increase was reversed. In this decade, decreases were still possible without drastic depression, and price stability was the characteristic pattern during expansion.

The 1950's began with a recovery from recession, accentuated by Korean War expenditures, so it is hardly surprising that prices increased rapidly in 1951-52. From that point, the growth of the economy slowed down and unemployment crept gradually upward. The consumer price index held steady until 1955. It went up in that year under the influence of strong demand and temporarily high economic activity, but it then kept on going up right to the end of the decade despite two recessions and high average unemployment. Measuring from 1955 to 1960, a period of subnormal industrial growth and excessive unemployment, the consumer price index increased 11 percent.[3] This increase could rightly be consid-

[2] Board of Governors of the Federal Reserve System, *Historical Chart Book 1965* (1965).

[3] For a thorough description of price movements in the 1950's, stressing the role of costs for services and construction in particular, and suggesting less of a

ered modest if the period had been one of rapid growth, but hardly so for one of deepening unemployment and falling investment. It suggested an upward bias in the pattern of price movement that had not been customary during peacetime years in American economic history.

Another new consideration that had a good deal to do with the presentation of the guideposts arose at almost the same time. The United States balance of payments deteriorated to the point at which it became a major concern of economic policy. The "basic balance," defined to exclude special transactions and short-term capital movements, fell to a deficit of $3.7 billion in 1958 and $4.7 billion in 1959.[4] Gold reserves decreased from $22.9 billion at the end of 1957 to $19.5 billion two years later, and then to $17.0 billion by the end of 1961. The growth of exports, previously just a shade slower than the growth of world exports as a whole, was suddenly interrupted. Merchandise exports fell from $20.9 billion in 1957 to $17.9 billion in 1958, and remained at that lower level in 1959 despite a rise of 6 percent in aggregate world exports.[5]

While a great many factors other than prices entered into this disappointing export performance, it became a matter of concern that the prices of American exports were increasing relative to those of other major industrial countries in a period in which most other nations were operating much closer to full employment than was the United States. Table 1, shown on page 6, summarizes changes in unit values for exports of manufactured goods for the United States and six of the countries with which it is most directly competitive for such exports. It will be noted that American export prices rose relative to those of all the other countries listed during both subperiods. The American share of total exports of manufactured goods by this group was 30 percent in 1957, just as it had been three years before, but it then fell to 25 percent by 1959, and 24 percent by 1961.[6]

problem than that indicated here, see *Economic Report of the President, 1962,* together with Council of Economic Advisers, "Annual Report," Chap. 4.

[4] Walter S. Salant, "A New Look at the U.S. Balance of Payments" (Brookings Institution Reprint 92, 1965), Table 1, p. 6.

[5] International Monetary Fund, *International Financial Statistics,* Supplement to 1966/67 Issues, p. xvi.

[6] Bela Belassa, "Recent Developments in the Competitiveness of American Industry and Prospects for the Future," Joint Economic Committee, *Factors Affecting the United States Balance of Payments* (U.S. Government Printing Office, 1962), p. 31.

TABLE 1

Indexes of Unit Values of Exports of Manufactured Goods, 1953–60
(1953 = 100)

Country	1953	1957	1960
United States	100	112	119
Belgium	100	102	95
France	100	101	96
Germany	100	103	103
Italy	100	90	83
Japan	100	97	98
United Kingdom	100	108	113

Source: Bela Balassa, "Recent Developments in the Competitiveness of American Industry and Prospects for the Future," Joint Economic Committee, *Factors Affecting the United States Balance of Payments,* U. S. Government Printing Office, 1962), p. 40.

New Empirical Inquiries into Factors Determining Prices

The behavior of prices in the second half of the 1950's provoked many collective inquiries and individual research studies, some of them directly related to the formulation of the guideposts in 1962. Of the major investigations in the United States, three that stood out were the Kefauver Committee Hearings on administered prices, which began in 1957; the 1959 session of the American Assembly on wages, prices, profits and productivity; and the study of employment, growth and price levels, directed by Otto Eckstein for the Joint Economic Committee in 1959-60. In Europe, widespread concern with the same set of issues led to a large-scale committee study for the OECD, launched in 1959 and published in 1961.[7]

These efforts succeeded in organizing an enormous range of factual material and generating a number of interesting suggestions. It can hardly be said that they achieved any consensus on theoretical interpretation or policy prescription, but they did help clarify two conflicting lines of thought which have been central to debates about the guideposts.

[7] *Administered Prices,* Hearings before the Subcommittee on Antitrust and Monopoly of the Senate Committee on the Judiciary, 85 Cong. 1 sess.; American Assembly, *Wages, Prices, Profits and Productivity* (Columbia University Press, 1959); Joint Economic Committee, *Employment, Growth and Price Levels,* 86 Cong. 2 sess. (U.S. Government Printing Office, 1959); Organization for Economic Cooperation and Development, *The Problem of Rising Prices* (Paris, 1961).

The first of these two ideas is that it is possible for prices and wages to be pushed up in enough industries, despite unemployment and conditions of general excess capacity, to affect the general price level perversely. This proposition does not represent any challenge to the argument that runaway price increases are unlikely to occur in the United States in conditions of weak aggregate demand, or that really serious and prolonged depression could bring prices down. Rather, the new discussion served to emphasize that the textbook dichotomy between full employment and its absence was a flagrantly oversimplified framework within which to discuss problems of price stability.

Given the ability to prevent major depressions, and general agreement on the desirability of doing so, the economy is likely to operate most of the time under conditions in which unemployment is not so severe, and market prospects not so bleak, as to eliminate the possibility of rising prices. The new examinations of particular industries readily showed cases in which prices increased despite idle capacity or even falling sales, and in which wages increased despite falling employment in the industry concerned combined with rising unemployment in the economy as a whole. The effect of the evidence was to strengthen the belief that factors other than the pressure of demand on limited supply must be considered in order to explain wage and price trends adequately. Furthermore, an ingenious effort to trace through the interaction of the steel industry's prices on the costs of other firms showed that in this case, and presumably in some degree for other industries supplying inputs for further production, a single center of increasing prices can raise costs for a wide range of consuming industries and set in motion a chain of pressures affecting significantly the general level of prices for the whole economy.[8]

Emphasis on the importance of discretionary behavior in particular markets leads directly toward the guideposts. It also leads to questions about the relationship of guideposts to the main stream of economic analysis bearing on inflation, and to conflict with traditional preferences for generalized economic policy avoiding entanglement in specific markets.

Modern interpretations of inflation center on the relation between aggregate demand and productive capacity. Under conditions of severe un-

[8] Otto Eckstein and Gary Fromm, "Steel and the Postwar Inflation," Study Paper No. 2, Joint Economic Committee, *Employment, Growth and Price Levels.* The technique used and the conclusions of the study have been extensively debated; cf. the comments by W. Brainard and M. C. Lovell, and reply by Eckstein and Fromm, in *American Economic Review*, Vol. 56 (September 1966), pp. 857-68.

employment and idle plant capacity, increases in demand lead to rising production; they need not result in higher prices because supply can be increased to match demand. As the economy approaches full employment, it becomes more difficult to raise supply. Further increases in demand are then likely to lead to shortages and higher prices, calling for aggregative deflationary restraints to hold demand within the limit of productive capacity. The course of prices thus depends primarily on changes in demand and in capacity to produce, rather than on the exercise of discretion by price makers. But there remains a margin of uncertainty; the idea that aggregative factors are of greatest importance may be pushed to an extreme suggesting that discretionary decisions are of practically no relevance, or may on the contrary allow for the possibility that they can make a significant difference.

The position that discretionary price changes are of little or no importance as an explanation of inflation is often linked to one, or some combination, of three plausible arguments. The first is that monetary restraint can keep prices from rising no matter what is done by particular price makers; the second is that firms with market power set the prices that pay best for them and then have no interest in any process of continuing increases; the third is that the fundamental factor is the trend of production costs, which is in turn determined by the degree of unemployment.

If monopolistic industries were to raise prices, but aggregative monetary and fiscal restraint were applied to keep total expenditures constant in monetary terms, the general effect would be to divert expenditure away from more competitive industries. Prices in these industries would be expected to fall, offsetting to some extent the initial increases. There is no particular reason to believe that the balance need work out to keep employment and average prices unchanged. It might do so, but the more likely adjustment would be a fall in production, with a price level somewhat higher than existed in the first place. The monetary authorities would then have a choice: to raise the money supply in order to keep up expenditures in real terms despite higher prices, or to restrict the money supply to the degree necessary to bring the average price level back down. Whether the industries causing the trouble in the first place give any ground, as long as there are some market-determined prices in the economic system, they can be made to come down enough to keep the average stable. Monetary restraint holds a veto power. It cannot prevent distortions, inequity, and inefficiency, but if pursued relentlessly, it can keep down inflation.

The second suggestion is that abuses of market power cannot account for rising prices. The idea is that firms will set the prices that are most profitable for them, and having once done so have nothing to gain from any further increases. Monopoly power can explain high profit margins, but not increasing prices. The validity of this point would seem to depend on the existence of some clear optimum to which discretionary price makers can go and expect indefinitely to stay. As discussed at length in Chapter 9, it would seem more useful to consider both firms and unions as active explorers in continuously changing markets, trying to go from wherever they are at the moment to better positions. On this view, any new restraints changing the degree of ease with which they can increase charges might have some effect in moderating the general pace of price and wage increases.

These two logical presumptions against the relevance of discretionary price making as an explanation of inflation seemed to gain support from a new set of statistical investigations beginning in the late 1950's. The familiar idea that wage behavior is related to the degree of unemployment was given new status, and nearly converted to a form of rigid determinism, by A. W. Phillips' demonstration of a persistent long-term relationship between levels of unemployment and rates of wage change in the United Kingdom.[9] On the basis of the association he found, which came to be called the "Phillips curve" relating wage changes to unemployment, he showed that wage behavior in the 1920's could be predicted from behavioral relationships in the period 1861-1913. Differences in levels of unemployment seemed to explain most of the differences in rates of wage change, and minor deviations from this result could be attributed to a secondary influence coming from the rate of change in unemployment.

Phillips' investigation suggested that movements of demand will determine the level of unemployment, and thereby the rates of increase of wages and prices, in a fairly inexorable pattern. "If, as is sometimes recommended, demand were kept at a value which would maintain stable wage rates, the associated level of unemployment would be about 5½ percent." Or, in terms noticeably similar to those used later in presenting the guideposts, "assuming an increase in productivity of 2 percent per year, it seems from the relation fitted to the data that if aggregate demand were

[9] "The Relation Between Unemployment and the Rate of Change of Money Wage Rates in the United Kingdom, 1861-1957," *Economica,* Vol. 25 (1958), pp. 283-99.

kept at a value which would maintain a stable level of product prices the associated level of unemployment would be a little under 2½ percent."[10]

The proposition that higher employment will normally be associated with a faster rate of increase in wages is reasonable enough, and fits American experience as well as that of the United Kingdom.[11] The question, examined from many angles since Phillips' study, is the nature of the relationship. Is it at best a rough approximation, subject to change? Or is the relationship simple, direct, and nearly immune to influence from other factors?

Most of the answers have rejected the idea of any fixed relationship. In England, Richard Lipsey provided a clear demonstration that the long-term association derived from data for 1861-1913 did not give a good basis of prediction for wage behavior in the 1930's or later periods.[12] He also showed that additional variables were necessary to get accurate prediction of wage behavior, and made a good analytical case for the belief that the degree of uniformity of changes in unemployment among industries is an important factor. A more nearly balanced expansion should yield a slower rate of increase in wages than would otherwise occur.

Attempts to test similar questions using American experience reinforced Lipsey's evidence that factors other than the degree of unemployment may have significant effects on the rate of change of wages.[13] More complex analysis using several variables is necessary to get good explanations of wage changes for any given period, and when a good regression relationship is established for any one set of years, it nearly always turns out that the coefficients change significantly in the next period. One of the most important findings, demonstrated by Bowen and Berry for American

[10] *Ibid.*, p. 299.

[11] Cf. especially Albert Rees and Mary T. Hamilton, "Postwar Movements of Wage Levels and Unit Labor Costs," *Journal of Law and Economics,* Vol. 6 (1963), pp. 41-68.

[12] Lipsey, "The Relation Between Unemployment and the Rate of Change of Money Wage Rates in the United Kingdom, 1862-1957: A Further Analysis," *Economica,* Vol. 27 (1960), pp. 25-31.

[13] William G. Bowen, *The Wage-Price Issue* (Princeton University Press, 1960), pp. 223-25; William G. Bowen and R. Albert Berry, "Unemployment Conditions and Movements of the Money Wage Level," *Review of Economics and Statistics,* Vol. 45 (1963), pp. 163-72; Otto Eckstein and Thomas A. Wilson, "The Determination of Money Wages in American Industry," *Quarterly Journal of Economics,* Vol. 76 (1962), pp. 379-414; George L. Perry, *Unemployment, Money Wage Rates, and Inflation* (Massachusetts Institute of Technology Press, 1966); Paul A. Samuelson and Robert M. Solow, "Analytical Aspects of Anti-Inflation Policy," *American Economic Review,* Vol. 50 (May 1960), pp. 177-94.

data, was that changes in the rate of unemployment can provide a better explanatory factor than the level of employment itself. Discussions in terms of the Phillips curve tend to suggest that some particular range of unemployment ratios, such as 4 percent or below, is critical in that going below this level will generate rising prices. If the main question is instead the rate of change in unemployment, it might be that a gradual decline to a ratio of 4 percent would cause less trouble than a sudden drop from 8 to 6 percent. That is, attention is directed toward the speed of change, with at least the suggestion that steady decreases in unemployment could be consistent with price stability even at levels much lower than usually considered to be safe.

For American data, the independent role of profits in explaining wage changes also seems to be significant. Practically all investigations using profits as an explanatory variable have found this to be relevant, though one interesting study defends the alternative idea that the real determinant operating through profits is value added per hour.[14] On this hypothesis, the basic factor explaining the pace of wage change is the rate of increase of the value of output per hour, because this determines the worth of workers to firms. Statistical tests using an indicator of average value productivity, along with lagged measures of the proportion of the labor force employed, worked out well. The effect of the level of unemployment did not disappear, but became clearly secondary.

None of these investigations destroyed the idea that rising demand, if sufficient to reduce the degree of unemployment, could be expected to generate greater pressure for wage increases. What the more exact quantitative studies demonstrated was that the association between unemployment and wages is complex and subject to change, and thereby possibly open to influence from restraints acting on discretionary decisions.

Policies to Counter Price Increases, 1957-60

Faced in the late 1950's with a combination of rising prices and balance of payments difficulties, the government relied on monetary deflation and relatively restrictive budget policies as the main line of defense. This approach did brake the upward trend of wholesale prices. After an increase

[14] Edwin Kuh, "A Productivity Theory of Wage Levels—An Alternative to the Phillips Curve," *Review of Economic Studies* (forthcoming).

of 1.4 percent between 1957 and 1958, they stopped going up. Labor costs per unit output in manufacturing stabilized at the same time.[15] Consumer prices continued rising without significant change of pace. There is little doubt that they could have been stopped too, if the deflationary policies had been pushed more aggressively. The problem was that the degree of deflation being followed was already enough to kill off the weak 1957-58 recovery movement and allow a new recession to develop in 1959. Unemployment for 1958-60 averaged 6 percent of the labor force. The idea of tightening restrictions still further lacked universal appeal.

One possible reaction to this situation could have been to hold unemployment at this level or perhaps slightly higher, and hope to drive home to everyone eventually that the cost of efforts to raise wages and prices would be so unpleasant that it would be better to exercise more self-restraint. Such a policy, if sufficiently prolonged, might work out to permit reconciliation of higher employment with continued price stability. Then again, it might not.

The Kennedy Administration entering office in 1961 took the opposite path, toward expansion of demand and higher employment, but not without misgivings. The problem then, and probably for many administrations to come, was to find a course of action to cope with wages and prices less costly and less defeatist than aggregate deflation. On all the available evidence, a greater rate of economic expansion and higher levels of employment could be expected to stimulate wage claims and to reduce the restraint on price increases that may have come from the existence of widespread idle capacity. Since the new administration was explicitly determined to raise production and employment, it was under an obligation to seek some means other than deflation to restrain price and wage increases. The answer attempted, or perhaps more accurately the proposal offered for public debate, was the system of wage-price guideposts.

[15] Rees and Hamilton, *op. cit.*, Table 11, p. 58.

II

Formulation and Presentation of the Guideposts

THE GUIDEPOSTS WERE presented in the January 1962 annual report of the Council of Economic Advisers, at the end of the first year of the Kennedy Administration.[1] They were preceded by more overt action on the part of the President himself and by some official statements pointing in this direction, but not by any general public discussions of possible alternative ways to formulate the proposals.

The Immediate Background

In September 1961, prior to presentation of the guideposts, the President wrote to the heads of the twelve largest steel companies, urging them to resist the temptation to raise prices at the time of the wage increase scheduled to take effect on October 1. The belief that price increases might occur had been suggested by newspaper accounts of statements by executives of a number of the steel companies to the general effect that they thought this would be a good time for prices to go up. The President's letter gave evidence of more active attention to such signs and of a new willingness to try to forestall business decisions rather than wait for something to happen and then deplore it. The letter stated that,

[1] *Economic Report of the President, 1962*, pp. 185-90.

13

The steel industry, by absorbing increases in employment costs since 1958, has demonstrated a will to halt the price-wage spiral in steel. If the industry were now to forego a price increase, it would enter collective bargaining negotiations next spring with a record of three and a half years of price stability. It would clearly then be the turn of the labor representatives to limit wage demands to a level consistent with continued price stability.[2]

The letter to the steel companies was followed a week later by another addressed to the president of the United Steelworkers of America, urging that 1962 wage negotiations seek a "settlement within the limits of advances in productivity and price stability."[3]

It will be noted that these two letters remained in the tradition of the appeals to business and labor that had become common in the latter part of the Eisenhower Administration, but also that they introduced a note of greater specificity. Instead of requesting responsible behavior, they asked the steel companies not to implement a possible price increase being discussed for October 1961, and asked the labor side to limit claims for wage increase to the rate of advance in productivity.

The idea of restricting the rate of wage increases to that of improvement in productivity was further explained and emphasized as administration policy by one of the members of the Council of Economic Advisers, James Tobin, in a speech during October to officials of the AFL-CIO. The position was not enthusiastically received.[4]

The Guideposts

The principle underlying the guideposts was that the economy would work more efficiently if discretionary price and wage decisions were brought more in line with the results that would be expected in competitive markets. Prices could rise in response to changes in demand conditions in the short run, but would in the longer run move toward average costs of production. Wages would tend toward equality for similar types of work, or at the very least above-average wages associated with strong bargaining power would not continue to rise faster than the rest. The Council of Economic Advisers said it better:

[2] From *ibid.*, p. 182.
[3] *Ibid.*, p. 183.
[4] *New York Times,* Oct. 7, 1961.

The general guide for noninflationary wage behavior is that the rate of increase in wage rates (including fringe benefits) in each industry be equal to the trend rate of *over-all* productivity increase. General acceptance of this guide would maintain stability of labor cost per unit of output for the economy as a whole—though not of course for individual industries.

The general guide for noninflationary price behavior calls for price reduction if the industry's rate of productivity increase exceeds the over-all rate—for this would mean declining unit labor costs; it calls for an appropriate increase in price if the opposite relationship prevails; and it calls for stable prices if the two rates of productivity increase are equal.[5]

Four specific modifications were spelled out in the original statement:

(1) Wage rate increases would exceed the general guide rate in an industry which would otherwise be unable to attract sufficient labor; or in which wage rates are exceptionally low compared with the range of wages earned elsewhere by similar labor, because the bargaining position of workers has been weak in particular local labor markets.

(2) Wage rate increases would fall short of the general guide rate in an industry which could not provide jobs for its entire labor force even in times of generally full employment; or in which wage rates are exceptionally high compared with the range of wages earned elsewhere by similar labor, because the bargaining position of workers has been especially strong.

(3) Prices would rise more rapidly, or fall more slowly, than indicated by the general guide rate in an industry in which the level of profits was insufficient to attract the capital required to finance a needed expansion in capacity; or in which costs other than labor costs had risen.

(4) Prices would rise more slowly, or fall more rapidly, than indicated by the general guide in an industry in which the relation of productive capacity to full employment demand shows the desirability of an outflow of capital from the industry, or in which costs other than labor costs have fallen; or in which excessive market power has resulted in rates of profit substantially higher than those earned elsewhere on investments of comparable risk.

Even this amplified statement leaves potentially important considerations out of account. The Council noted several of them, which will be discussed subsequently. The proposals were thus fairly complex, providing two apparently simple touchstones but then adding a series of shadings and possible corrections that make their application anything but mechanical. The exceptions were not given any quantitative limits and no weights were suggested by which to balance considerations that could easily conflict with each other. The package therefore did not provide determinate answers for specific cases. It was not presented as a set of solu-

[5] *Economic Report of the President, 1962,* p. 189.

tions, but as a basis for public discussion of what the operative strategy should be.

Were the Guideposts a Radical Innovation?

It is possible to make the guideposts sound as if they were a totally new thrust at traditional values by people determined to change the nature of the economy. Alternatively, they can be presented as a simple rephrasing of familiar statements previously accepted by a wide range of opinion. The latter seems closer to the truth, but not close enough.

The frequency with which President Eisenhower and other officials of his administration appealed to business and to labor for responsible behavior indicated clearly that they did not consider that all price and wage decisions are uniquely determined by competitive market forces. Nor do most people who have studied the operation of the American economy in detail. There are a great many industries in which competitive pressures dominate decisions, and there are no industries in which they are wholly absent, but the fact that market power exists in many areas has been so conclusively demonstrated that there can be little room for surprise at yet another assertion to this effect.

The guideposts did introduce a new element by attempting to be more precise about the meaning of responsible behavior. A quantitative criterion was implied for the permissible rate of wage increases, even though the question was left open as to which of several relevant measures might be most appropriate. The criterion itself was not new; it was a fairly common-sense and widely accepted observation. If hourly earnings increase 3 percent, while output per man hour rises 3 percent, labor costs per unit remain constant and do not exert any pressure on prices. Who could quarrel with that, or regard it as a disconcerting statement in an official document?

Furthermore, the proposition was not that all prices should remain constant, or that all wage rates should advance at the same pace as the long-term trend in overall productivity. The main modifications have been quoted, and they alone could provide a home for a vast array of familiar considerations not included in the two central guides. It might conceivably be argued that the step from generalized exhortation in the preceding administration to explicit guidance in the new was of such modest proportions as to be nearly imperceptible to all but the most zealously suspicious.

Still, there was a new note involved. People did take the guideposts more seriously than the earlier, more generalized, appeals for good behavior. One reason they did so was the historical context: a determined president, clearly willing to consider more active policies in this field; evidence from the letters to the steel industry and union that the government was ready to take more initiative; a difficult balance-of-payments situation that could not be ignored if economic policies were to be directed toward greater employment and investment; and a realization on all sides that a burst of inflation in the early stages of expansion would jeopardize all the new ideas for social reform being considered or submitted to Congress for action.

Finally, what was new was the framework. Although the guideposts themselves did not provide precise answers for particular cases, they were set up in a form well designed for increasing precision. If the overall rate of gain in productivity were considered an unsatisfactory guide for wage increases to be accepted in the case of a union whose members had unusually low earnings, why not suggest that the deviation be made up by a series of annual increases equal to some specified fraction above the rate indicated by the general guide? The system was conceived in such a way that systematic suggestions for progressively more complex cases could readily be proposed, if the country chose to follow the indicated approach.

What was new was not the general idea, nor the publication of governmental advice on such questions, but the official presentation of a more specific set of principles, consistent with efficiency and pointing toward a more active role by the government in shaping the evolution of prices and wages.

Technical Advice and Public Participation

One of the continuing criticisms of the guideposts has been that they were formulated by a small group of economists and presented as a set of specifications about desirable behavior without prior consultation among the groups affected. Two answers have been made to this complaint. One is explicit in the presentation itself: that they were not intended as administrative orders, but as a contribution to discussion of a problem. The second is that a central issue, the rate at which wages can be increased without leading to rising labor costs, is a technical matter to be handled by professional inquiry and not something which can usefully be debated by the general public.

As long as the guideposts are considered as topics for discussion rather than rules for action, there is not much basis for complaint that they were proposed by the Council of Economic Advisers. The Council's job is one of seeking and proposing methods for achieving high levels of employment with a minimum of offsetting difficulties. It would be a sorry organization indeed if it never proposed anything that did not already enjoy general public acceptance.

The grounds for criticism are stronger if one takes the guideposts more seriously, not as one set of ideas among many but as the specific suggestion of the particular officials providing advice on economic policy to an active president. Whatever the legal situation, an agency in this position cannot propose something without expecting, or at least hoping, that it will in fact influence behavior.

The more weight one chooses to attach to this way of looking at the matter, the more unfortunate it appears to be that no way was found to hold open discussions with the main parties interested prior to publication in the Council's annual report. This would not have bound the Council to change its views. It might have added valid considerations to the package. It might even have achieved some measure of support, or at least taken some of the resentment out of subsequent attacks.

In other countries with somewhat similar policies, including England and Holland, considerable effort was made to work out some measure of agreement with representatives of labor and industry prior to any public presentations of policy. Professor Phelps Brown, one of the best informed economists concerned with these problems in the United Kingdom, has placed considerable stress on the government's success in getting not only general consultation but even formal mechanisms to facilitate cooperation from the British Trades Union Council.[6] It may well be judged that the

[6] Henry Phelps Brown, "Guidelines for Growth and for Incomes in the United Kingdom: Some Possible Lessons for the United States," George P. Shultz and Robert Z. Aliber, eds., *Guidelines, Informal Controls and the Market Place* (University of Chicago Press, 1966), pp. 143-63.

consequences in practice have not so far proven greatly different, but it is still probable that the tone of debate and willingness to explore solutions have been somewhat improved by these efforts. It was a hopeful step forward in this connection when the President reactivated the Labor-Management Advisory Committee in 1966 primarily to bring both sides into active discussion with the government on these issues.

The argument that there is not much point in public discussion, because the keystone of the system is the technical question of the rate of growth of productivity and thereby that of wage increases, has been stressed in particular by Robert Solow, one of the most penetrating economists involved in the debate as a defender of the guideposts.

The parties to collective bargaining are likely to resent being presented with a figure they have no part in setting. That is understandable. The trouble is that the parties' mutual relationship is naturally a bargaining one; presented with an opportunity to set or influence the guidepost figure, they will naturally bargain over it. But that would destroy any claim that the guidepost figure might have to being an objectively determined number. . . . In principle the guidepost figure is not something one sets, it is something that one finds out.[7]

Solow went on to note that there are other questions involved which might be better handled by exchange of opinion among the interested parties, which indeed there are. They include such issues as the degree to which wage increases for higher-wage groups ought to be held below average productivity improvement to compensate for faster increases by the lowest-paid workers; the proper distribution of the burden among active groups when social benefits to the retired or disabled are increased; and the question that became particularly troublesome in 1966: what to do when supply and demand factors in fields outside manufacturing generate rising prices despite stable unit labor costs in that sector. Scientific measurement is essential to clarify what is involved in such matters, but it is not a sufficient basis for making the essentially political decisions involved.

Considering the original proposals themselves, with their series of qualitative modifications selected from a conceivably extensive list, it is clear that the technical operation of measuring productivity changes is a small part of the matter. With multiple valid criteria, exchange of opinion on which rank highest and how much any one ought to weigh against any other would be a vital part of a workable system. This could come either

[7] "The Case Against the Case Against the Guideposts," *ibid.,* p. 53.

in the form of a series of case resolutions or as a systematic ordering of alternative considerations. It would be consistent with objective technical measurement of productivity change. Public debate on inflation in general, or on such matters as cost-of-living adjustments in wage and other contracts, does not interfere with the efficient measurement of the cost-of-living by the Bureau of Labor Statistics. A complex society needs and must rely on honest measurement by objective technicians, but it does not have to hand over to them the decision on what to do about the facts they establish.

It would be unfortunate if the guideposts were to be distrusted and disowned as some sort of technocratic scheme. They were not expressed that way. They were on the contrary presented as a stimulus to public discussion and accomplished an accurate formulation of complicated issues for that purpose. The idea was not that some central group should weigh all the issues, reconcile differences, and announce conclusions. It was rather that all interested parties, through business associations, union organizations, educational institutions and professional forums, should consider seriously the possibility that relatively simple rules for restraint on the exercise of market power can serve to promote widely shared goals of greater employment and price stability; that all of them should seek more workable means of reconciling the individual group's interest in higher money incomes with some sense of the way things must add up.

The President's Labor-Management Advisory Committee provides a particularly appropriate forum for high-level exchange of ideas and objectives. Not for establishing rules, but for making sure that the multiplicity of valid interests involved are properly considered in clarifying standards of reference for the exercise of discretion by decision-making groups. Such clarification would have more meaning if the main parties interested were involved in formulating it, and this would seem to be a necessary condition for any commitment on their part to give weight to the suggested standards in making their own decisions. If the guideposts or successor techniques are to be pursued seriously, it would seem not only more equitable but also more effective to ensure continuous communication among government officials, business, labor, and professional groups.

III

Evolution of the Concept

THE GUIDEPOSTS HAVE the happy characteristic of being difficult to pin down because they can evolve freely with successive restatements and case applications. The main lines as presented in 1962 have remained intact, but some difficulties might be encountered if one were to attempt to reconcile in a single statement both that version and the one given in the 1966 annual report of the Council of Economic Advisers. Further, the question of what the guideposts really mean must be answered in part by reference to actions in specific cases which have helped make clear which parts of the general idea are operative and which are not.

Strengthening the Central Rules, 1964-66

The main line of evolution in official explanations has been one of decreasing attention to possible complications and increasing stress on the two central guideposts. The first modification came in the 1964 annual report of the Council. The original discussion stated that the concept of productivity intended as a guide for noninflationary wage settlements was that of the long-term trend for the nation as a whole, but it did not give any numerical measure of this trend. Instead, it pointed out that problems of judgment were involved in selecting among a variety of defensible measures. The 1964 statement was more specific. It introduced a single figure to serve as a basis for judgment of acceptable wage increases.[1]

The measure used in the 1964 discussion was the five-year moving average of output per man-hour in the private economy. This technique had the advantage of providing a relatively stable result, moderating the effects of cyclical changes while avoiding complex statistical methods for separating the trend from cyclical variations. But it turned out to be a bad choice.

Prior experience suggested that any period of five years would include more than one phase of a cycle. (The five years from 1956 through 1960 managed to include two recessions.) But the improvement in aggregative economic policy from 1961 onward resulted in five years of expansion, with no interruption to average things out. The rate of growth of productivity went much above that calculated for postwar experience as a whole. In 1966, when recalculated to drop out the weak results of 1960, it showed an increase in the calculated trend from 3.2 to 3.6 percent. But in 1966, with the economy operating close to its upper limit, the Council's expectation of productivity gains for the year was that they would fall below the preceding rate rather than rise above it. Wage increases of 3.6 percent would almost surely overshoot productivity gains. So the council decided that its own measure was an overstatement and that it would be better to stick to the 1960-65 calculated rate of 3.2 percent.[2] This switch caused considerable, and understandable, irritation.

Apart from the question about the particular measure chosen, the interesting point is the strength imparted to the central guidepost rule for wages by assigning a number with which to apply it. Given a range of possibilities, as suggested in 1962, unions could be fairly open-minded about the whole thing. Given a numerical limit in 1964, it became clear that customary targets were being rejected. The guideposts became a subject for more intensive debate because they became more specific.

The 1964 annual report is explicit on the decision to strengthen the central rules at the expense of possible exceptions. It states that the modifications originally suggested "still apply but it must be emphasized that they are intended to apply to only a relatively few cases. Particularly at a time when our national capabilities for responsible price and wage

[1] *Economic Report of the President, 1964,* pp. 114-15.
[2] *Ibid.,* 1966, p. 92. See the discussion of reactions by labor spokesmen in Chap. 5 below.

making may undergo a more serious test than in recent years, the most constructive private policies in the great majority of situations would be to aim at price decisions and wage bargains consistent with the general guideposts."[3]

The 1965 discussion continued this tendency. It listed three possible situations in which above-average wage increases might conceivably be warranted: cases in which an industry is unable to attract enough labor to meet demand for its product, of unusually low wages to start with, or of major changes in work rules which create the possibility of large gains in productivity but imply substantial human costs of adjustment. The third exception was to some degree new, or at least a noticeable amplification of the original brief reference to incentive pay. But the widening of criteria in this sense was more than balanced by an important reservation relative to the first two exceptions. "Because the industries in which market power is concentrated are largely high wage industries with a relatively low long-term rate of increase of employment, the first two of these exceptions are rarely applicable."[4]

The Council's 1966 report amended the working of this new reservation slightly, but kept the point. It also introduced reservations to previously stated exceptions envisaging possible grounds for price increases in industries for which labor costs are not rising. These exceptions referred to cases in which costs other than labor had risen, or in which higher profits are necessary to attract capital. The 1966 presentation somewhat undermined both. With respect to the first, price increases "may occasionally be appropriate to reflect increases in unit material costs, to the extent that such increases are not offset by decreases in other costs and significantly impair gross profit margins on the relevant range of products. . . ." With respect to the possible need to raise profits to attract capital, the 1966 statement was emphatic: "The large firms to which guideposts are primarily addressed typically have ready access to sources of capital; moreover, the profits of virtually every industry have risen sharply and are at record levels as a byproduct of the general prosperity in the economy. The second exception is thus not widely applicable in the present environment."[5]

The 1966 statement dealt with a new economic situation, not

---

[3] *Ibid.*, p. 119.
[4] *Ibid., 1965*, p. 108.
[5] *Ibid., 1966*, p. 91.

specifically discussed in the original presentation, and defined what was in effect an extension of the guideposts' applicability. As first presented, they were concerned with holding down price increases while moving from high levels of unemployment down toward a rate of about 4 percent. The objective was to prevent "premature" inflation under conditions in which a competitive economy would not generate rising prices. The 1966 version, while forecasting correctly that unemployment would go below 4 percent in the course of the year, and noting that scattered labor shortage and operation of plant close to capacity in some industries would result in greater pressures for wage and price increases, reacted by underlining "the increasing importance of the guideposts."

Finally, the 1966 statement selected a sensitive nerve for an incidental but telling comment. Where do profits come from anyway? To the people who own and run business firms, they come from private investment and personal effort. If they have gone up a great deal in the period in which the guideposts have existed, this is because of hard work, good management, reinvestment of profits, and so on. The Council's 1966 report introduced a haunting thought, already quoted but perhaps worth repeating: "the profits of virtually every industry have risen sharply and are at record levels as a byproduct of the general prosperity of the economy."

Restatement, 1967

From the point of view of efforts at price and wage stabilization, 1966 was a bad year. The initial reaction of the government was to defend the guideposts but then—following defeat in the airline strike in midsummer —they had seemingly been given up for dead. The January 1967 report recognized more explicitly than before some of the main objections being raised about application of the guideposts, and retreated slightly in the sense of admitting greater complexity than had been suggested in immediately prior years, but did not abandon the idea. What it did abandon was the presentation of a specific numerical guide for wage increases.

Real Wages and the Cost of Living

The original idea of balancing increases in wage rates with the trend of productivity improvement was calculated to yield, on average, constant labor costs per unit output. The expectation was that this would result in approximately stable prices, so that real wages would rise at the same rate as money wages and productivity. The process worked out well enough on the manufacturing side—unit labor costs remained stable until mid-1966[6] —but prices in other sectors kept on going up and undermined the rise in real wages. The previously slow rise in the consumer price index speeded up from the middle of 1965, and outpaced the rate of gain in productivity during 1966. Money wage increases equal to the gain in productivity during 1966 would have left real wages at the end of the year lower than they were at the start.

To keep the rate of gain in real wages equal to that in productivity, it would be necessary to add the increase in consumer prices to the productivity gain. But this in turn would mean that unit labor costs in money terms would rise and exert added pressure on prices. Price stabilization would call instead for holding down the rate of increase of wages in periods in which the cost of living was rising. This would come close to asking the impossible in a voluntary program: labor would have to be willing to accept slower increases in real wages in order to compensate above-average gains in real incomes by other groups.

The Council took a compromise position, without quite coming to the point of stating where the balance ought to go.

While it can be expected that many wage settlements in 1967 will exceed the trend increase in productivity, it is obvious that if, on the average, they should exceed it by the amount of the recent increase in living costs, price stability could never be restored. If the average wage increase in 1967 were to include a full allowance for productivity plus an additional margin to "compensate" for past increases in living costs, unit labor costs would rise at a rate which would require living costs to continue their rapid rise.

In 1967, the national interest continues to require restraint in wage settlements; indeed, it is more essential than ever that restraint be practiced in order to turn the trend of prices back toward stability. If restraint cannot mean an average wage advance only equal to the rise in productivity, it surely must mean wage advances which are substantially less than the productivity trend plus the recent rise in consumer prices.[7]

This statement nicely defined the issue, and left it to be settled elsewhere. This means that the solution was left in effect to the exercise of

---

[6] U. S. Department of Commerce, *Business Cycle Developments* (February 1967), p. 30.

[7] *Economic Report of the President, 1967,* pp. 128-29.

bargaining power in particular markets, subject to whatever deflationary constraints might be imposed through aggregative policies.

The Council's decision not to present a specific wage norm for 1967 was understandable. The issue involved a highly political choice affecting relative welfare, plus a strategy decision on how to weigh preference for price stabilization against the necessity of obtaining voluntary agreement in an unbalanced situation. The path toward adjustment ought to be chosen in a forum in which all interested parties could participate. But the underlying problem came from a set of economic relationships which cannot be wished away. Given stable unit costs in manufacturing, high employment is quite likely to continue to generate rising consumer prices. This is partly because demand trends are focused on services for which supply is not expanding sufficiently rapidly, and partly because of the failure of prices to fall in some of the areas in which unit costs are decreasing. If these factors continue to operate, the wage norm consistent with price stability must be set below the rate of gain in productivity. The question calls for a more explicit reconciliation of the wage guideline with analysis of expectations as to price trends outside the manufacturing sector.

Exceptions for Above-Average Wage Increases

Another thorny problem tackled in the 1967 report was that of arguments for exceptions warranting above-average wage increases. The three familiar arguments considered were those involving shortages of particular skills, ability to pay in the industry concerned, and abnormally low initial wage levels. The discussions of the first two possibilities were essentially restatements of prior positions; that concerning exceptionally low wages added significant clarification to the original point.

None of the Council's statements on wages has undermined the original exception in favor of above-average wage increases where there are shortages in particular labor markets. The new one reemphasized the position, adding that the role of differential wage increases in allocating labor takes on even greater importance in a high-employment economy such as that of 1967. It also suggested an interesting clarification of the idea of what a shortage is. "An exception to the guideposts for workers in a shortage occupation should be claimed only where the union involved stands ready to lift every artificial barrier to entry into the occupation, and to cooperate fully in public and private efforts to train whatever numbers of workers may desire to enter the occupation."[8]

Concerning arguments for above-average wage increases in those industries in which firms have unusually high ability to pay, the 1967 statement remained in line with previous explanations that this could not be considered a valid exception. If high profits lead to rapid wage increases, the consequence will be more generally rising prices; the workers in the particular field gain in real income, but the rest of the labor force, and the community, will lose. The conclusion leads to the necessity of price reductions by firms with falling unit costs; the difficulty in application is that this is not a characteristic form of voluntary behavior. Prices come down with falling costs where they are forced to by competitive pressure or by administrative ruling, not by choice. At least, this has been the general result so far. The 1967 statement left the problem in the same unsatisfactory position in which it had been before.

On arguments concerning initially low wages, the 1967 statement stressed the distinction between wages that are low relative to comparable occupations and wages that are far below the average for all occupations. The former type of comparison—"catching up" between unions—is a murderous weapon. It has been one of the major plagues hampering stabilization efforts in the United Kingdom. Any group in any field can always find some other people earning higher incomes for reasons that do not seem to involve greater skills or to merit greater recognition. There is always someone to whom it is only right and just to catch up. And each time that the gap is narrowed, the higher group considers that its historically established rights are being undermined, so that it is necessary to widen the difference again. On this road, there is no resting point.

The 1967 report restricted the meaning of the exception explicitly to those wages near the bottom of the national wage scale. The fact "that few strong unions exist among low-wage workers gives the exception only limited relevance for collective bargaining. . . . Indeed, the productivity arithmetic suggests that, if an exception for low-wage workers is to be meaningful in permitting low-wage workers to receive increases in *real* wages, high-wage workers who have profited in the past from exceptionally strong bargaining power must respect the counterpart proposition that their wage increases should be less than average."[9]

[8] *Ibid.*, p. 130.
[9] *Ibid.*, p. 130.

Profits: Cyclical and Long-term Norms

Official statements concerning the guideposts have focused on wages and prices, not on profits. The implication of the system is that profit could vary cyclically, but would in the longrun be expected to rise at the same rate as national income. The few criticisms directed at profit behavior have been those referring to particular industries in which above-average productivity increases were only used to raise profits and not to reduce prices. There was no suggestion that profits in the aggregate were increasing too fast, or that they should be limited to any specified level. The 1967 report remained circumspect on such questions, but added an interesting discussion of the type of profit behavior that would be desirable for longer-term growth.

The point of the discussion was that price stability requires business to settle for profit rates lower than those typical for cyclical peaks. In the immediate context, firms with discretion in pricing should not aim at protecting the record rates of return achieved in the first half of 1966. Rising unit costs could be expected in many industries in 1967, but they should be considered as reestablishing more sustainable profit margins rather than as justifying price increases. "If public and private policies now succeed in maintaining a steadily expanding economy, it follows that the profit margins which were feasible only in the boom stage of a boom-bust economy—and therefore may have been appropriate in that stage—are inappropriate in a steadily prosperous economy."[10]

In conjunction with the proposition that labor should forgo attempts to raise wages by the full total of productivity gains plus increases in the cost of living, the suggestion that business should absorb part of impending increases in unit costs pointed toward a conceivable way of calming down the pace of price increase set in motion during 1965-66. If followed to any degree, the advice would clearly lessen the danger of a costly interaction between attempts by labor to catch up and attempts by business to pass on all resulting cost increases through higher prices, stimulating still greater wage claims.

The advice to these two groups was aimed very much in the right direction, but it left out of account some of the main problems behind rising consumer prices in the first place. The pressure had come less from orga-

[10] *Ibid.,* p. 133.

nized labor and business than from services and food. As of the beginning of 1967, the problem of rising food prices seemed to be lessening through a process of corrective market response, but that of rising service prices was not. It would seem necessary, as discussed in several contexts in following chapters, to widen the range of direct concern before cooperation by organized labor and business could be counted on to add up to a stable aggregative result.

Restatement or Admission of Defeat?

Many people outside the government regarded the guideposts as a lost cause by the beginning of 1967. Several of the industries previously willing to accept pricing restraints, such as aluminum, copper, and molybdenum, went ahead with increases that had been blocked before. Labor unions began to carry through much higher settlements, more on the order of 5 to 6 percent, without much outward sign of governmental attempts at restraint. The January 1967 report was the first in several years to avoid specifying a wage guidepost. Its tone could be interpreted as a good deal less activist than those of the statements from 1964 through 1966.

Despite the signs of lessened effort at direct restraint, the 1967 statement cannot be regarded as a denial of future intent. It moved toward greater precision on several particularly tough issues, notably on adjustments to the fact of increasing consumer prices, on wage comparability, and on profits. It gave new attention to the importance of restrictions on entry in some labor markets. It set up the framework for a possible reconciliation of choices calculated to restore greater stability. It advanced the discussion at the same time that it retreated from immediate operational pressure.

One might easily doubt that the advice to labor and to business would have great effects on behavior in the climate of the moment. But general failure to heed the suggestions could cut in either of two ways: it might make the advice look pointless, or it might—by demonstrating the adverse consequences of ignoring it—strengthen the case for eventually greater precision and more active enforcement.

PART TWO

EXPERIENCE WITH IMPLEMENTATION

IV

Years of High Unemployment, 1962-64

IF THE GUIDEPOSTS HAD NOT BEEN invented, many of the government's actions and statements concerned with price and wage stability during the 1960's would have been much the same. The actions were responses to troublesome problems, not to issues invented by the Council of Economic Advisers. What the guideposts did was to provide a coherent background, without which the steps chosen might have been more hesistant and differently directed. In return, the actions gradually defined the applicable content of the principle, and got it taken seriously. General policy and specific action grew together.

The Collision with the Steel Industry

The first and most dramatic effort to change a particular business decision was the head-on conflict between President Kennedy and the leading firms in the steel industry in April 1962, less than three months after presentation of the guideposts.

It will be recalled that the President had written letters to the twelve major companies the preceding September, asking them to avoid increasing prices at the time of a scheduled wage increase in October. This was followed up with a letter to the union asking for restraint in the new wage negotiations to be held in March 1962. Steel prices were not raised in 1961. The administration, through Secretary of Labor Goldberg, then publicly took an active role in persuading the steel workers to accept a noninflationary settlement in 1962. The limit was defined as an increase of 12 cents per hour in combined wage and fringe benefits, intended to match an estimated 3 percent rate of gain in productivity. This ceiling was below the pace of the 1950's: total employment costs per hour had risen at a rate of 5.3 percent per year from 1953 to 1961.[1] In the last preceding contract, when officials of the Eisenhower Administration intervened to settle a long strike, the settlement yielded an increase of about 3.7 percent in hourly compensation.[2]

The union initially requested a 1962 package that would have cost approximately 17 cents per hour, then quickly settled on terms that left wage rates unchanged for 1962 but gained fringe benefits worth about 10 cents. The increase in hourly compensation was about 2.5 percent. The contract thus cost the companies less than the preceding settlement, and was also within the limits suggested by the guideposts as consistent with stable unit costs. The President and much of the financial press expressed their relief at the apparent success in moving toward greater price and wage stability in this crucial industry. The next week, the United States Steel Company announced a general increase of 3½ percent on all its products.

The increase announced by United States Steel was followed the next day by five other of the twelve largest companies, led by Bethlehem. All of them matched the same general increase, with no distinctions as to region, to any possible differences in product costs, to marketing conditions, or to company profitability.

It would have been difficult to design a clearer confrontation than that provoked by these decisions. In terms of judgment of the public interest, the executives of United States Steel declared emphatically that their behavior was responsible, restrained, and necessary for national welfare. The guideposts presented a flatly contradictory answer from the same facts. In terms of traditional spheres of authority, company officials seemed almost to be seeking a showdown to demonstrate that such decisions were properly theirs. The government acted on newly stated criteria to challenge established relationships and create new ones. Seldom does such a public-relations conscious society have the chance to watch a dis-

---

[1] *Steel Prices, Unit Costs, and Foreign Competition*, Hearings before the Joint Economic Committee, 85 Cong., 1 sess., April-May 1963, p. 52.

[2] Council of Economic Advisers, *Report to the President on Steel Prices* (April 1965), p. 42; Roy Hoopes, *The Steel Crisis* (Day, 1963), pp. 39-50.

pute between business and government so free of the screening techniques that normally sheer off the sharp edges and transform conflicting positions into mushy ambiguity.

The company's stated position was curiously similar to that of the typical public utility requesting a rate increase.[3] It was a justification in terms of profit levels and the need to attract capital for long-run expansion. It did not make any concession to current market conditions nor any reference to possible demand pressures. This was not surprising since industry operations were below two-thirds of capacity at the time.

Since our last over-all adjustment in the summer of 1958, the level of steel prices has not been increased but, if anything, has declined somewhat. . . . The price increase of 3½ percent announced today clearly falls considerably short of the amount needed to restore even the cost-price relationship in the low production year of 1958. In reaching this conclusion we have given full consideration, of course, to the fact that any price increase which comes, as this does, at a time when foreign-made steels are already underselling ours in a number of product lines, will add—temporarily at least—to the competitive difficulties which we are now experiencing. But the present price level cannot be maintained any longer when our problems are viewed in long-range perspective. For the long pull, a strong, profitable company is the only insurance that formidable competition can be met and that the necessary lower costs to meet that competition will be assured.[4]

The company and the government seemed to be far apart on measurements of productivity gains and costs. The problem was in part that most company statements referred to its individual position, while the government's statistical evidence showing that improvements in productivity had fully offset rising wages since the last general price increase referred to the industry as a whole. It was not the industry that announced the price increase, it was the United States Steel Company. And it is possible that, for this particular company, labor costs per unit had increased. Its profits and cash flow available for investment had definitely fallen.

A comparison of profits in 1958 and in 1961 for eight of the largest companies showed that those of U.S. Steel had decreased by 37 percent,

---

[3] Cf. Richard Austin Smith, "Behind United States Steel's Price Blunder," *Fortune* (August 1962).

[4] From text of statement released by Leslie B. Worthington, President of the United States Steel Corporation, in announcing the price increase, *New York Times,* April 11, 1962. See also Roger M. Blough, "My Side of the Steel Price Story," *Look,* Jan. 29, 1963, and the transcript of Mr. Blough's radio-television presentation of April 12, reprinted in Hoopes, *op. cit.,* pp. 118-36.

while the total for the other seven companies had gone down only 2 percent.[5] Since operations were at very low levels in 1961 and were climbing in 1962, the government's argument that the trend of profits for normal rates of operation was upward seemed solidly based for the industry as a whole. But it was less clear for U.S. Steel. The *Fortune* study of the case emphasized that the company's market share had been falling persistently, chiefly because of failure to move its product mix in directions of relatively favorable market growth.[6] The industry as a whole did not have a good basis for any price increase when judged by the criteria of the guideposts, but the same criteria applied to an individual firm unable to raise efficiency and grow as fast as the rest might yield a different answer.

In general, it appears undesirable to apply the guidepost concept to an individual firm, unless it is actually "the industry" in the sense of controlling all or nearly all of the supply of the product concerned. In the case of the increase by U.S. Steel, there were alternative sources of supply. If the majority of the other large firms had not moved their prices up so quickly to match the initial increase, the case against the company's action might have looked weak. It would not have mattered anyway, because the company would have been forced by the market to come back down again. But the steel industry has not usually acted this way. If it had, there probably would never have been any guideposts in the first place.

The first reaction of the rest of the industry was all too familiar. Despite the evidence of determined government opposition, and their own prior expressions of misgivings about foreign competition, most of the larger firms followed the increase. More than 80 percent of the industry's capacity was placed at the new price level within 24 hours.

Three of the twelve largest producers, Armco, Inland, and Kaiser Steel, delayed action. It would be interesting to know why they held back. The possibility that they might reject the increase was picked out immediately by the Council of Economic Advisers, thinking in terms of the way a competitive industry might act. Although this industry had never been renowned for independent pricing behavior, it clearly was divided internally about the advisability of increases at the time. Joseph Block, Chairman of Inland Steel, had spoken out publicly on the necessity of concentrating on cost reduction rather than price increases as the way to raise industry profits. His company was doing notably better than United States Steel in

[5] *Steel Prices, Unit Costs, and Foreign Competition*, Hearings, p. 58.
[6] Smith, *op. cit.*

terms of profits and rate of growth. All of the holdouts could have gained business rapidly if the others held to the higher level of prices, though it is unlikely that they gave this a great deal of weight since it was readily foreseeable that the others' prices would come back down again if they stayed put. They might simply have estimated that foreign competition made demand so elastic that industry profits as a whole would be greater if prices were not increased.

The government did not sit still to see which way the remaining companies might judge the market. Government officials personally friendly with executives of the companies called them up to state the case against the increases; more pointed action was taken to make sure that purchasing contracts would be directed insofar as possible to companies which had not raised prices; critical statements by the President, senators, governors, and the Council of Economic Advisers rained down; and some people closely linked to both the government and executives of the largest steel companies were found to initiate direct diplomacy on a quieter basis.[7]

Something worked. Inland and Kaiser stated publicly that they had decided against an increase. Bethlehem then again displayed its rapid reactions by leading the way back down. United States Steel followed, retracting its stimulating decision three days after the initial announcement.

No one can be sure that the existence of the guideposts affected the outcome. They did provide important ammunition during internal discussions prior to moves by the government, and in forceful public statements during the interval in which it seemed possible that the price increases would stick. The one fairly sure conclusion is that they gained weight as a factor to be taken into account in pricing decisions, at least for as long as a determined president takes them seriously himself.

The conflict was the first to raise a troublesome issue left unmentioned in the presentation of the guideposts. What happens if they are ignored? The original discussion suggested that public opinion would be made a more effective force by the availability of criteria for judgment. To the steel companies, if anyone looked back at the discussion, this must have seemed an understatement. To many others, it has remained a source of great irritation that an undefined threat is involved.

[7] For a fascinating summary of everyone's moves from April 11 to 13, see the article by Wallace Carroll in the *New York Times,* April 23, 1962. More detail is provided in Hoopes, *op. cit.,* and Grant McConnell, *Steel and the Presidency, 1962* (Norton, 1963).

In the steel case of 1962, the actual techniques used to exert pressure could hardly be regarded as ferocious infringements on private rights. The main method used was persuasion, apparently free of any dire hints about drastic action, applied to the companies which had not joined the increase right away. It might have helped to warn publicly that government orders would not go to firms raising prices, but such action is not totally foreign to private firms in their role as buyers of supplies, and is not in principle any worse when followed by the government. Still, a decidedly disagreeable note was introduced by the use of Federal Bureau of Investigation agents to check on the accuracy of statements attributed on April 10 to the president of Bethlehem Steel.[8] For many people, publicized use of the Federal Bureau of Investigation is an emotion-charged matter. Headlines about grand jury indictments and the serving of subpeonas also carried connotations quite different from typical efforts by The Great Atlantic and Pacific Tea Company to beat down the prices of its suppliers. None of this was necessary, and all of it made for bitterness on issues which must be fought out in the long-run through argument and compromise.

Relatively Peaceful Coexistence, 1963-64

Either the emotional costs of the 1962 conflict with the steel industry were so great, or the lesson so firmly driven home, that no further conflicts over price increases occurred during the next two years. The steel firms did not hesitate to raise some prices in 1963 and subsequently, but they no longer tried to repeat the practice of across-the-board increases on all products by all firms. Instead, some products went up and others down, with different patterns among companies, suggesting careful study of differential costs and competitive conditions rather than a mechanical upward march.

The net result of these more discrete price changes in the steel industry was not to accomplish quietly what had been blocked publicly. The wholesale index of iron and steel prices at the end of 1963 was exactly where it had been at the end of 1961. Even by April 1966, four years after the attempt to institute the 3.5 percent general increase of April 1962, the index was only 2.0 percent above its level at the end of 1961.

[8] Carroll, *op. cit.*

Price and wage increases remained restrained for a period of expansion such as that experienced in 1963-64, but official statements picked out two important problem areas. These were the construction and the automobile industries.

Construction

Construction was a special difficulty in the 1950's and has remained so despite the guideposts in the 1960's. The Council of Economic Advisers pointed out in 1962 that construction costs had increased relative to wholesale prices in all years since the Korean War, regardless whether the economy was expanding or contracting. They have continued to do so, and it seems doubtful that any action similar to that taken in the steel industry can provide a solution.

The average rate of increase in hourly wages for the construction industry between 1960 and 1965 was 3.8 percent, and gains in fringe benefits probably brought the rate of increase in payments per hour above 4 percent. According to the Council, estimates of productivity, though not very accurate for this field, "suggest that the annual increase in output per man-hour is below the economy-wide average, and substantially below the annual increase in employee compensation."[9]

A major part of the problem in this sector is that there is no central decision group with which a confrontation can accomplish anything. The labor force is highly organized, but in terms of particular craft groups in limited areas. The national leadership has not been eager to be cooperative, but even if it were, it has no power to make California plumbers moderate their claims.[10]

Decentralization of decision-making is, of course, a common characteristic in American labor markets. It is often allied with low bargaining power due either to the necessity of dealing with firms facing severe competitive restraints or to lack of organization on the labor side. Neither of these limiting factors is potent in construction. There certainly can be

[9] *Economic Report of the President, 1966,* p. 85. Cf. Douglas C. Dacy, "Productivity and Price Trends in Construction Since 1947," *Review of Economics and Statistics,* Vol. 47 (November 1965), pp. 406-11, who concludes that the rate of gain in output per man-hour in contract construction has been approximately 3 percent per year.

[10] Cf. William Burke, "Hammering on Guideposts," Federal Reserve Bank of San Francisco, *Monthly Review* (April 1966), pp. 87-94.

local competition among contractors, but if costs for a particular type of labor go up for all of them at once, these cost increases are translated into higher prices because each contractor knows that the others will be forced to raise prices too. The situation is not the same as that for the local shoe factory or cannery facing higher wages: for them, price increases can be disasterous because the firm must export its products to other areas, and must sell locally against outside firms. The contractor is not subject to this crucial restraint.

On the union side, there is a considerable advantage deriving from the very fact that the labor force is fragmented. Each small group can convince itself, and perhaps even the contractors, that an increase in its wages will not drastically raise total costs, and most of the separate groups are capable of stopping the whole construction process by striking. In New York City in July 1966, a construction industry employing nearly 200,000 workers was seriously slowed down by strikes of 800 hoisting engineers and 4,000 plumbers.[11] Since the cost of giving in at any particular time are likely to appear lower than the costs of resisting, settlements for wage increases far above the values that would be indicated by the guideposts have been common. The persistent problems of the general situation have been further aggravated by attempts of the Defense Department to rush through large-scale construction projects in areas unable to supply the required labor readily. This has resulted in extraordinary wage increases that spread by example even to sections in which the labor supply is adequate.

Possibilities for dealing with the above-average pace of wage increases in the construction industry are discussed below. As far as the guideposts are concerned, they drew attention to the issues in this sector but have not so far proven to be of much help in solving them.

Automobiles

The other problem area given special attention in 1963-64 was the automobile industry. This was not an instance of increasing prices. Rather, it was a focus for demonstration of a troublesome weakness in the operation of the guideposts. While they may help to restrain price increases, they have not accomplished much if anything to get prices down in instances in which full application of the concept would require a decrease.

[11] *New York Times,* July 28 and Aug. 2, 1966.

The system envisaged that prices would increase where low rates of productivity improvement resulted in rising labor costs, and that these increases would be balanced by declining prices in those industries for which productivity gains were fast enough to reduce unit costs. The automobile industry presented a case in which productivity had increased at above average rates during the early 1960's as output expanded rapidly. As a result of the fall in unit costs, profits increased markedly.

The 1964 annual report of the Council of Economic Advisers, in a passage aimed at the automobile industry, emphasized the threat to stability created by the evidence of sharply rising profits in situations where decreasing costs were not reflected in falling prices. The United Automobile Workers followed with the argument that they would restrain wage claims if prices were cut, but would not be bound by the guideposts if the companies were not. Reportedly extensive negotiations behind the scenes did not obtain any price reductions, seriously undermining the case against high wage increases, and the final result was a settlement decisively breaking the recommended ceiling.[12]

It was possible to argue that the guidepost concept had helped somewhat to induce moderation in the wage settlement, especially since it was clear that the companies' profit margins were not placed under any significant pressure and might well go on increasing. But it remained true that the episode fairly well consecrated defeat for the idea of getting price reductions in industries for which productivity gains are above average.

The Market as an Ally of the Guideposts

Although the government did not manage to force reductions in prices under the guidepost policy, this did not mean that all prices either stayed constant or increased. Rather, market forces continued to operate in many industries as they always have, bringing down prices in the fields in which costs were reduced and competitive pressures were strong enough to carry these savings through to prices. The chart of price and productivity trends for nineteen manufacturing industries reproduced on the next page, from a study by the Council of Economic Advisers, indicates a general tenden-

[12] Cf. Myron L. Joseph, "Requiem for a Lightweight," University of Pennsylvania Conference on Pricing Theories, Practices, and Policies, October 1966 (Mimeo.), pp. 15-17.

FIGURE 1

Price and Productivity Trends, Nineteen Manufacturing Industries

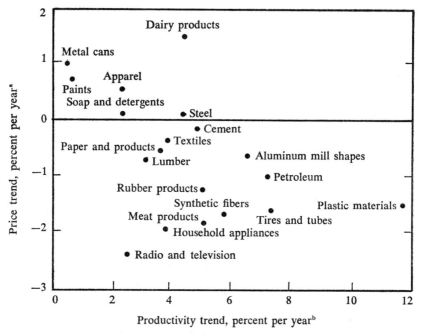

Source: *Economic Report of the President, 1965,* p. 58, Chart 8.
ª Average annual percentage change in wholesale price index, 1959-64.
ᵇ Average annual percentage change in output per employee man-hour, 1959-64.

cy toward decreasing prices for those industries in which productivity gains were above average. Between 1959 and 1964, prices decreased by at least 1 percent per year for seven of the nineteen cases considered. A more general survey of changes in wholesale prices between 1961 and 1965 for broadly defined industrial groups showed that they had decreased in five of the thirteen categories used.[13]

On the basis of the fact that prices had come down in many cases in which costs had decreased, the Council was able to state in 1965 that, "Despite occasional exceptions—as in automobiles and construction—the general pattern of recent wage and price changes has closely approximated the Government's wage-price guideposts."[14] It would also be possible

[13] *Economic Report of the President, 1966,* p. 66.
[14] *Ibid., 1965,* p. 58.

to describe the same events by saying that the market system continued to work much as it had before the guideposts were invented, bringing down prices without direct intervention in many industries for which cost reductions made this possible. To the extent that the guideposts deserve credit for decreases in prices, it was not a matter of direct policy implementation in the areas in which the decreases occurred. Their contribution was rather in restraining pressures on costs emanating from the pricing practices of concentrated industries, and possibly in moderating the pace of increase in wages, so that those industries which are competitive might more readily realize decreasing unit costs as their own productivity improved.

V

Attempts to Limit Wage Increases, 1965-66

THE EXPANSION OF 1961-65 raised gross national product in real terms at a rate of 5.4 percent per year, but productivity increased so fast in the process that the rate of unemployment did not come down rapidly. From an average of 5.6 percent of the civilian labor force in 1962, it decreased to 5.2 percent for 1964. The expansion finally began to dig seriously into the rate of unemployment in the course of 1965, bringing it down to 4.1 percent by the end of the year. The behavior of prices changed simultaneously. After six years in which the wholesale price index had remained stable, a steady succession of monthly increases began to occur in mid-1965.

The Johnson Administration made an attempt to restrain wages in the automobile industry negotiations of 1964, but accepted a final settlement above the guidepost ceiling without any strong reaction. This relatively mild policy continued until the general price level began to go up seriously in the second half of 1965, but then began to move toward more direct pressure on wage negotiations and pricing decisions. As the administration attempted to apply the brakes more strongly, the previously negative attitudes of the major labor unions became more intense. The opposition from union leaders was reinforced by that of the government's negotiators in the mediation services. It quickly became clear that the price of insistence on the guideposts was likely to be a greater rate of breakdown in the negotiation process, implying either more frequent strikes or new legislation to prevent them.

44

Negotiating Procedures and Union Attitudes

The great majority of the thousands of wage settlements negotiated each year do not involve the government in any direct way. If the guideposts affect these decisions, it can only be through examples of effective intervention in a few important cases, through their possible influence in moderating inflation and thereby the pressure to raise money wages more rapidly to keep up, and through encouraging the idea that moderation on the part of officials of a particular union will not be made to look foolish by everyone else's more aggressive behavior.

The administration did take an active role in bringing the guideposts into the picture in a number of important negotiations, but there has always been a touchy question as to the degree to which government mediators should back up this effort. Officials of the mediation services have usually managed to restrain their enthusiasm for the whole idea.

The tradition of the mediation services has been to aim at peaceful settlements, not at limiting wage increases. The mediators believe that their usefulness depends on the conviction that they are neutral in the bargaining process. To bring in the wage guideposts in a situation where the union is asking more would be in effect to side with the employer. The mediator would be helpless if the range of claim and offer was above the guidepost figure in the first place, and would be lessening the chances of a settlement to insist on this limit if it did not happen to be near the center of the bargaining positions. Besides, experienced mediators are profoundly aware of the complications of particular cases, and tend to be highly critical of single-number solutions for complex problems.[1]

The administration never succeeded in defining its own position in the matter very clearly. Despite many public statements about the desirability of following the guideposts, the government has been exceedingly wary about backing them up when it seemed likely that a strike might result, or might be prolonged by insisting on them. Federal mediators were not requested to follow any rigid line on the point, and in general continued to stress settlements rather than wage limits. To some people within the ad-

---

[1] Cf. The address of William E. Simkin, Director of the Federal Mediation Service, "The Role of the Government in Collective Bargaining," University of California Annual Labor-Management Conference, San Francisco, May 25, 1962.

ministration, this behavior was apparently considered to be a form of treason. To those in the mediation services, it was simply that their primary function required them to put the guideposts in the background. The government is interested in both wage stability and peaceful settlements, and their job is to promote the latter.

If the government were to decide that the only objective was to hold settlements within guidepost limits, that it would be better to put up with more frequent or longer strikes than to weaken the principle, the mediation services and everyone else could be directed to follow a consistent line. No such decision was ever taken. It is easy to see why it was not. The government does care about labor peace, for both political and economic reasons. The unions never accepted any commitment to support the guideposts. The firms involved might often prefer themselves to offer higher wages rather than to risk strikes. A tougher position would not work without a higher degree of consensus. And a tougher position which lost sight of the true multiplicity of objectives could involve extremely high costs.

Labor leaders do not all agree any more than government officials do. Most public statements on the subject of the guideposts have been highly critical of the idea, particularly on the ground that its practical effect is to limit wages rather than prices. On the other hand, Walter Reuther's testimony for the AFL-CIO in congressional hearings on the 1964 *Economic Report of the President* specifically accepted the general framework. "Although the guideposts for wage and price decisions first set forth by the Council of Economic Advisers in 1962 and reiterated in the Council's more recent reports may have contributed, as a result of misinterpretation, to a negative emphasis on wages as costs, there is actually no conflict between the guideposts and the kind of dynamic wage policy which the AFL-CIO has been urging."[2]

The union policy as explained by Reuther emphasized the exceptions to the central guide for wages that had been included in the Council's original presentation. One of them was the justification for larger increases in cases in which workers were receiving unusually low wages in the first place.

But the Council's recognition of the need for flexibility went beyond the point of specific exceptions. It recognized that unbending adherence to the

[2] *Economic Report of the President,* Hearings before the Joint Economic Committee, 88 Cong. 2 sess., Pt. 2 (1964), p. 29.

general rule would permanently freeze the shares of a firm's income going into wages and profits. It therefore went on to make clear that it was not proposing that income shares remain fixed. There is nothing sacred about the existing distribution of income.[3]

Reuther proposed the creation of a public review board to investigate pricing decisions, to require decreases when profits are exceptionally high, and to prevent unwarranted increases. He suggested that such a board could be directed to review pricing in those particular cases in which a single firm accounts for more than 20 percent of the sales of a basic commodity.[4] He was not too explicit on the way that such external control should bear on wages, but the approach suggests the acceptance of a limit on the rate of justifiable wage increases, provided that it is set high enough to allow an increase in labor's share of national income. It points in the direction of comprehensive planning of incomes in relation both to equity and to the promotion of growth in aggregate demand.[5]

As the leader of a strong union seeking wage increases in a profitable industry, Reuther's position has been simpler. The month following the above testimony on the 1964 *Economic Report,* the United Automobile Workers declared that its target for wages and fringe benefits in contracts coming up during the year would be an increase of 4.9 percent. To criticism by the Chairman of the Council of Economic Advisers, Reuther commented that "nothing Walter Heller says can change our position at the bargaining table."[6]

The generally negative attitude of the unions turned toward sharper hostility in 1966. One of the causes may have been irritation at the fact that, although money wages were not rising faster than the guidepost rate, consumer prices began to go up with increasing speed. Gains in real wages fell behind the rate of growth of productivity, and the government did not take any new step to adjust for this in its recommendations on wages. In fact, the Council of Economic Advisers made a decision which seemed to the unions to be deliberately unfair. As discussed in Chapter 3 above, the system of measuring productivity gains by a five-year moving average indicated that the rate had gone up from 3.2 percent to 3.6 percent per year, when the average was extended to include 1965. But the Council con-

[3] *Ibid.*

[4] *Ibid.*, pp. 29-31; *New York Times,* Jan. 18, 1966.

[5] See especially testimony in *Economic Report of the President,* Hearing before the Joint Economic Committee, 87 Cong. 2 sess. (1962), pp. 715-816.

[6] *New York Times,* March 24, 1964.

cluded that its own measure overstated the true long-term trend, and recommended that the 3.2 percent guideline be maintained. While the decision made sense in terms of the fundamental objective, it struck the unions as a change of tactic aimed at them, and probably contributed to the aggressive flavor of the official AFL-CIO statement on the guidelines issued in February.

By discarding its own rules for calculating the wage guideline, in a flagrant effort to keep it low, the Council of Economic Advisers has destroyed the guideline's credibility, has helped to accelerate the shift of incomes away from wage and salary earners to other groups in the economy and has added to imbalances that can undermine healthy economic growth. . . . This action is nothing less than an attempt to short-change workers—an effort to impose the burden of the price level on wage and salary earners, who do not set prices, while there is no effective guideline for prices and no guidelines at all for profits and dividends.

We do not believe that price stability is a top priority goal to which workers' equity must be sacrificed.

. . . There is no evidence of general wage-cost pressures on the price level. In his recent Economic Report, the President stated that unit labor costs in the national economy "have largely offset moderate increases in hourly labor costs." In addition, in the key manufacturing sector, unit labor costs have been in a declining trend since 1960 and the Economic Report shows that such costs declined eight-tenths of one per cent last year.

Despite this record of relatively stable unit labor costs . . . the level of consumer prices has risen over 1 percent per year in recent years—washing out part of the value of wage and salary gains. But the wage guideline takes no account of the rise in living costs, a factor of major importance to workers. . . .

While workers' buying power has been lagging behind the increase of productivity, profits and dividends have been rising much faster than employee compensation. In 1965, for example, corporate profits rose 15 percent before taxes and 20 percent after taxes. . . . However, there are no government guidelines for profits or dividends.[7]

In succeeding months, several unions sounded as if they cared almost as much about smashing the guideposts as about getting wage increases. The Communications Workers of America ran a newspaper advertising campaign against "the decimal point" (that is, the idea of a 3.2 percent norm), as a prelude to their 1966 contract negotiations with the Bell Sys-

[7] Report of the Economic Policy to the AFL-CIO Executive Council on "The Wage Guideline," Feb. 26, 1966, Bal Harbour, Florida (Mimeo.).

tem. The airline machinists, victorious over the administration in a decisive struggle discussed below, celebrated by claiming that they had demolished the guideposts once for all.

In their Washington role as participants in discussion of national economic policy, union spokesmen were much less dogmatic. When the President's labor-management advisory committee faced the subject, union officials joined in a report that included proposals to make applications of the guideposts more effective. These recommendations requested a quarterly evaluation by the Council of Economic Advisers of the operation of the guideposts, asked the Council to identify causes of difficulties, and specified that the Council should take up discussions with the advisory committee "to determine whether any appropriate corrective action can be recommended."[8]

The committee's report was somewhat less than a dramatic call for tougher enforcement, but it did accept the approach. It almost suggested that more cooperative methods of setting the guideposts, and more flexibility in their application, could lead to more sympathetic consideration by the unions.

Wage Negotiations Involving the Guideposts

As the labor market tightened in 1965, and the shower of belligerent statements from union officers continued, the prospects for accomplishing anything through the wage guideposts appeared murky. They were not improved by the results of an important union election, for the presidency of the United Steel Workers of America.

The decision of the steel workers under David McDonald to settle their 1962 contract quickly for an increase within the guidelines had been a crucial factor in strengthening President Kennedy's position against the immediately following attempt of the steel companies to raise prices, and had thereby contributed to getting acceptance of the idea that the guideposts should be taken seriously. Within the union, cooperation with wage restraint became one of the arguments involved in criticism of McDonald. His opponent, I. W. Abel, promised to be tougher. The election involved

[8] From text of the Wage-Price Policy Report, *New York Times,* Aug. 19, 1966.

enough other issues to obscure the role of this one, but the general idea of cooperation on wage restraint gained little support when the election went against McDonald.

Steel Industry Wages, 1965

Bargaining over the 1965 wage contract with the steel industry was delayed by the union election, and an agreement was reached to push back a threatened strike deadline from May 1 until the end of August. The same union is one of two representing workers in the aluminum industry, and went ahead to reach a settlement with the aluminum companies in June. The increase in that contract was estimated at 4.1 percent, well over the guidepost ceiling. Government officials criticized the settlement as inflationary, after the event.[9]

The new president of the steel workers' union promptly announced that he would get a similar settlement from the steel industry. The government bore down to get a low settlement, this time aided by evidence of continuing interest in stability of steel prices, and by the fact that they had remained stable. The position did not suffer from the ambiguity of objectives surrounding wage negotiations in automobiles the preceding year.

After personal intervention by the President to postpone a seemingly inescapable strike deadline, negotiations were resumed in the Executive Office building next door to the White House. The Secretaries of Labor and of Commerce participated in the discussion, and the President repeatedly stressed the need for a noninflationary agreement. When the Council of Economic Advisers calculated the cost implications of the multiple claims and offers involved, it was able to demonstrate that an even compromise between the two sides would come out equal to a gain of 3.2 percent in wages and benefits.[10] It only remained for the President to make definite suggestions as to how the compromise might be implemented on a

[9] *New York Times,* June 3, 4, and 6, 1965. The estimate that the settlement involved an increase of 4.1 percent was used in published discussion at the time, without any official contradiction. Several months later, the correct figure was stated to be nearer 3.5 percent: cf. Press briefing of Secretary McNamara, Secretary Fowler, and Mr. Ackley, Nov. 10, 1965, in connection with aluminum prices and sales from the stockpile.

[10] *New York Times,* Sept. 4, 5, 6, and 10, 1965. The increase would be above 3.2 percent if estimated from the effective date of the settlement (September 1), to the conclusion of the contract. The Council based its calculations on the earlier deadline set for termination of work under the preceding contract, May 1.

few issues still in dispute, and an accord was reached that both avoided a strike and reasserted the government's interest in implementation of the guideposts.

The Maritime Strike and Settlement

East Coast and Gulf shipping was tied up by a seamen's strike, aiming at wage increases much above the guidepost rate, from June 15 until the end of August. The seamen had once been a relatively low-wage group, but had worked up fast from this to a favored position after the passage of the Merchant Marine Act of 1936. The purpose of that act had been to promote development of the American merchant marine, primarily through a system of subsidies to offset the excess of American over European costs of ship construction and operation. Under this system, any widening of the excess of wage rates for American seamen over wage levels abroad was in effect paid by the government. At the time the act went into effect, wages for American seamen were about 50 percent above those for foreign counterparts; by 1964 they were 3 to 5 times as high. As compared to American manufacturing wages, those of seamen moved from being slightly below average to about double the average.[11]

In 1965, the Maritime Commission made a determined effort to slow down the trend of wage increases for seamen by stating that the subsidies would not be increased to cover an excessive wage grant. What gave them a weapon with which to define an excessive wage increase was the guidepost norm of 3.2 percent. About two weeks after the strike started, the Commission cut subsidy payments scheduled according to several prior agreements going beyond this rate, and stated that it would continue to follow this norm. The Secretary of Commerce, with jurisdiction over the Commission, decided to overrule the decision because of its retroactive effect. But he simultaneously praised the Commission's approach, and reinforced the suggestion that it would be desirable to put a limit on the amount of wage increases which would be covered by future subsidies.[12] The strike continued for a month after these intrusions, but was then settled with a wage increase of 3.2 percent.

The unusually direct leverage applied to affect this particular wage set-

[11] Samuel A. Lawrence, *United States Merchant Shipping Policies and Politics* (Brookings Institution, 1966), pp. 91-94.

[12] *Ibid.*, pp. 151-52; *New York Times,* July 6, 14, 15, 24, 25; Aug. 5, 19, 30, 1965.

tlement is not often available, but the interest of the case is considerable because somewhat similar possibilities are open in many fields. Wherever federal agencies determine conditions of entry to a market, as in airlines, trucking, railroads, or broadcasting, the possibilities are evident. Profits can be affected by new decisions on import quotas as in oil, sugar, or textiles; on regulations affecting the flow of bank credit or depreciation rulings affecting particular industries; and so on almost indefinitely. These are directions of action bearing on profits rather than directly on wages, but the maritime case helped show that measures which make it more difficult for firms to pass on the costs of high wage settlements can help limit the settlements themselves.

Construction: A Test Case and An Impasse

A case which was given especially pointed publicity in early 1966 as a test of the ability to apply the guideposts to labor was that involving the New Jersey Engineers' Local 825. The government was not looking for a way to break into a particular negotiation in the construction industry; it was rather driven in by criticism implying that inability to act here was a confession of defeat for the policy of restraining wages.

The situation was in a difficult stage when action was taken. The union and the contractors had announced, though they had not yet signed, a new three-year agreement. The accord would have raised the hourly earnings of the operators of large cranes to $7.75 an hour, publicized widely as a new record for the field. The increase for the first year included 35 cents per hour in additional wages and 30 cents additional benefits. The contractors estimated that the annual rate of increase in earnings for the life of the contract would be from 13 to 17 percent per year. The head of the union local said that it really "would not be much more than 3.2 percent."[13]

Discussions in Washington among the contractors, Secretary of Labor Wirtz, and the Council of Economic Advisers, led to appeals to both sides to reopen negotiations. The union rejected the request for further discussions and went out on strike March 21 because the pay increase had not come through. Five days later, an agreement was reached under which the union got the 35 cents increase in wages, but not the added fringe benefits. These benefits, and all terms for the next two year, were held up pending reconsideration by outside arbitrators. The arbitration committee, which

[13] *Ibid.,* Jan. 20 and March 27, 1966.

included the Secretary of Labor, appointed a private consulting firm to prepare a report on the New Jersey labor market as a basis for analysis.[14] On the basis of this report, the committee recommended a new employer-financed system of compensating workers for seasonal unemployment. The contractors rejected this alternative. In September, a settlement was reached which gave the union substantially what it had tried for in the first place. The record of mediocre results from requests for voluntary cooperation in the construction industry was preserved.

Throughout the negotiations on the New Jersey dispute, there was an active circulation of rumors, denied by the administration, that expenditures on construction involving federal funds would be held up unless a noninflationary accord were reached. By analogy with the steel industry, such steps would seem to be a plausible part of government strategy if it were necessary to exert pressure on the construction industry. The analogy is a little weak: the government cannot turn to midwestern contractors and unions to build the roads or hospitals that have been decided on for New Jersey. Given that the projects involved were chosen because of their public benefits in the first place, it would be doubtful strategy to block them as a bargaining move in the process of seeking a different public goal.

On the other hand, it is possible that the total amount of public and private construction scheduled for any particular area may exceed the possible rate of implementation in a period of tight labor supply, as in 1966. If that is the source of the trouble, if the contractors are willing to meet any offer because they have too much work on their hands, the solution might include a review and rescheduling of the work intended for the area. In principle, this is a matter of adjusting demand to supply and not a matter of bargaining with an industry. In practice, the two may be hard to separate.

In February, Secretary Wirtz presented a proposal for a new approach to bargaining in construction to a meeting of the leaders of the AFL-CIO Building Trades Department. The part of the proposal that became public centered on the idea of establishing a national review board for wage negotiations, to which local unions were to report disputes before taking any strike actions. The union leaders rejected it categorically.[15] The president

[14] *Ibid.,* Feb. 8 and 28; March 17, 27, 29 and 30; April 7, 1966.
[15] William Burke, "Hammering on Guideposts," Federal Reserve Bank of San Francisco, *Monthly Review* (April 1966), pp. 87-94; *New York Times,* Feb. 18, 1966.

insisted particularly that the apparently high hourly wage rates in construction were misleading because of the seasonal nature of the work. In his view, an increase of 4.1 percent in hourly earnings, as reported for the field, was probably not above an increase of 3.2 percent in annual earnings. The basis of the argument about percentage increases was not made too clear. The rejection was.

The Government as Employer, 1966

Two lines of policy which had been proceeding on independent paths intersected in 1964, and collided head-on in each of the two following years. One of them was the long-term program of improvements in pay scales for civilian employees of the federal government initiated in 1962 under the Federal Salary Reform Act of that year. The leading principle of that act was that the government employees would receive pay and benefits comparable to those performing similar types of work in the private sector. Since federal salaries were at the time well below those for the private sector, particularly in the technical and professional ranks, it was intended that they be raised faster than private salaries during the next few years. They did go up faster than private sector wages through 1965, but did not fully catch up to comparable levels as calculated by the Bureau of Labor Statistics because the administration began to delay the movement on the ground that it ran counter to another important principle: the guideposts.

In October 1965, the President used the threat of a veto to get congressional agreement to keep civilian pay increases voted that year within the guidepost limits. In early 1966, several congressmen introduced bills aiming at a general increase of 7 percent in federal salaries. They and the representatives of associations of government employees used the occasion for a direct attack on the guidepost concept.

In opposition to the bills for a wage increase of 7 percent, the administration proposed a schedule of pay increases averaging 2.9 percent, plus improved fringe benefits bringing the total up to a gain of 3.2 percent. The bill followed the principle of comparability by proposing varied rates of increase by job classifications, related to the width of the gaps between public and private salaries. This would have meant increases of only 1 percent at the lower clerical levels, and up to 4.5 percent in the middle-level technical jobs. The bill stipulated a ceiling of $485 million per year for the allowable rise in total compensation, and recommended that the increase not begin until January 1967. The President's message urged Congress to take into account both "the wage-price guideposts which are key weapons in our defense against inflation, and sound and responsible Federal fiscal policy."[16]

The administration's presentation by the Chairman of the Civil Service Commission used the guideposts as the main line of defense for the limit proposed.

In adjusting the compensation of its employees, the Government is acting as an employer, and as the country's largest employer. It is essential that the Government's action in this capacity conform with national policies which other employers are expected to follow. The President's Federal pay proposals have been carefully drawn so as to be within the economic guidepost that total compensation increases in private enterprise are expected to follow in the interest of a stable economy.[17]

Perhaps the fundamental reason for the government's determined effort to hold down salary increases was that the economy was bordering on outright inflation. Government salaries do not raise unit labor costs for firms producing goods, but they can affect aggregate demand. They were running at a rate of about $20 billion per year for civilian employees in mid-1966. In contrast to the situation through 1964, the possibility of excess demand was genuine, and an increase in government expenditures without a corresponding rise in taxes was awkward. In this context, the microeconomic criteria of the guideposts became an instrument of macroeconomic policy; they were used not so much to restrain costs as to hold down aggregate demand.

The employee representatives argued that the guideposts had always envisaged allowing pay increases above the average for workers with subnormal wages, and that they were entitled to catch up with the private sector both according to this principle and because of the stated purposes of the Federal Salary Reform Act. The Director of the Budget, Charles L. Schultze, was given the honor of answering this for the administration. He tried two different approaches.

One of the answers constituted a redefinition of what the escape clause

[16] *Federal Salaries and Fringe Benefits,* Hearings before the Subcommittee on Compensation of the House Committee on Post Office and Civil Service, 89 Cong. 2 sess. (1966), p. 4.
[17] *Ibid.,* p. 7.

in the wage guidepost meant. "It isn't really catch-up, it has to do with employees who are grossly underpaid. It is a need basis, not a comparability exception."[18] The Council had never made this point completely clear, and Schultze went on to say why it needed to be clarified. The idea of catching-up can be either reasonable or explosive, depending on how it is applied. "As sure as I am sitting here there isn't a union leader in the country worth his salt who couldn't find for his union some other relevant group of employees whom he didn't have to catch up with."[19]

The other suggestion in the same connection is of great interest as a possible clue for adjusting the guidepost criteria to conditions of aggregate demand. This is the idea that steps to establish comparability should be systematically delayed in times of high employment and strong inflationary pressures, and then speeded up when aggregate demand is not pressing strongly on capacity to supply.[20] This parallels the actual course of increases for government employees, speeding up from 1962 to 1965 and then slowing down. It could be made more specific and might lead to a real improvement in the package of guidepost policies.

The federal employees drew freely on the whole range of AFL-CIO complaints about the guideposts, with particular emphasis on the fact that profits were not being limited by any similar rule and were rising much faster than wages. They also threw in a new twist: the guideposts were being given legislative force in their case, but not for workers in the private sector.

The administration's answer to the argument that the guideposts do not limit profits distinguished sharply between unit margins and absolute profits. The guideposts are meant to prevent widening of unit profit margins by increasing prices, but not to restrain absolute profits arising from greater volume.

Just as the guideposts are not designed to limit profits *per se,* we are not attempting to control the total wage bill in the economy; that is, we are not attempting to say that you can't pay in the aggregate more wages. . . . Weekly earnings can rise because hours of work rise. In other words, volume rises.

---

[18] *Ibid.,* pp. 271-72.
[19] *Ibid.,* p. 271. Cf. the testimony of the president of the National Association of Letter Carriers, *ibid.,* p. 67: "A number of years ago, pay for letter carriers in our larger cities equaled and even exceeded that of policemen. This is no longer true, as the chart you have before you will demonstrate. We are not saying that policemen are overpaid—but we are saying that letter carriers are underpaid."
[20] *Ibid.,* p. 264.

Just as in the case of corporation and industrial activities, it is the price part of it and not the profit part of it that the guideposts seek to control.[21]

The administration did not present a direct reply to the complaint by the federal employees that it was only in their case that the guideposts were being given legislative force. It was pointed out that the difference in treatment had not prevented a faster increase of wage and fringe benefits for government employees than for workers in the private sector from 1962 on.[22] In effect, the market forces and bargaining pressures which play roles in the private sector similar to that of legislation for government employees had proved to be a more potent restraint than the legislation. But that is somewhat less than a complete answer. Market forces do impose severe restraints for the great majority of workers in the private sector, but not for all of them. Where they do not act, neither does legislation impose a ceiling. This is, of course, the problem at which the wage guideposts were aimed.

Congress reacted to all these arguments by passing bills which adhered to the 2.9 percent increase specified for wages, but which broke away from the comparability principle by making the increase standard for all categories rather than adjusting to the structure of differentials between the public and private sectors, and which also rejected the President's overall limit for fiscal year 1967 by stipulating that the increases should go into effect as of the first of July 1966. The outcome could hardly be considered a clean-cut victory for the administration, but the guideposts did survive one of their roughest tests in a struggle that helped bring out some interesting issues, particularly the possibility of linking up wage adjustments to conditions of aggregate demand.

The Strike of the Airline Machinists

The guideposts met outright defeat in the airline machinists' strike of July-August 1966. The government first ensured that the struggle would take place on almost hopeless terms, then stuck tenaciously to a position it had already undermined, and finally went out of the way to repudiate the fundamental ideal of the wage guidepost in the course of giving up.

In the airline industry, the government's possibilities of leverage to

[21] Charles L. Schultze, *ibid.,* pp. 262-63.
[22] Issues posed by alternative ways of measuring these changes were discussed at length; see particularly *ibid.,* pp. 33-34, and 260-69.

guide decisions are exceptionally high. The carriers are subject to extensive regulation in both economic matters and technical operations. Some of the smaller lines are subsidized, as all of them were until their improving profitability made it possible to take them off subsidy in the course of the 1950's.

The Civil Aeronautics Board has the authority to decide which carriers, and how many, can fly on any given route. The Board can also delay and investigate proposed changes in airline fares and can order inquiries into existing fare structures. These powers have been used to block some proposed increases, as in 1965, and also to order increases in fares deemed to be too low. The Board has not used them to order decreases. It has frequently made suggestions that the airlines try to find ways of expanding traffic through lower fares, but without requiring them to do so.

The CAB decided that airlines need higher rates of return than conventional public utilities, and set 10.5 percent as a reasonable average for the industry. More specifically, it calculated a desirable rate of 10.25 percent for the four largest carriers, and 11.125 percent for the rest of the domestic trunklines, in both cases referring to net after taxes and before interest charges on long-term debt.[23] Earnings have usually been below these rates and were especially low from 1960 through 1963. They began to go up fast in 1964, reached an average rate of return of 11.1 percent in the fiscal year through June 1965, and then went on up to 12.3 percent for the year through June 1966.[24] The earnings of the four largest carriers remained below the 10.5 rate prescribed for them, but those of the other trunklines (except Northeast), went far above the Board's recommended level. Braniff, Continental, Delta, and National earned from 16 to 24 percent returns in each of fiscal years 1965 and 1966. The CAB made a number of suggestions on the desirability of considering decreases in fares, but did nothing very emphatic about it. Neither did the airlines.

The machinists and ground service personnel of five of the national airlines took advantage of the companies' profit positions in 1966 by presenting a set of claims for increases in wages and benefits that, while going far beyond the guidepost, could be defended as consistent with adequate rates of profit without any increase in airline fares. They thereby adopted

[23] Richard E. Caves, *Air Transport and Its Regulators* (Harvard University Press, 1962), Chap. 7; Clair Wilcox, *Public Policies Toward Business* (Irwin. 3d ed., 1966), pp. 423-24.

[24] Civil Aeronautics Board, *Reports to Congress, Fiscal Year 1966*, App. 1, p. 77.

the traditional approach, used successfully by the automobile workers in 1964, of relating their wage claims to the individual industry's ability to pay instead of the national trend in productivity. They might very well have made the same requests in any event. Their position was strengthened by the fact that no action had been taken by the government to bring down airline fares even though it was indicated both by the CAB's standard for adequate profits and the guidepost idea that prices should decrease for industries with falling unit costs.

The airlines in effect allowed the government to direct negotiations, first offering an increase in line with the guideposts and then raising it to the 3.5 percent recommended by mediators. When the union went out on strike in July, it was a strike against the government as well as against the companies.

The CAB, like the Maritime Board earlier, then began to use some fairly mild measures to back up the position of the rest of the government. These included rulings which allowed increased flights by the carriers still in operation in order to replace some of those blocked by the strike, and authorization for the carriers which had been shut down to lend planes to those still operating. Taken together with an agreement among many of the airlines under which those gaining traffic from the strike would compensate the companies shut down, moves of this type could conceivably have had considerable effect. They were not pushed aggressively.

As irritations caused by the strike mounted, Congress began to debate legislation that would either directly require the workers to return or give the President authority to make such a decision. The administration was clearly divided on its own position. Senator Morse, speaking for the government's special board of negotiators, took an increasingly hostile attitude toward the union and became the main proponent of legislation to force the workers to return. The Secretary of Labor systematically avoided encouragement of such drastic action, and just as systematically avoided discouraging it. The President consistently linked his statements in favor of early settlement with calls for restraint. As the incompatibility of the two goals became evident, the emphasis on the latter progressively decreased. When the negotiators offered and the union leadership accepted a settlement going above the guideposts, to about 4.3 percent, the President announced that the agreement was noninflationary in the sense that the increase would be more than compensated by the high rate of productivity gain in the industry.[25]

[25] *Ibid.*, July 31, and Aug. 1, 1966.

Administration sources estimated the industry productivity improvement rate to be on the order of 8 percent per year, so that unit labor costs could continue to decrease even with the new offer. But the position thus taken publicly by the government cut the ground from under the premise of the guideposts. It suggested the acceptability of wage increases linked to the individual industry's ability to pay, and gave up the idea that prices should decrease in those cases in which productivity gains are particularly high. The proposed settlement would not force airline fares up, but it would prevent airline fares from coming down. It moved back in the direction of higher wage rates for the workers who have the good luck to be in industries which can pay higher wages more readily. It lost track of, or abandoned hope for, the idea that price increases in those industries which have rising unit costs could be offset by decreases in those with exceptionally rapid gains in productivity. The reward for abandonment of principle was prompt: the union membership rejected the settlement for which the President had publicly taken credit.

The strike was finally settled with an increase evaluated by the Council of Economic Advisers at 4.9 percent. The Secretary of Labor commented that the attempt to enforce the guideposts had prolonged the strike. The president of the machinists' union stated that the agreement "completely shatters" the guidepost concept. The President, and his Labor-Management Advisory Committee, meeting shortly thereafter, concluded that some new approach to wage restraint had become necessary.[26]

Storm Signals

While it is possible to find a number of instances in which the wage guidepost was used succcessfully to help restrain increases in 1965-66, and reasonable to assume that these cases had some wider influence both through example and through lessened pressure on prices leading to further cost of living adjustments, it must be recognized that acceleration of the general rise in wages as unemployment decreased was not prevented. From 1960 to 1965, average hourly compensation in manufacturing, including fringe benefits, increased at a rate of 3.5 percent per year. Between 1965 and 1966 the increase was 4.8 percent.[27]

[26] *Ibid.*, Aug. 6 and 16-21, 1966.
[27] *Economic Report of the President, 1967*, p. 83.

The rate of rise in wage rates between 1965 and 1966 was higher in many fields than it was in manufacturing. Manufacturing wages rose 3.6 percent, wholesale trade 4.6, contract construction 4.9, hotel and motel 5.9, and laundry and cleaning 5.3 percent.[28] All these increases refer to wages alone, not including fringe benefits.

It is particularly striking that wage increases in 1966 were greater in trade and services than in manufacturing, despite the low degrees of union organization in most of these fields. These are areas in which wages have long been far below the average for manufacturing, but which are more directly responsive to changes in demand pressure. Their wages are bid up in periods of high demand by firms which are trying to expand and have to induce workers to leave prior jobs because the pool of unemployed labor is insufficient, or by their old employers who suddenly find that laundry workers, store clerks, hotel and hospital workers, and everyone else, now can find better openings more easily. Even within manufacturing, recent gains have been greater for workers in the nondurable branches, where wages are generally lower than in durable goods production.

The timing of contract negotiations in the major industries can make a considerable difference to such comparisons, but it seems clear that the recent trend has been relatively favorable to the less well-organized and lower-paid workers. From many points of view, such a pattern is one of the greater blessings of pushing close to full employment. The less privileged get the greater gain because the society is able to put their capacities to better use.

From the standpoint of concern with price stability, the process is not so helpful. It raises costs when the wage gains in these fields exceed improvements in productivity, which has been the usual case, and it lessens the willlingness of the more organized groups to consider cooperation with restraints that leave their increases below those of the rest of the labor force. Added to the more fundamental problem raised by the acceleration of price increases, this change in relative wages did a great deal to intensify union opposition to the guideposts in the course of 1966, and to threaten rough weather for efforts at voluntary constraint for some time to come.

[28] *Ibid.*, p. 82.

VI

Intensified Pressure on Prices, 1965-66

FROM THE CONFLICT WITH THE steel industry in April 1962 until November 1965, the government avoided public confrontation with business over pricing decisions. When wholesale prices began to rise in the spring of 1965, more determined efforts to implement the guideposts were at first limited to wage negotiations. The calm on the side of prices was interrupted when the aluminum producers, who had already implemented a series of increases without any trouble, took one more small step upward.

Return to Direct Action: Aluminum and Steel

The aluminum companies had the misfortune to be considered a cooperative group capable of exercising discretionary control over the price of a basic commodity. While there are many firms engaged in fabricating aluminum products, the basic aluminum reduction process involves such high costs of investment and advantages of large scale that entry is difficult, and the number of firms small. Primary reduction was a monopoly of Alcoa up to World War II; there are only seven producers now, and the three largest account for 85 percent of total capacity.

Like the steel industry, the aluminum producers raised prices persistently from the late 1940's until 1957 and then began to run into trouble with import competition. The basic price of ingots moved from 15 cents a pound in 1948 to 26 cents in 1957, in twelve successive upward steps.[1] Trouble began in 1958 when the Canadian producer tried to develop sales in the United States by undercutting the going price. New disruptions kept hitting the market, and the price worked downward gradually to a low of 22.5 cents by the end of 1962. As the expansion of the economy brought the industry's capacity more fully into use, the downward pressure stopped. Reynolds Metals led an increase to 23 cents in September 1963, with all other firms quickly following. In March 1964, all prices went to 24 cents. No trouble arose when the price went up again to 24.5, but when it went to 25 it touched off the first open conflict over pricing between business and the Johnson Administration.

Two related issues got tangled together in this confrontation. One was the price increase itself. The other was the question of the conditions under which the government might properly use its stockpiles of strategic materials to affect prices.

The stockpiles were originally designed to meet possible defense production emergencies, and were built up for a great variety of commodities including aluminum. During the 1950's, when some of the industries producing strategic materials were unable to utilize their capacity fully, purchases were made for the stockpiles partly for the purpose of supporting these industries. Changing conceptions of potential military requirements and lessened concern with any need to support producers as the economic expansion got under way led to review of the situation and a decision to classify some of the stocks as being in excess of military needs. The government began to sell off these excess supplies, usually in close cooperation with producers and users of the commodities in order to avoid disrupting markets.

Negotiations for disposal of excess aluminum were being carried out with the producers for eight months prior to the dispute over prices. The producers were attempting to limit the rate of disposals below the pace preferred by the government, and to establish firm controls over the manner of disposition. The question was critical for the industry, since the part of the aluminum stockpile considered to be in excess of military needs was about 1.4 million tons, compared to an annual rate of domestic consumption running about 2.5 million. The producers were operating close to capacity, but there was no actual shortage.

[1] Merton J. Peck, *Competition in the Aluminum Industry, 1945-58* (Harvard University Press, 1961), Table 5, p. 42.

Negotiations on the stockpile were proceeding intermittently when the storm broke over prices. In terms of the price guidepost, there might well have been trouble earlier. When the industry's labor contracts were settled in June, the Council of Economic Advisers was quoted as saying that productivity in the industry was rising approximately 6 percent per year and should permit decreasing prices despite the higher wages.[2] At that time, charges on some fabricated products were raised but the price of primary ingot was not changed. As in the case of the automobile industry in 1964, administration comments were limited to pointing out that the guidepost for prices called for a decrease; no active pressure was attempted.

In October, one company after another moved the basic price up to 25 cents, an increase of about 2 percent. A confusing series of denunciations, and denials that any denunciations were intended, began to stream out of Washington. When Alcoa confirmed the increase by joining it, apparently interpreting the confusion to mean that there was no firm government position on the issue, Washington statements became much more emphatic. A distinct effort was made on all sides to avoid the impression that the steel conflict of 1962 was being repeated, but the Secretary of Defense announced that sales from the stockpile would go ahead at a rate of perhaps 200,000 tons per year, well above that preferred by the industry. It was explained that these sales were meant to help meet military production requirements, and to reduce imports; they could also be expected to "reduce price pressures."[3]

Spokesmen for the industry insisted that they had no intention of rescinding a rise that still left the price of primary aluminum below that prevailing in 1960, and that the rate of return on capital was so much below those prevailing in other branches of manufacturing that it was impossible to finance adequate expansion without the increase. Once again, the manufacturers succeeded in sounding much like the typical public utility arguing for a justified rate increase.

Neither government nor industry spokesmen seem to have made much point of an interesting difference between this case and that of the steel industry in 1962. In the earlier conflict, the attempt to increase prices was made while the industry was operating at less than two-thirds of its capac-

---

[2] *New York Times,* June 3 and 6, 1965.

[3] Press briefing of Secretary McNamara, Secretary Fowler, and Mr. Ackley, Nov. 6, 1965, p. 10.

ity. In 1965, the aluminum producers were running close to full capacity and demand was increasing rapidly. In a competitive industry, prices might well have gone up under these conditions.

After five days of discreet implications by both sides that facts were being distorted, positions misquoted, and understandings violated, an amicable agreement was announced. Alcoa rescinded its price increase, forcing the other producers to follow. The government agreed to dispose of its surplus stocks on terms close to those sought by the industry. The score for the guideposts was ambiguous: where they called for a decrease, an attempted increase was blocked, at the cost of a restriction on the government's right to sell its excess stocks in a strong market.

In the steel industry, prices changed frequently from 1962 to 1966, without conflict with the government. These changes were selective, often mixed in some decreases with the increases, and raised the index of wholesale prices for the sector by only 1.8 percent in the four years to December 1965.

At the end of December, another flareup occurred when Bethlehem Steel announced an increase of $5 per ton on structural steel. This accounts for about 7 percent of total industry deliveries, but is particularly important for Bethlehem. The increase was not accompanied by any conciliatory gestures such as prior consultation or acccompanying decreases on other products.

Within a few hours of Bethlehem's announcement, the Chairman of the Council of Economic Advisers had issued an analysis and statement denouncing the move. According to the Council, labor costs per ton had fallen persistently in the preceding five years, and there was no basis for a price increase under the guidepost policy. Company officials met with the Council, at the President's request, but rejected a proposal that the increase be delayed until the reasons for it could be studied thoroughly.

The conflict was suddenly resolved by the intervention of a conciliatory industrial statesman, disguised as the U.S. Steel Company. U.S. Steel suggested that it would like to implement increases of $2.50 a ton on structural steel, and also to reduce prices on other products of no great importance to Bethlehem. Both sides accepted the suggestion, and Bethlehem kept one-half of the increase it had originally announced.

This new tone in the industry was strengthened the following month, when U.S. Steel presented another package of increases and decreases on its own. The Council of Economic Advisers had suggested repeatedly that companies considering possible increases on important products notify the Council in advance and discuss the issues when the case seemed doubtful. U.S. Steel became the first company, so far as has been made known publicly, to accept the suggestion. Its decision to increase extra charges for some types of plate steel was accompanied by the statement that quoted prices for nails and some forms of wire rod subject to particularly intense import competition were being dropped to free the company to cut prices more readily against such competition. The set of changes was then blessed with an official statement of approval by the Council.[4]

The new harmony was jarred in August, when Inland Steel announced, without prior consultation, a straight-forward increase of $3 a ton, or about 2 percent, on sheet steel. This increase hit an important product without any compensating decreases to mitigate the blow. The Council did not denounce the company but immediately sent requests to the other major producers to delay action on the matter until they had discussed the issues with the government. Some replied, some did not. All, including U.S. Steel, followed the increase. The Chairman of the Council then issued a critical statement, but no further action followed, and the increase went fully into effect.[5]

Although the issues were not debated, it is probable that the companies would have made a forceful case about the effects of previous forbearance on their profit margins. Most of them had within the previous weeks issued financial reports showing that their sales had increased substantially in the first half of 1966 but that their total profits had fallen. Most of them could argue that their rates of return in 1965 had been far down on the list for manufacturing industries, despite operations at a high level in excellent market conditions. They could make these arguments because the guideposts had worked when the case for price increases was more doubtful. It might have helped move the implementation of the guideposts in more flexible directions if the companies had used the occasion to discuss the issues beforehand rather than to reassert their lack of interest in negotiation.

[4] *New York Times,* March 1, 1966.
[5] *Ibid.,* Aug. 4 and 5, 1966.

More Doubtful Cases: Copper and Hides

In late 1965 copper became involved in negotiations concerning sales from the stockpile and the reversal of an announced price increase, but the outward similarity to the aluminum case confused some important differences. This instance involved a step beyond participation in the administrative decisions of a small number of firms with considerable control of the market. The copper case was a more complex arrangement to stabilize prices for a product previously supplied on a fairly competitive basis. It was a move from attempts to share in existing management of markets toward the creation of greater market control.

Most of the American copper supply is provided by a few large firms, both through domestic production and through imports from their mining properties abroad. But these companies can hardly be said to control the market. They are subject to competitive pressure from independent customs smelters who buy scrap and process it for resale, from alternative metals, and, at least potentially, from noncontrolled imports. Outside the United States, there is an active world market for which demand and supply conditions are continuously indicated by quotations on the London Metals Exchange. This is not to imply that the world price is immune to deliberate action by producers: a series of export cartel arrangements, or informal decisions by some producers to build inventories and purchase supplies for withholding in order to keep up the London price, has made the latter somewhat less than perfect as an indicator of current demand and cost relationships.[6] But such efforts have always broken down after varying periods of succcess in establishing an arbitrary world price, just as the pressure of the customs smelters has invariably undermined efforts at arbitrary pricing within the United States.

The major American producers have frequently expressed a preference for greater price stability, even at the cost of foregoing increases in periods of shortage. They have explained this in terms of the belief that widely fluctuating prices shift preferences of industrial buyers toward inputs with

[6] Olin T. Mouzon, *Resources and Industries of the United States* (Appleton-Century-Crofts, 1966), pp. 406-17.

more stable prices, and in particular that periods of sharply higher costs for copper stimulate efforts to find substitutes which may become permanent even though copper prices come back down again. Besides, there is not much prestige in the industrial hierarchy for big companies which do not seem able to maintain some degree of order in their markets.

Although the producers fix quoted prices and try to adhere to them, the market forces acting to maintain flexibility have remained strong. When demand is weak, the customs smelters shade the quoted price of the mining companies, and can sell sufficient quantities to bring the price down. When demand is strong, the customs smelters charge a premium over the primary quotation.

The major producers have shown on several occasions, notably in 1955-56 and again in 1964-66, that they value stability so highly as to sacrifice current profits by holding the quoted price down and resorting to rationing among their customers while secondary copper sells at a premium. Still, there is a limit to patience in all things. The primary price in the U.S. market crept up from an average of 30.0 to 32.6 cents a pound between 1961 and 1964, then moved more impressively to 36 cents in May 1965 and 38 cents in November.[7]

Quotations on the London exchange moved up in parallel with the American price between 1961 and 1963, then more swiftly than the American in 1964-65. As indicated by futures quotations for deliveries one month ahead, the price for secondary copper in the American market moved more like the London price, well ahead of that quoted by the primary producers. At the time that the first primary producer announced a move from 36 to 38 cents, the secondary price was about 57 cents and the London quotation close to 70. The major producers were rationing deliveries of their production and imports, and perhaps one-third of the market was being supplied through purchases from others at premium prices.[8]

As the rest of the major domestic producers shifted from 36 to 38 cents, government officials declared that an increase was not warranted, and arranged meetings with the companies. On November 17, the Secretary of Defense announced that at least 200,000 tons of copper would be sold from the stockpile to alleviate a shortage for defense production. The

[7] Averages from U.S. Bureau of Mines, *Minerals Yearbook, 1964,* p. 415; other price quotations from the *New York Times.*

[8] *Ibid.,* Nov. 2 and 18-21, 1965.

decision and the industry reaction had different tones than had been the case with respect to aluminum. This was not a bargaining threat but an offer of supplies that would ease rationing problems. It would possibly bring the price of secondary copper down toward the primary quotation but was hardly likely to put any pressure on the latter. The government also suspended the tariff on copper imports and instituted controls on exports, to assure adequate supplies and in the process to provide a protective device for a policy of maintaining domestic prices below the world market level.

On November 19, the two leading producers cut their quotation back to 36 cents. They were followed down by the others, while the secondary market and the London price remained far higher. The producers made no public complaints. They were assured in any case of good profits by high volume and by a price 20 percent above the average of 1961. But the relevant test of such a decision can hardly rest on the question of whether or not the companies accept it easily. A competitive market solution would surely have dictated a higher price, as it was doing in the secondary market.

Although the new situation was accepted by the American producers, another party at interest was resentful about it. This was the government of Chile. Copper is Chile's main source of foreign exchange earnings to pay for the imports it needs and is also a major part of the domestic tax base. Most of these exports come from mines owned by the American companies and go to the United States, for sale at the controlled domestic price. Chile was being asked to subsidize American users of copper by accepting lower export earnings than could be obtained by sales at London market prices. In partial compensation, the American tariff on copper was temporarily suspended, with the effect of raising the net return to the producers by the difference of 1.7 cents a pound. Chile maintained its previous rate of exports to the United States and sold additional output in the world market at a temporarily fixed price of 42 cents.

The official Chilean export price to world markets stayed at 42 cents until April 1966, but at that point the government ordered that it be increased to 62 cents, bringing it further out of touch with the American market and closer to the London quotation. This led to a new set of agreements among the companies and the two governments, including a loan from the United States to Chile, a new tax arrangements for the mines there, the opening up of some export sales to other markets at 62 cents.

continued suspension of American tariffs, and continued deliveries to the United States at the controlled American price.[9]

A complex system of prices resulted from the agreement. Chilean exports other than those to the United States remained at 62 cents for some time, with the London market moderately above this until the Chileans decided to accept the London price in August; the secondary price in the United States continued below the London quotations, falling slowly from 60 cents to 48 in August; and the official primary price stayed at 36. All this for a standardized commodity on which prices had previously been determined by competitive forces.

One explanation suggested for the tenacity of the government's effort to hold the price down in the context of persistent rationing is that the shortage was expected to be over fairly quickly. At 36 cents, profits were high and incentives to expand production were strong. Further, the shortages in 1965-66 could conceivably be eased by the solution of strikes and political obstacles to sales in several important producing countries. If the pattern to be expected were such that an uncontrolled market would shoot the price upward for a few months and then let it fall back down again, not a great deal would be lost by controlling it in the meantime. This could avoid building in higher costs and accentuating signs of inflation in the interval, while not destroying incentives.

The problem is, of course, the difficulty of knowing how future demand and supply will work out. It is rarely easy to distinguish between a temporary swing and a movement to a new situation that may persist. The implied forecast in this case, that copper supply would quickly become plentiful at 36 cents, was an interesting case of contrary forecasting between the government and the copper purchasers. The latter were paying premiums on the order of 50 percent for deliveries under future contracts for a full year ahead. One year after the November agreement the government forecasters seemed to be better than the industrialists: secondary prices had fallen more than half-way back to the primary level. They remained well above the price of 38 cents which the government had rejected as too high. In January 1967, the major producers tried again to move to 38 cents, and this time there was no reaction.

As long as a system of multiple prices remains in effect the possible abuses of rationing as practiced by the primary producers at fixed prices, of diversion from the primary to the secondary market, or even of illegal

[9] *Ibid.*, Jan. 21, 26, and 31, March 22, April 15 and 23, 1966.

exports, involve evident difficulties that could become progressively more troublesome. The solution reached would not appear to be one that could or should be maintained for very long.

Something happened in March 1966 to make this a particularly lively month for efforts to restrain particular prices. Various forms of intervention were publicly reported, some as new cases and some referring to earlier private negotiations, for hides and shoes, residual fuel oil, cigarettes, and newsprint. Of these, the mixture of gains and losses from the point of view of economic efficiency seemed to be particularly negative for hides and shoes.

Neither hides nor shoes constitute markets in which there is any high degree of private control. Organized markets provide competitive channels for pricing and distributing hides. The shoe industry is not tightly organized either on the company or on the labor side. New entry to the industry is not unusually difficult. Bain considered in his study of entry barriers that they were of some significance for higher-priced shoes, but that entry was so easy as to lead to persistently excessive numbers of firms and excess capacity for standard shoes.[10] There has been a steady attrition among the smaller firms in the last decade, but there are still a large number of producers. Some of them are not unionized. As might be expected in this context, wages are well below the average for manufacturing in general.

The reason that the shoe industry became involved in negotiations with the Council of Economic Advisers seems to have been that prices were going up very fast. The wholesale price index for footwear had been steady from 1962 through 1964, but it then increased 4.4 percent in the year to December 1965. The rise accelerated in 1966, reaching by March a level 8.8 percent higher than that of a year earlier.[11] The companies blamed this on the cost of hides for producing leather. Prices of hides and skins had fallen steeply between 1962 and 1963 without bringing shoe prices down, but when they went back up in 1965, they were cited as the main reason for higher shoe prices. They did go up fast in 1965, rising 47 percent in the course of the year. The cause seemed to be the effect of high demand for domestic and export sales impinging on limited supply.

Labor costs were given less attention than the price of hides, perhaps because wages were not rising particularly fast. Gross hourly earnings

---

[10] Joe S. Bain, *Barriers to New Competition* (Harvard University Press, 1956).
[11] U.S. Office of Business Economics, *Survey of Current Business* (May 1966), Table S-8.

went up at a rate of 2.8 percent per year from 1961 to 1965.[12] But this is an industry in which the rate of gain in productivity is below average. The long-term rate of increase in production per man-hour for all employees, measured from 1947 to 1964, was about 2.1 percent. From 1959 to 1964, the rate of gain was only 1.0 percent, less than one-third that of all manufacturing.[13] In terms of the guideposts, this is an industry in which prices should be expected to rise.

On March 10, the government announced that a ceiling would be placed on the export of hides in order to alleviate domestic shortages. Exports were limited to the volume realized in 1964. The price of hides for July delivery fell promptly from 26 to 21 cents a pound. Representatives of the shoe industry met with the Council of Economic Advisers and the Secretary of Commerce, and promised to restrain shoe prices if controls were kept on the exports of hides. Almost immediately thereafter, leading shoe companies announced increases ranging from 2 to 7 percent on their lines for the fall of 1966. They explained that the increases were due to preceding cost pressures, and would have been greater in the absence of the export limitation.[14]

It would be difficult to defend this operation in terms of its economic effects. In the copper industry, the restriction placed on exports applied to a commodity in which the United States is a net importer. Any ability to prevent exaggerated swings in copper prices could conceivably aid exports of products using this input. In the case of hides and shoes, an export was blocked to prevent it reaching the levels it would in an open market, for the purpose of restraining prices of a commodity aimed almost exclusively at domestic consumption. Exports were sacrificed to permit higher consumption. Not many exports, it is true. But something is at times worse than nothing.

Extension of the General Approach

As if to make up for misdirected effort in the case of hides and shoes, the stabilization program led to an important improvement in foreign trade

[12] U.S. Bureau of Labor Statistics, *Monthly Labor Review*, Vol. 89, No. 4 (April 1966), Table C-1.
[13] "Output per Man-Hour in the Footwear Industry," *ibid.*, pp. 401-04, Table 1.
[14] *New York Times,* March 11, 26, and 29, 1966.

policy when applied to fuel oil. The change here is of great interest as an indication of the way in which efforts to limit inflation by investigating the causes of pressure on particular prices may widen out from the range originally suggested by the guideposts. No question of analyzing productivity trends, employment levels, or labor costs was involved; the objective was simply to forestall an expected increase in a specific price. The result, accomplished with an ease that must have astonished those who had fought over the issue for a decade, was to reverse a policy that had seemed permanently entrenched.

Oil imports had become a highly significant factor in the domestic market after 1945, as American companies found and developed oil abroad at costs much below those possible in the United States. The imports were profitable to the companies which developed the new supplies, and had the effect of keeping oil products cheaper in the domestic market. The latter aspect was not welcomed by those producers who continued to depend on domestic supplies. These were in general smaller companies, well-organized through the Independent Petroleum Association.

A coalition of the domestic oil producers and the coal industry convinced the Eisenhower Administration to impose restrictions on oil imports in 1957. Total imports were to be held to a fixed fraction of domestic consumption, and licenses were reserved for those companies which had been importers in 1957. The rationalization given was that the limitations would, by reducing supplies and holding up prices, make it more profitable to explore for new sources in the United States and thus to build up reserves for possible wartime emergencies. The peculiar logic involved in forcing greater use of American oil reserves and preserving Middle Eastern supplies in peacetime, in order to prepare for possible future interruptions in access to foreign supplies, has been particularly well dissected by James Nelson.[15] The operation was essentially a means to raise the incomes of domestic oil producers, and perhaps to some extent of the coal industry, at the expense of the rest of the economy.

The import restrictions hit New England particularly adversely. The region does not produce any of its own fuel for space heating or electric power generation, and was now denied the right to buy from the cheapest

---

[15] "Prices, Costs and Conservation in Petroleum," *American Economic Review*, Vol. 48 (May, 1958), pp. 502-15. See also Melvin de Chazeau and Alfred E. Kahn, *Integration and Competition in the Petroleum Industry* (Yale University Press, 1959), Chap. 9, and Sebastian Raciti, *The Oil Import Problem* (Fordham University Press, 1958).

source of supply. The limitations frequently meant that fuel costs took a major upward jump when requirements rose in the winter. It was regarded as probable that such an increase would be forthcoming in December 1965, as so often before, but the government's intensified interest in price stabilization came to the rescue. The Secretary of the Interior decided to add an extra quota for imports of residual fuel oil from December through March 1966. This was followed up in March by a decision to open licenses to all importers who could obtain contracts for domestic sales, thereby effectively removing the controls instituted in 1957. The policy of trying to restrain particular prices thus broke down a stubbornly defended system blocking market forces in order to maintain special privilege.

Again in the context of efforts to get at the causes of specific problems rather than as any direct application of the guideposts, the Council of Economic Advisers, in reviews of the price situation, has given a great deal of attention to the costs of medical care. The reason for concern is that the cost of medical care, which now accounts for 6 percent of all consumer expenditures and is growing continuously in relative importance, has risen about twice as fast as the average of all other consumer prices in the postwar period.[16] The major factors underlying this striking disparity were summarized by the Council as "the inadequate supply of personnel and facilities, the sharply rising cost of hospital construction and of continually more complex medical equipment, the rapid increases in salaries of medical personnel relative to productivity gains as presently measured, and the expanding demand for medical services."[17]

The rate of increase in the cost of medical care slowed down slightly after 1960, but then increased again in the first half of 1966. The impending start of Medicare, expected both to raise demand and to change traditional methods of charging for medical services, stimulated revisions of fees at the professional level and pressures for major improvements in salaries by long-underpaid nurses and other hospital personnel. With costs rising sharply again, even prior to any significant increase in the number of patients, governmental concern with the area intensified. This took the outward form of a novel antitrust suit against the American College of Pa-

---

[16] *Economic Report of the President, 1966,* p. 86. For a detailed review of earlier data and of factors determining costs, see Markley Roberts, "Trends in the Supply and Demand of Medical Care," Study Paper No. 5, Joint Economic Committee, *Employment, Growth, and Price Levels,* 86 Cong. 1 sess. (1959).

[17] *Economic Report of the President, 1966,* p. 87.

thologists for practices believed to be forcing charges up artificially, and then of a directive from the President to the Secretary of Health, Education, and Welfare to begin a thorough study of medical costs in general.[18]

The impending study of medical costs was not presented as having any connections with the guideposts, and it is possible that it will not have. But it is also conceivable that the issues encountered will include such questions as "catching up" by the lower-paid hospital personnel, and the pace at which professional fees might legitimately be increased, as well as entry conditions affecting long-term income trends for everyone involved. Labor unions have repeatedly objected to the idea of limiting the rate of increase in wages without trying to do anything about professional incomes. Perhaps the effort to negotiate limits will be given up in both directions; it is hard to see how, or why, they might be pushed on one side without complementary treatment on the other. The general strategy of the guideposts, with all its unanswered questions, would seem to be intimately involved. The fact that the guideposts have been given a trial may even alter the probabilities that something will be done to limit the rate of increase in the cost of medical care.

Quieter Negotiations and Continuing Questions

Behind the scenes of periodic public confrontations, the administration continuously endeavored to keep in touch with business and labor about impending decisions, and sometimes took an active role in calling meetings to underline interest in making them conform to the objective of greater price stability. Especially during 1963-64, and again in the latter part of 1966, outward evidence of conflict was strenuously avoided in favor of informal discussion. This approach has evident merits in any program emphasizing voluntary cooperation, but also makes it somewhat frustrating to try to describe what has happened and how much it may have amounted to. In the latter part of 1966, the Council of Economic Advisers was apparently receiving several inquiries a week from business officials, and was engaged from time to time in organizing informal conferences. As the Council states, "The outcome of these activities cannot be fully known."[19]

[18] *New York Times,* July 8 and Aug. 23, 1966.
[19] *Economic Report of the President, 1967,* p. 127.

Negotiations did come to light with respect to cigarettes in March, some indirect influence of the guideposts was suggested by the press as relevant to gyrations in newsprint prices in the same month, and a successful accord after a brief clash was reported for molybdenum in July. These cases may represent a small sample of many quiet successes, or they may constitute all the success that was achieved during this period.

The episode with the cigarette industry involved another concentrated group of firms with a long record of price leadership and cooperation serving to moderate competition.[20] Labor costs are of relatively minor importance, but the companies have to cope with rising costs of tobacco under governmental price support programs. Using the argument that prices for leaf tobacco had risen 10 percent in the 1965-66 season, the American Tobacco Company announced on March 15 an increase in cigarette prices equal to .8 cents per pack. All the other companies followed quickly.

With the new level of wholesale prices established and moving into effect at retail, Reynolds Tobacco surprised everyone by backing out. Company spokesmen stated that they had made this decision in response to appeals by the President to avoid consumer price increases, after talking to government officials about it. American Tobacco had talks with government officials too, and then announced with some irritation that they would take back half of the price increase but no more. The other companies lined up, or down, with American. Reynolds held to a lower price for a while, then joined the rest. For better or worse, direct negotiations seemed to have succeeded in making cigarettes cheaper than they were apparently destined to become.[21]

Prices of newsprint went through somewhat similar convolutions at the same time. Leading Canadian and American producers announced increases of $10 a ton, provoking a great deal of complaint by the American Newspaper Publishers Association and a number of regional newspaper groups. Amid much talk of appeals to Congress about this outrage, some of the companies which had not taken part in the price rise came out with alternative increases of $5 a ton. Some firms tried $7 for a time, but all eventually settled on a rise of $5. No reports of intervention by government spokesmen were made public, but press discussion gave credit to the

[20] Joe S. Bain, *Industrial Organization* (J. Wiley and Sons, 1959), pp. 126, 306-08.

[21] *New York Times*, March 16, 19, and 22, 1966.

guideposts as an inspiration by example for the compromise settlement.[22]

The chairman of the Council of Economic Advisers made a public statement in July opposing an increase of 5 percent in the price of molybdenum announced by the American Metals Climax Company. This company accounts for more than half of total supply for the countries outside the Soviet bloc. The other two major producers are Kennecott Copper and the Molybdenum Corporation of America. The metal is used as an alloying agent in producing stainless steel, and has several other important applications. Despite a severe shortage, the price had been constant since April 1964. The government had already sold its supplies to alleviate the shortage, with the approval and cooperation of the industry.

The Council's criticism of the increase by American Metals Climax pointed particularly at the company's high rate of profit on its molybdenum operations, estimated to be in excess of 30 percent on net worth.[23] The criticism did not deter the Molybdenum Company of America from following the increase, making the case look like a clear defeat for the government. Nevertheless, after talks with the Council of Economic Advisers, American Metals Climax announced that it was voluntarily taking back its announced increase. The company apparently accepted the administration's argument that higher prices and profits in this field could have serious effects on future wage negotiations as well as on prices in other industries.

The success in molybdenum was almost immediately overshadowed by the government's abandonment of efforts to defend the wage guideposts in the airlines settlement of August, and utter failure to affect the increase in steel prices led by Inland Steel at the same time, as discussed above.

The generally quieter negotiations which apparently continued on a variety of fronts provoke serious questions about government-industry relations. In particular, conferences bringing together representatives of leading firms in an industry to discuss prices might seem doubtful practice for a government committed to enforcement of the antitrust laws. Maybe there has been nothing to worry about; maybe there has.

Apart from the possibility of introducing more cooperation on prices than would otherwise have occurred, such conferences lead to doubts regarding what the government may give to the business community in re-

[22] *Ibid.*, March 1, 7, 8, 16, 17, and 19, 1966.
[23] *Ibid.*, July 12, 14, and 16, 1966.

turn for cooperation. The limitation on exports of hides to aid the shoe industry was a bad sign. No good purpose is served by a state of warfare between government and business, but neither would it be desirable to extend favors to particular groups through this process without open hearings for all interested parties. The wage guidepost itself tends naturally to line up government and industry on the same side in wage negotiations. The possibilities of cooperation to a point unduly favorable for particular groups is hard to rule out when the content of negotiations is not made public.

Enough cases of successful limitation on prices were obtained through July 1966 to establish a firm claim that the guideposts were not being applied exclusively to labor. On the other hand, arrangements such as those reached in copper, shoes, and molybdenum pose questions about the reality of the economic advantage achieved.

Finally, a widening of the techniques involved in seeking more stable prices made it more than ever uncertain what might properly be considered an implementation of the guideposts, as distinct from general strategy against inflation. Perhaps it is not helpful to try to make any such distinction. It might be more illuminating to consider the guideposts as a point of reference for a much wider strategy of trying to give greater coherence to the whole range of administrative choices which bear on specific prices.

VII

Impact of the Guideposts

THE FIRST FOUR YEARS of the guideposts' existence were characterized by a change toward greater stability of prices and wages. As compared to the immediately preceding four years of slower growth and
higher unemployment, the rate of increase in prices was closely similar
and the rate of increase in wages was less. As compared either to the
whole postwar period from 1947 to 1961, or to 1953-61, both prices and
wages were more nearly stable.

It is impossible to prove or to disprove the hypothesis that the guideposts were an important factor in this achievement. This is because no one
can be completely sure of what would have happened if they had not existed. Comparison to past relationships indicates simply that the period in
which they were applied was one of considerable gain.

From mid-1965, both prices and wages began to rise more rapidly.
This does not prove that the guideposts ceased to have any relevance.
Neither prices nor wages went up as fast as might have been expected in
terms of earlier relationships. Still, they went up too fast for continued
public acceptance, despite intensified efforts to apply administrative restraints. Table 2 summarizes some of the main indicators.

It is evident that the period 1961-65 started with an advantage, given
the decision to abandon previous deflationary policies and promote expansion, in that the level of unemployment at the start was exceptionally
high. This made it easier to get rising output per man-hour as increased
production enabled firms to use existing equipment and employees more
effectively, and it meant that there were few if any bottlenecks in labor or

79

TABLE 2

Rates of Increase in Prices and Wages, and Average Rates of
Unemployment, Selected Periods from 1947 to 1966

Period	Average Annual Increase, Percentage				
	Wholesale Prices	Consumer Prices	Hourly Earnings in Manufacturing Excluding Overtime	Total Compensation per Hour in Private Economy	Average Percent of Labor Force Unemployed[a]
1947–61	1.5	2.1	4.8	4.9	4.8
1953–61	1.0	1.4	3.7	4.2	5.4
1957–61	0.3	1.5	3.1	3.9	6.2
1961–65	0.5	1.3	2.7	3.6	5.3
1965–66	3.2	2.9	3.6	6.5	3.9

Sources: *Economic Report of the President, 1965*, p. 109; *1967*, p. 83 and Tables B-20, B-29, B-42, B-44.
[a] Unemployment percentages refer to simple averages of annual figures for unemployment as a percent of the civilian labor force, excluding the base year and including the terminal year of each period.

materials. Any attempt to find underlying changes in price or wage behavior must take into account differences in the degree of unemployment and idle capacity, as has been done in various ways in the studies discussed below.

Changes in Prices

A relatively simple and suggestive review of price changes by the Federal Reserve Bank of Cleveland serves to bring out the fact that, for any given level of unemployment, wholesale prices were more nearly stable in 1961-65 than they had been in preceding years.[1] The Bank's study relates changes in wholesale prices to concurrent levels of unemployment, without bringing in any other explanatory variable.

Plotting increases in the index of wholesale industrial prices against quarterly averages for the percentage of the labor force unemployed, the study shows that prices for the period 1954-60 tended to go up when unemployment was below 6.5 percent and to go down when it was higher than that rate. For 1961-65, the unemployment rate consistent with stable

[1] Federal Reserve Bank of Cleveland, "Prices: Patterns and Expectations," *Economic Review* (April 1966).

FIGURE 2

Industrial Wholesale Prices and Rate of Unemployment

(Quarterly, 1954-65)

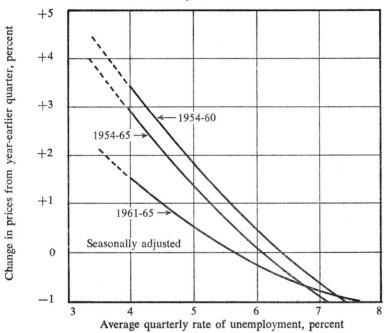

Source: Federal Reserve Bank of Cleveland, *Economic Review* (April 1966), p. 4.

wholesale prices appeared to have been reduced to approximately 5.8 percent.[2]

The schedule relating increases in wholesale prices to the percentage of unemployment shifted downward between 1954-60 and 1961-65, as shown on the Figure 2. A quarterly average rate of unemployment equal to 4 percent corresponded to a price increase of about 3.4 percent in the earlier period, and about 1.5 percent in 1961-65. The lower the rate of unemployment, the greater the difference in price behavior.

More elaborate statistical tests by Frank Brechling and by Robert Solow, using two different approaches, came to the same conclusion that the rate of price increase was reduced as compared to earlier relationships. Brechling examined the behavior of the GNP deflator and of wholesale prices for manufacturing products for the period from 1954 to the

[2] *Ibid.,* p. 4, Chart 2.

first quarter of 1966. He tried to predict quarterly changes in the GNP deflator on the basis of deviations of GNP from its trend rate of growth, plus hypothetically exogenous changes in farm prices. He found a significant break in the series after 1961, with a gradual rise thereafter in the excess of predicted over actual price increases.[3] A similar test applied to wholesale industrial prices gave a corresponding result, except that the reduction of actual below predicted prices remained constant instead of growing progressively.

A possible difficulty with both the Brechling and Cleveland Bank studies is that they do not separate out the contribution to price stability which may have come from more rapid improvements in productivity. Comparing the two time periods used in the latter analysis, there was a significant difference in the rate of growth of output per man-hour in manufacturing. It was 2.8 percent per year from 1954 to 1960, and 4.2 percent from 1960 to 1965.[4] Whether this difference might have accounted for part of the change in price behavior is an open question. Productivity improvements may act chiefly to permit rising factor prices, and differential productivity gains need not be associated systematically with changes in the price index.

As a test of the relevance of differences in the rate of growth of productivity, annual changes in output per man-hour may be introduced, along with the level of unemployment, in a joint regression attempting to explain annual changes in wholesale industrial prices by the two independent variables. The resulting regression equation, fitted to data for 1947-61, proved to be statistically significant at the 5 percent level.[5] It is

---

[3] "Some Empirical Evidence on the Effectiveness of Price and Incomes Policies," paper presented to the Canadian Political Science Association, June 1966, p. 16 (mimeo.). The dummy variable introduced to catch changes in behavior after 1961 proved to have a negative coefficient three times its standard error.

[4] *Economic Report of the President, 1963,* p. 209, Table C-32, and "The State of the Economy and the Problem of Price Stability" Aug. 30, 1966, (mimeo.).

[5] Where P stands for the percentage change in wholesale industrial prices, u for the level of unemployment, and v for the percentage change in output per man-hour in manufacturing, the regression equation is:

$$P = 13.100 - 2.112u + 0.002v$$
$$(0.632) \quad (0.394)$$
$$R^2 = .51; \quad F \text{ value} = 5.685$$

The regression coefficient for the unemployment variable is significant at the 1 percent level. The productivity variable turns out to be irrelevant.

Sources: prices and unemployment from *Economic Report of the President,*

not impressive as a means of explaining price changes, because it accounts for only 51 percent of the year-to-year variation. But it does help answer the question about the effect on prices of changes in productivity: they do not seem to play any systematic role.

The purpose of using data for 1947-61 to fit the preceding regression equation is that it permits another check on possible change in price behavior after 1961. The test is similar to that used by the Cleveland Bank, but applied to annual changes rather than quarterly, and for a different period. This method predicts price changes for 1962-65 averaging 1.6 percentage points above actual increases. Extended to 1966, the indicated deflection in price behavior increased to 2.8 percentage points.

An alternative method used by Robert Solow also takes productivity changes into account, by relating changes in wholesale prices for manufacturing to measures of the degree of capacity utilization and to changes in unit labor costs. This approach differs from the preceding in that it does not rely on unemployment data, and that it abstracts from any possible changes in wage behavior. He estimated that the actual rate of price increase after 1962 was 0.6 to 0.7 percentage points per year less than expected from earlier relationships.[6]

The Behavior of Wages in Manufacturing

Frank Brechling, Otto Eckstein, and George Perry carried out independent statistical investigations of the behavior of wage rates in manufacturing, and all concluded that there was a significant shift in the schedule relating wage increases to levels of unemployment after the introduction of the guideposts. All of them relied on the official series for unemployment as one of the key variables explaining the rate of changes in wages. Norman Simler and Alfred Tella introduced an alternative measure of pressure in labor markets, adding to the number of those officially reported as

---

1967; productivity in manufacturing from Jerome A. Mark and Elizabeth Kahn, "Unit Labor Costs in Nine Countries," *Monthly Labor Review,* Vol. 88 (September 1965), p. 1058, Table 2.

[6] The "Wage-Price Issue and the Guideposts," in Frederick Harbison and Joseph Mooney, *Critical Issues in Employment Policy* (Princeton Manpower Symposium, May 1966), p. 67. The stated result, "just fails of statistical significance."

unemployed an estimate for reserves of potential workers who voluntarily withdraw from the labor force when demand is low. This method leads to a lower estimate of expected wage change for the period 1961-66, and thus less of a gap between expected and actual wage increases. The conclusion is in the same direction as the others: actual wage increases in the period turned out to be less than predicted on the basis of prior relationships.

Brechling explained changes in wages by the level of unemployment and its change in the preceding year, plus the rate of change in the consumer price index. The estimated rate of increase in wages began to overshoot actual increases by a widening margin after 1961. By the end of 1965, the annual rate of increase in money wages was 1.6 percentage points below the prediction based on preceding behavior.[7]

Perry used four explanatory variables: the rate of unemployment during the year preceding each quarter's change in wages, the immediately preceding change in the cost of living, the rate of return on capital in manufacturing industries, and the rate of change in profits. Together, these four factors accounted for 88 percent of the variation in quarterly rates of change for manufacturing wages from 1947 to 1960. Each of them had a significant independent effect in explaining changes in wages, as measured by the degree to which each reduced the percentage of variance left unexplained by calculations using the other three.[8] (See Table 3.)

Using these same explanatory variables, Perry tested the behavior of wages in the 1920's, for 1947-60, and for the subperiods 1947-53 and 1953-60. The tests showed that wage behavior was anything but rigidly determined; the coefficients changed in each of the periods. In contrast to Phillips' conclusion from his study of the United Kingdom, wage behavior seems to alter in response to many factors other than the rate of unemployment.[9]

---

[7] Brechling, *op. cit.*, pp. 15-16.

[8] The reduction in unexplained variance attributed to each variable (the square of the partial correlation coefficient for each) is as follows:

lagged change in consumer price index	.508
lagged change in percentage of unemployment	.501
lagged rate of profit	.456
rate of change in profit	.316

Unemployment, Money Wage Rates, and Inflation (Massachusetts Institute of Technology Press, 1966), p. 52, Table 3.2.

[9] Ibid., pp. 70-77, 80-84.

TABLE 3

Differences Between Actual Increases in Manufacturing Wages and Increases Estimated on the Basis of Relationships Established for Preceding Years, 1962–66

Quarter	Actual Percentage Increases Minus Those Estimated from Relationships for 1947–60	Actual Percentage Increases Minus Those Estimated from Relationships for 1953–60
1962–I	0.84	0.75
–II	0.07	0.08
–III	−0.52	−0.59
–IV	−0.71	−0.71
1963–I	−0.97	−0.96
–II	−0.37	−0.48
–III	−0.19	−0.22
–IV	−0.18	−0.31
1964–I	−0.27	−0.53
–II	−0.77	−0.97
–III	−0.73	−0.95
–IV	−1.72	−1.77
1965–I	−1.68	−1.82
–II	−1.63	−1.75
–III	−2.11	−2.35
–IV	−1.61	−1.88
1966–I	−2.48	−2.79

Source: G. L. Perry, "Wages and The Guideposts," *American Economic Review*, forthcoming.

The method used to check on the possible role of the guideposts was to estimate the way wages would have behaved from 1961 to 1966 on the basis of the relationships established for earlier years and to compare these estimates to actual changes.[10] Perry used both his relationships for 1947-60 and for 1953-60, and they gave the same answer. Wages in manufacturing increased less rapidly from 1961 to 1966 than movements in unemployment, consumer prices, and profits would indicate as likely on the basis of preceding behavior. The differences widened through the period. Compared to what would have been expected from 1954-60 wage be-

[10] Tests on data subsequent to that available at the time of publishing of his book are reported in "Wages and The Guideposts," *American Economic Review*, forthcoming.

havior, the downward deflection averaged about 0.9 percentage points per year for the whole period, and 1.5 percentage points for 1965.

Both Brechling and Perry tested the behavior of wages, and not that of total compensation. This left open the possibility that part of the observed change in wage behavior may have been offset by a shift toward greater emphasis on fringe benefits. It has been true throughout most postwar years that hourly compensation has increased faster than hourly wages. This would not pose any problem about the conclusions of these studies if the relationship between the two rates of increase were unchanged in the 1960's, but would do so if the rate of gain in compensation had speeded up relative to that of wages.

For the whole period 1947-65, hourly compensation in manufacturing increased at a rate of 5.1 percent per year, and average hourly earnings at 4.3 percent.[11] Compensation thus increased 19 percent faster than wages. From 1960 to 1965 compensation increased 3.5 percent per year, and average hourly earnings 2.9 percent. The increase in the rate of gain in compensation was then 21 percent faster than that of wages. Increases in compensation apparently did not shift downward quite as much as increases in wages. The difference is small. It could account for about 0.1 percentage points per year. That is, Perry's measure of the downward deflection in wage behavior, averaging 0.9 percentage points through 1965, would suggest a deflection of about 0.8 percentage points in compensation.[12]

Both Brechling and Perry worked with quarterly data. This concentrates attention on the response of wages to current market conditions, but the results are subject to possible distortion from long-period wage contracts. Such contracts provide for periodic increases that are independent of market conditions at the time they go into effect, thus doing their bit to make statistical testing of wage determinants more difficult. Otto Eckstein and Thomas Wilson developed a framework of analysis in terms of three-year wage rounds intended to deal with this problem, and Eckstein subsequently applied the same technique to test changes in wage behavior after the introduction of the guideposts.[13]

The system as originally developed gave highly precise estimates of

[11] Economic Report of the President, 1967, Table 12, p. 83, and Table B-27, p. 245.

[12] Results for tests going through 1966 would require more serious correction: the relative rate of gain in compensation speeded up markedly.

[13] "The Determinants of Money Wages in American Industry," Quarterly Journal of Economics, Vol. 76 (1962), pp. 379-414; Eckstein, "Money Wage Determination Revisited," March 1967 (Mimeo.).

wage changes in manufacturing through 1960. Applied to a new wage round from December 1960 through December 1963, for durable goods manufacturing industries, the method gave estimated average wage increases of 2.0 percent. The actual rate of increase was above this, averaging 2.5 percent. Eckstein's conclusion was that the downward wage deviations calculated by Brechling and Perry for this period are explicable in terms of the restraining effects of prior multiyear contracts.

For the next three-year period, through 1966, the wage round method applied to durable goods manufacturing industries gave expected wage increases of 6.7 to 7.0 percent, in contrast to an actual average of 2.7 percent. Eckstein concluded that there was a significant change in wage behavior in this group of industries, consistent with the degree of change indicated by Perry's short-period tests for all manufacturing. Finally, he noted that long-period wage contracts signed from mid-1966 onward began to move back toward the values suggested by the wage round system of prediction.

All three of the above sets of tests use the officially reported figures on unemployment as one of the key variables explaining wage behavior. As an indicator of the degree of slack in labor markets, the unemployment figure is always an understatement. It includes only those people actively looking for work, and not those who might switch from school to jobs, or from domestic to outside employment, if it became easier to find jobs they liked at sufficiently attractive wages. This reserve of potential workers usually moves in the same direction as the unemployment rate itself, but not necessarily in close parallel. A study by Norman Simler and Alfred Tella shows that the reserve supply of idle labor not looking for work increased relative to stated unemployment in the 1960's. This means that greater wage restraint, relative to stated levels of unemployment, should have been expected whether or not there had been any guidepost policy.[14]

Applying their measure of the degree of slack in labor markets, Simler and Tella predicted wage changes for the period 1962 through 1966, and contrasted their results with Perry's. For 1962-63, their method showed no downward deviation. For 1964-66, it showed a growing deflection from expected behavior, parallel to but lower than that indicated by Perry. For these last three years, they estimated a downward deflection averaging 0.9 percentage points per year, as compared to an average of 1.8 points indicated by Perry's method.

[14] "Labor Reserves and the Phillips Curve," April 1967 (Mimeo.).

Simler and Tella also applied their technique to a test of wage behavior for the whole private economy, as distinct from manufacturing. They found no downward deflection in 1962 (agreeing with Perry), but an average downward shift of 0.5 percentage points per year for the period 1963-66 (compared to an average of 1.2 indicated by Perry's method). All their tests scaled down the measure of the degree of change in behavior, but agreed with the others on the direction.

While there is no reason to doubt the relevance of the concept of a corrected unemployment figure bringing the voluntarily unemployed into the picture, it does not necessarily follow that the Simler-Tella estimates are more meaningful for predictions of manufacturing wages than those of Perry and Brechling. The reserve labor force which accounts for the difference in results consists mainly of female workers, and males who either are very young or who are over 54. It includes little representation of male workers in the prime age group who constitute the great majority of the labor force in manufacturing. This group is almost entirely in the active labor force at all times, and availability of these workers is thus measured reasonably well by the official unemployment index. If the two groups were entirely noncompeting, in the sense that the reserve labor force could not substitute for adult male workers in manufacturing, the official index would be a better basis for prediction than the adjusted measure including the reserve labor force.[15] Any assumption of complete non-substitutability is surely wrong, but any idea that the two sets of workers are completely interchangeable is wrong too. That is, the Simler-Tella estimates show that the other measures of the degree of wage change are probably too high, but their own results are probably too low.

Perry also tried a different method of checking on changes in wage behavior, involving a separation of industry groups into a set of more "visible" industries and a set of "invisibles." The former were the industries in which large firms or unions were considered to be particularly important, and thus likely to attract more explicit attention under the guideposts. The separation was done on the basis of external judgment, not measurable criteria. He compared the rates of wage increases from 1954 to 1957, and from 1963 to 1966, separately for the two groups. For the more visible industries the average annual wage change from 1963 to 1966 was 2.1

---

[15] Cf. Otto Eckstein, "Economics Conditions and the Success of United States Policies Against Inflation, 1961-65," paper prepared for the Expert Council on German Economic Development, November 1966 (Mimeo.), pp. 6-7.

percentage points lower than from 1954 to 1957; for the less visible, the slowdown between the same two periods was only 0.5 percentage points.[16] The difference of 1.6 percentage points matched fairly closely the net deflection downward in wage behavior for all manufacturing as estimated for 1965 by both Perry and Brechling.

This comparison of behavior between highly organized industries and those more subject to market forces is particularly interesting as an approach to the type of desegregation which could reveal some of the vital workings of a heterogeneous economy. If the economic system were thoroughly competitive, the guideposts would have no useful role and might do a great deal of harm. If it were completely an administrative system run in terms of discretionary rules, the guideposts could help alter the rules in directions more nearly consistent with the general public interest. The actual situation mixes in all shades of variation between these two extremes, making it possible to get either good or bad results out of the same set of policies, depending on where they are applied. Perry's test is in a sense reassuring. Guideposts did not seem to make much difference to behavior in the labor markets considered to be more open to competitive forces, while they did in the more organized industries.

It must be recognized that this last test, while going toward a crucial question, is not much more than a fascinating suggestion. The division into two broad groups on the basis of subjective judgment, using two-digit industrial classifications which lump together industries of highly different characteristics, is a rough approximation to the complex differences within the economy. The comparison of 1954-57 to 1963-66 uses about the best pair of periods offered by recent experience, but it is still open to objection because the periods were unlike in important respects. In particular, profits and employment in nondurable manufacturing were beginning to go down in 1957, while still going up for the durable goods industries, and this could have affected the comparison between visible and invisible industries quite strongly. Further, the more organized industries probably could be expected to react more slowly to factors determining wages than do the industries more open to pressure from market forces. In 1954-57, the expansion of profits and employment came early, giving the more or-

[16] "Wages and the Guideposts." The 1963-66 comparison actually refers to the rate up to April 1966. The differential slowdowns were not explicable in terms of different rates of change in employment; the latter suggested the opposite pattern of change in wage behavior.

ganized industries plenty of time to react; in 1963-66, the greatest rise in profits and fall in unemployment did not occur until 1965. The test of differential behavior, as compared to the 1950's, may come in 1967.

The preceding suggestions are not meant to contradict the general conclusion reached by all the studies discussed. Individual tests are subject to reservations, but they add up to a convincing case that wage behavior in manufacturing became more restrained in the four years following presentation of the guideposts than it had been in the preceding decade.

Comparisons Among Estimates

It would be a pleasant surprise if these diverse investigations proved to give comparable and consistent results. Some do, and some do not.

The tests of change in wage behavior by Brechling and by Perry come out very similarly. Eckstein's results support them for 1964-66, though cast doubt on their conclusions for 1962-63. The measures of change given by Simler and Tella are lower for an understandable reason—their conclusion that there was more slack in the labor force than indicated by the unemployment data—but they show the same direction and pattern.

For measures of changes in price behavior, Solow's test has a special advantage in that it does not use the debated unemployment measure. His figures indicate a slowdown of 0.6 to 0.7 percentage points per year, for wholesale manufacturing prices. Brechling reported a downward shift of about 0.5 percentage points. This seems to support Solow's result, but the question they asked is quite different. Solow abstracted from effects of changes in wage behavior and in the rate of productivity improvement by using unit labor costs as one of his independent variables. Brechling did not include these factors among his explanatory variables. His technique merged the effects of changes in productivity improvement, wage behavior, and pricing.

The results of the study by the Cleveland Bank, indicating a downward deflection of prices by about 1.2 percentage points at 5 percent unemployment, and about 1.9 points at 4 percent unemployment, are not inconsistent with Solow. Like the parallel test reported here, this approach combines changes in wage and price behavior, so should give a higher measure of deviation if there actually was any wage restraint.

The conclusions of Perry's tests for wage behavior, adjusted to refer to changes in total compensation, suggest an average downward deflection of about 0.8 percentage points for 1962-65. Taking wages to be 70 percent of national income originating in manufacturing, this factor should have been worth slightly under 0.6 percentage points in terms of unit costs. Adding this to Solow's result for price behavior suggests a net change of about 1.2 percentage points per year as an average for the period. For 1965, with the deflection in wage behavior widening to about 1.5 percentage points (or about 0.9 in terms of unit costs), the combined result would be nearer 1.5 percentage points.

The Simler-Tella tests of changes in wage behavior indicate downward deviations averaging 0.35 percentage points per year for 1962-65. Converted to unit costs, this is a reduction of about 0.2 points. Adding this to Solow's result for price behavior indicates a net change of about 0.8 percentage points per year. This may be taken as the lower end of the range of measures suggested by available studies.

While it is conceptually defensible to add the effects of changes in wage behavior to those in pricing relative to wage costs, it is a doubtful procedure because the tests did not use the same explanatory variables and may have picked up some of the results included in each other. A rough check is provided by the simpler measures used by the Cleveland Bank and the test of joint unemployment-productivity effects reported above. They combine price and wage effects, and suggest an average change of about 1.6 percentage points for 1962-65. The range of estimates thus runs from a low of 0.8 percentage points per year up to 1.6, with the Solow-Perry combination indicating about 1.2

There have not been so many attempts to work with employee compensation for the whole private economy, or with the deflator for gross national product rather than wholesale industrial prices. The Perry model and the Simler-Tella method have been applied to changes in employee compensation for the private economy, and the former suggests an average downward shift about three-fourths as large as that for manufacturing. Simler and Tella conclude that there was no downward shift for 1962-64, though there was an average reduction of 0.6 percentage points for 1965-66.[17]

Brechling's measure for changes in the GNP deflator, a downward shift which increased gradually to 0.8 percentage points in 1965, seems consistent with Perry's results for wages, but the Simler-Tella estimates make this seem too high. The latter are perhaps more relevant here than they

[17] *Op. cit.,* pp. 17 and 19.

are for manufacturing because the reservation noted above about limited substitutability between the reserve labor force and prime age male workers is much less meaningful.

Such comparisons can quickly generate headaches. They may serve to bring out the imprecision inherent in the statistical tests under discussion. Those for industrial prices and wages support the idea of a downward deflection, holding the increase in prices from 1961 to 1965 to less than half of what could have been expected from earlier relationships.

Alternative Explanations

While the evidence is good that wage and price behavior became more restrained after 1961, anyone determined to resist the suggestion that the guideposts were responsible for the difference can readily find alternative explanations. And it should be recognized that the statistical tests discussed above give good reason to expect that factors other than the guideposts might have acted to change wage and price behavior. The examinations by Lipsey in the United Kingdom and those in the United States suggest that change is normal; they contradict any idea of a fixed schedule of relationships between unemployment and wages or prices.

Among the more plausible reasons for expecting that wage and price behavior would have become more stable in the 1960's even without the guideposts, three may be singled out for consideration: (1) a lessening of inflationary expectations after the successive recessions of 1957-58 and 1960; (2) an increase in competitive pressure from abroad; and (3) a more even pace of expansion, both as to overall rate and as to balance among sectors.

Paul McCracken has made a particularly good case for the possibility that the immediately preceding recessions did a great deal to weaken expectations of inflation. This should have reduced somewhat the pressure for wage increases by labor, and the willingness of business to calculate on offsetting price increases as an easy solution for higher wage costs.[18] He

---

[18] "Price-Cost Behavior and Employment Act Objectives," *Twentieth Anniversary of the Employment Act of 1946: An Economic Symposium,* Hearings before the Joint Economic Committee, 89 Cong. 2 sess. (February 1966), p. 68. Cf. the similar point, supported by measures of changes in expectations, in the Cleveland Bank discussion of price behavior, *op. cit.,* pp. 11-12.

stresses that the particularly disturbing rate of price increases observed earlier in the 1950's began to calm down from mid-1958, well before the guideposts.

The idea that inflationary expectations tend to become self-justifying, as each group and firm tries to make sure it moves at least as fast as the rest, fits well with observed behavior in many countries. The deliberate deflation of 1959, following so closely after the recession of 1957, almost surely had a calming effect on price expectations. On the other hand, it might be recalled that a number of eminent economists, including the Chairman of the Federal Reserve Board, along with much of the financial press, were emphatic in their predictions of serious inflation as the government began to consider more expansionary policies in 1961-62. Were inflationary expectations really broken, or is it just that a few people are extraordinarily far-sighted?

It might be suggested that there were strong forces acting to mold public opinion toward the expectation of inflation in 1961-62, but that there was also one overt policy change acting to help calm things down. The change was the introduction of the guideposts. The government announced a new program that sounded sensible and not utterly impossible, providing a specific manifestation of concern for price stability. This might have had little effect as an abstract policy statement, but the idea that it could make a difference was almost immediately given weight by the President's successful actions to restrain steel wages and, most dramatically, steel prices. Far beyond any direct consequences of steel prices for industrial costs, this evidence of willingness to act must have had a significant effect in reassuring people that the government really did intend to restrain inflation.

With respect to the restraining force of increased import competition, it is clear that this became an important factor during the 1950's. Some of the direct impact of intensified foreign competition on American markets has been noted above in connection with pricing for aluminum and steel in 1957-58. New competition from smaller European automobiles probably also helped check prices in the American industry from about the same time. More generally, the evidence in Table 1 that American export prices for manufactured goods rose relative to those of other industrial countries from 1953 to 1960 is a strong indication that their exports must have been exerting increasing pressure on pricing in the American market itself. But all of this refers to a factor operating to restrain American prices in the period *prior* to introduction of the guideposts.

Comparing export prices of manufactures in the four years from 1961 to 1965 should give some clue to whether import competition in this sector intensified during the period after the guideposts were established. Between these two years, it turned out that the increase in average unit values of American manufacturing exports was exactly equal to that of the index for the eleven main industrial exporters. This was a marked change from the preceding pattern: American export prices had risen 6 percent relative to the index for the same group in the previous four years.[19]

Several interpretations are possible. It could be that the lower relative level of foreign export prices established by 1961 exerted more pressure on American prices than had been generated during the earlier period of falling foreign prices, because they had not previously gotten low enough to be really effective. This is not too appealing an argument, because American export shares of manufactures began to deteriorate seriously from 1957. If it be considered instead that falling relative prices imply increasing competitive pressure, and stable relative prices imply unchanging competitive pressure, then foreign competition played less of a restraining role after the guideposts were established than it did in the immediately preceding years. But this too is a doubtful argument. American export shares for manufacturing continued to deteriorate from 1961 to 1965, so it does not seem correct to conclude that competitive pressures were lessening. Or it could be that the comparison is not particularly relevant. Although the indexes would suggest lessening competitive pressure on American prices after 1961, many specific prices, notably including those of steel products, were much less free to move than they had been up to 1957-58.

Apart from competitive effects at the level of finished products, decline in prices for imported basic commodities could have had important effects on American costs of production. As indicated by the Commerce Department's index of unit value for United States imports, their average price changed hardly at all in either the 1950's or 1961-65. The index for 1960 was 3 percent below that for 1954, and that for 1965 was 2 percent above 1961.[20] These infinitesimal movements toward lower prices in the first period and higher in 1961-65 suggest that differential behavior of

[19] United Nations, *Monthly Bulletin of Statistics* (December 1966), Table D, p. xvi.
[20] U.S. Office of Business Economics, *Business Statistics,* 1963 Ed., p. 119, and *Survey of Current Business* (May 1966), S-23.

costs affected by import prices had little to do with the greater stability of domestic wholesale prices in the more recent period.

The third consideration, the steadier pace of the rise in national output and the greater degree of balance among sectoral rates of growth in 1961-64 as compared to the mid-1950's, should have been expected to yield slower price and wage increases even in the absence of the guideposts.[21] Steadier and more balanced expansion eases bottleneck problems and lessens the tendency for wages in particular sectors to shoot ahead and establish higher targets for succeeding negotiations elsewhere. When investment began to accelerate at the same time as military demands in 1965, the fabric of stability was destroyed. Prices and wages then began to move up much faster. But it should be noted that all the statistical tests of wage-price behavior which have been carried through 1965 and into 1966 suggest that the rise continued to be less than would be expected on the basis of behavioral relations in the 1950's. Unless these tests are wrong, the steadiness of pace and degree of balance among sectors up to 1965 were not the only factors operating to improve price-wage stability.

The observed increase in price stability may have been helped by the improvement in the rate of gain in productivity, though this factor does not seem systematically related to price changes. The more important connection may run rather from price restraint to productivity improvement. Insofar as it became more difficult in at least a few major industries to raise prices, pressure on firms toward cost reduction may have been raised. In a wider sense, the marked change of climate toward steady growth, with more stable prices than had been observed in preceding years, encouraged rising investment on the expectation that expansion could be continued. Insofar as the guideposts restrained false signals of inflation in cases in which there were no genuine shortages, they helped avoid the premature application of monetary restraints and contributed to the more efficient progress of the whole economic system.

[21] This balance was impressive up to about mid-1965, and then began to break down; cf. *Economic Report of the President, 1966,* pp. 67-72, and *ibid., 1967,* pp. 72-79.

VIII

Related Experience in Other Countries

THE ACHIEVEMENT OF FAIRLY STABLE PRICES without sacrificing economic growth and high employment has been pursued with policies similar to the guideposts in many countries. Some of these efforts have worked reasonably well in certain periods, some hardly at all. Neither the modest successes nor the failures can be taken as lessons directly applicable to the United States; each economy has its own organization and patterns of reaction. Still, it would be surprising if there were nothing for the United States to learn from these diverse efforts.

The following notes on experience abroad are highly selective, aimed at providing a somewhat wider background for interpretation of issues in American wage-price policy. They summarize a rich literature, hopefully without distorting the record beyond the oversimplification necessary to make some of the central points stand out for consideration.

The Netherlands

The Dutch were the modern pioneers of efforts to guide price and wage developments within the framework of an overall analysis of the economy. This program began immediately after World War II, and focused on the objective of restoring the country's competitive export position while carrying out postwar reconstruction. It was developed in close connection with a general economic plan, aimed at clarifying major options with respect to monetary-fiscal policy, resource use, and price-wage decisions.[1]

Nearly half of Dutch production is intended for export. Both labor and management federations have demonstrated their awareness that a rising standard of living depends on the ability to compete abroad. This recognition helped greatly to encourage cooperation with governmental attempts to restrain prices and wages. The unions accepted stringent limitations in 1945 because they believed, correctly, that this would help improve the chances of avoiding any return to serious unemployment. All three of the major unions and the employers' associations agreed in that year to establish the Foundation of Labor as a forum for joint discussion of national wage policy. It was a full decade before a conflict within the Foundation became so strong that the government had to intervene to keep the system going.

The unions agreed, for about six years, to a system under which money wages were held close to the rate of increase in the cost of living. Real wages in 1953 were only 1 percent above the level of 1947.[2] Business apparently accepted the continuation of price control with no great struggle until 1954. Under this set of controls, prices could be raised to the extent necessary to compensate for increases in costs of materials, but increases in wages were not considered to be a valid justification.

Dutch policy on wages and prices was worked out as part of an analytical system covering all forms of income and use of resources. The Central Planning Bureau, created in 1945, has concentrated on supplying short-run forecasts of what might be expected for employment, prices, and wages, the balance of payments, and domestic supplies, in the year immediately ahead. The forecasts have often missed. They have some-

[1] Cf. William Fellner and others, *The Problem of Rising Prices* (Organization for Economic Cooperation and Development, 1961), pp. 359-90; A. Kervyn, "Politique des Revenus: L'Expérience Hollandaise," *Revue d'Economie Politique*, Vol. 75 (1965), pp. 608-37; B. C. Roberts, *National Wages Policy in War and Peace* (Allen and Unwin, 1958), Chap. 8; C. A. Van den Beld, "Short-Term Planning Experience in The Netherlands" and Willem Hessel, "Quantitative Planning of Economic Policy in The Netherlands," in Bert G. Hickman, ed., *Quantitative Planning of Economic Policy* (Brookings Institution, 1965), Chaps. 6 and 7; Rhattan J. Bhatia and Arie C. Bouter, "A System of Governmental Wage Control," International Monetary Fund, *Staff Papers*, Vol. 8 (1961), pp. 353-79.

[2] Bhatia and Bouter, *op. cit.*, Table 1, p. 369.

times been swamped by unexpected events, and have in general betrayed a bias toward underestimation of possible export earnings and overestimation of the necessary degree of restraint. These errors of excessive pessimism have at times involved wasteful acceptance of more unemployment than necessary, and have made the unions increasingly restless about acccepting the advice of the Planning Bureau. Still, the explicit nature of the forecasting technique has made it easier to analyze conflicting estimates, to reduce the range of uncertainty in policy discussions, and to work toward a more accurate analytical system.[3]

The Planning Bureau does not make decisions on wages or any other economic policies. It simply presents advice on what might be expected in the absence of new decisions, or on what may follow from particular proposals. Its role is thus somewhat similar to that of the Council of Economic Advisers, except that it takes more public risk by working out and publishing detailed annual forecasts based on a complete planning model.

The organization which made direct use of the Planning Bureau's analyses with respect to wage policy in the early postwar years was the government's Board of Mediators. This board was given official authority in 1945 to make decisions for the government on the basis of recommendations by the Foundation of Labor. In 1950, a new tripartite organization was established bringing together labor, the employers, and representatives of the government. This was the Social and Economic Council, which has since served as the main arena for resolution of price-wage issues in the context of the overall economic situation. Private labor-management discussion continues in the Foundation of Labor, but major questions of changes in the institutional system or in economic policy bearing on wages are usually presented by the government to the Social and Economic Council for three-way debate.

The system allows the government great flexibility. The government can initiate proposals, participate in discussions without committing itself to the recommendations made by the Council, and finally decide for itself whether to accept these recommendations. As a general rule, the private negotiations within the Foundation of Labor and the tripartite recom-

---

[3] Willem Hessel has been particularly critical of the occasionally wide margins of error and the conservative bias in the Planning Board's forecasts; Van den Beld has worked out statistical tests of accuracy indicating that the range of error has gradually decreased with growing experience; *op. cit.* See also Kervyn, *op. cit.,* pp. 633-34.

mendations prepared by the Social and Economic Council are accepted as the basis of the government's policy.[4]

The power of the Dutch approach to produce negotiated restraints to help in particularly difficult situations has been demonstrated several times, notably at the beginning of 1951 and in 1957. In the former case, the Korean War had raised import prices and the cost of living sharply, creating a serious problem with the balance of payments. Under the existing practice of allowing wage increases in line with changes in the cost of living, a rise of 10 percent would have been called for. Given the balance-of-payments situation, the government proposed a reduction in real wages rather than full compensation. The unions agreed, settling on an increase of 5 percent in money wages, and an equal reduction in real earnings.[5]

Following this agreement in 1951, the balance-of-payments deficit on current account decreased greatly, then changed to a substantial surplus through the next four years. A study of price levels in 1955, comparing eight European countries and the United States, showed Dutch prices to be below those of all the other countries except Italy.[6] As the balance-of-payments surplus and rising demand continued through 1955, first the employers' associations and then the unions began to express increasing dissatisfaction with the restraints imposed on prices and wages.

The employers were unhappy with restrictions on wages as well as those on prices. Many of them wanted to be allowed to bid higher for workers in order to expand production more rapidly. Officially negotiated wage rates went up swiftly, including increases of 16 percent agreed upon in 1954 and again at the end of 1956. On top of this, a residual known as "wage drift," common to experience in most European countries operating at low levels of unemployment, pulled up earnings faster than the statutory rates. This took such forms as upgrading of workers and rapidly spreading fringe benefits, both within the legally established system, and then gradually began to include outright "black" wages offered by employers in excess of legally authorized rates. The OECD study of the

[4] Fellner and others, *op. cit.,* pp. 364-65.

[5] *Ibid.,* p. 374; Kervyn, *op. cit.,* p. 615.

[6] Milton Gilbert and associates, *Comparative National Products and Price Levels* (Organization for European Economic Cooperation, 1959), p. 31, Table 6. On binary comparisons against the U. S., Dutch prices appeared lowest of all when using American quantity weights, or second lowest after Italy when using the quantity weights of the individual European country.

Dutch experience estimated the rate of wage drift from 1953 to 1959 at about 2 percent per year, on top of a rate of increase of 5.6 percent in officially negotiated rates.[7]

By 1956, the current account of the balance of payments had gone back into deficit. The Central Planning Bureau forecast deepening trouble if greater restraint were not exercised, and the government asked the Social and Economic Council to formulate a program distributing the burdens of reducing domestic resource use in order to improve the external balance. The Council developed a comprehensive plan which was accepted by all sides. Within the framework adopted, the unions agreed to measures raising unemployment slightly in order to help hold down wages and consumption. By 1958, the balance of payments on current account had again changed to such a large surplus that the program was criticized for having been excessively restrictive. Looking back, it clearly would have been desirable to have been less deflationary, but the comment of an official of the Planning Bureau seems defensible and relevant: "The important point is that agreement on a program of action *could* be reached on the basis of the planning methods and techniques now traditional in the Netherlands."[8]

Since 1958, and with particular intensity since 1961, the Dutch economy has had such low levels of unemployment that the apparatus of restraint has progressively lost acceptance. Major employers have overtly refused to hold their wage offers within the legal ceiling. The situation has become such that employers exercising restraint are likely to lose the workers they need to others bidding more freely, and the price of labor has raced up because it has been in continuously short supply.

In 1959, it was decided to allow wage increases to be determined more by productivity and earnings in particular industries, with greater freedom for departures from any national norm. This worked badly in the sense of encouraging leap-frog raises, and led to questionable estimates of industry productivity data to justify large wage increases. "One had the impression that the employers and the unions reached agreement on a wage increase and then arranged output data in such a way as to bring out a corresponding increase in productivity."[9]

Attempts to patch up a compromise system averaging national productivity data with individual industry results merely complicated a situation

[7] Fellner and others, *op. cit.,* pp. 366-71.

[8] Van den Beld, *op. cit.,* p. 155.

[9] Kervyn, *op. cit.,* p. 617

getting out of control. The difficulty was probably less with the mechanics of the method than with a genuine labor shortage. From 1959 through 1964, unfilled vacancies exceeded the number of unemployed workers and unemployment averaged at or below 1 percent of the labor force.

Despite extremely low unemployment and rapid wage increases, the balance of payments stayed in good shape for several years. The guilder was revalued by 5 percent at the same time as the German mark in 1961, and prices continued to rise despite this braking effect, but the balance of payments on current account remained positive through 1963. The explanation seemed to be that the Dutch had still not lost a price advantage established in the period of severe restraint from 1947 to 1953. Although wages and internal prices began to go up faster than in most other European countries after 1953, export prices remained stable through 1960. As of 1961, Dutch prices and hourly wage costs still compared favorably with those in competing countries.[10] By 1964, their upward movement overshot. An external deficit reappeared then and became progressively more difficult through 1966. A "target" rate of wage increase of 6 percent was set for 1966 as the upper limit consistent with stability, but settlements began to overshoot this so seriously in the early part of the year that the government resorted to a complete wage freeze in July. The position had clearly become such that elimination of aggregate excess demand was necessary to give negotiated restraint even a minimal chance of success.

Dutch policy originally included emphasis on change in the structure of wages, as well as restraint on the rate of increase. The objective was to get away from inequalities based on ability to pay in particular firms or industries, toward equal pay for similar work and narrower differentials between skill levels. The program did not succeed in altering skill differentials among industrial workers,[11] but agricultural wages were raised relative to industrial, and a thorough program of job analysis was carried out to provide an objective basis for wage setting. This study of job characteristics has been credited with an important side benefit, in that it "probably contributed a great deal to the considerable rise in productivity achieved in the Netherlands during the past few years. Whenever a systematic job analysis is done, it always brings to light inefficiencies that were not obvious, even though suspected."[12]

[10] Kervyn, *op. cit.*, pp. 623-28; Murray Edelman and R. W. Fleming, *The Politics of Wage-Price Decisions* (University of Illinois Press, 1965), pp. 269-72.

[11] Bhatia and Bouter, *op. cit.*, p. 378.

[12] Roberts, *op. cit.*, p. 130.

The negative side of this attempt to base wages on national standards was that employers wanting to bid for labor they needed, and workers with skills in greater demand, were blocked from using the market mechanism freely. Both sides became progressively more dissatisfied with the system. It was effectively abandoned in 1959, and subsequent attempts to patch up some form of compromise between national standards and local market criteria have not proven successful.

So far as effects on productivity are concerned, it is not clear that either the centralized rules up to 1959 or their collapse since have made much difference to the rate of improvement. Output per man-hour in manufacturing during the period of more centralized control, from 1951 to 1959, increased 3.4 percent per year. This was below the rates of improvement in Italy, West Germany, or France in the same years, but distinctly better than those of Belgium, Canada, the United Kingdom, or the United States, none of which was over 2.5 percent.[13]

The Dutch experience has been cited as a leading example of the failure of negotiated agreements to hold down wages in conditions of excess demand, despite all the advantages of centralized bargaining, recognized concern for the balance of payments, and sophisticated economic forecasting.[14] The point cannot be disputed. From 1953 on, wages rose faster than in most other European countries, and general willingness to cooperate with the system fairly well broke down in 1964-65. This is an important lesson, but perhaps less helpful than one might wish with respect to the question of identifying the point at which demand becomes so excessive as to make negotiated restraint useless. The unions accepted a voluntary cut in real wages in 1951, with unemployment at 3.2 percent of the labor force, and all sides managed to agree on an effective program of restraint for 1957, when unemployment was under two percent.[15] Efforts at restraint failed in those years in which very low unemployment was combined with an external surplus, but the error then may have been that of trying for more restraint than was either necessary or desirable. Under such conditions, wages ought to go up more than in other countries.

The Dutch experience was in a sense the opposite of the normal one.

[13] Richard N. Cooper, "The Competitive Position of the United States," in Seymour E. Harris, ed., *The Dollar in Crisis* (Harcourt, Brace, and World, 1961), p. 158.

[14] Roberts, *op. cit.*, pp. 130-34; F. W. Paish and Jossleyn Hennessey, *Policy for Incomes?* (London, Institute of Economic Affairs, 2d ed., 1966), pp. 50-57, 69.

[15] Unemployment percentages from Van den Beld, *op. cit.*, p. 150.

The more common difficulty seems to be that domestic prices go up too fast for external balance, leading to restraints on demand and employment in order to keep down deficits, or eventually to devaluation. The Dutch went the other way around: domestic wages and prices were held back so well that excess demand came from the outside, leading to internal inflationary pressures despite a slight appreciation of the currency. By 1964, the end result looked familiar. But up to then, the path followed by the Netherlands seemed to pay off unusually well in terms of high employment, fast productivity growth, and a strong competitive position in external markets.

The United Kingdom

The United Kingdom has managed to combine a high rate of employment with a low rate of increase in production. From 1949 to 1959, gross domestic product rose only 2.4 percent per year, more slowly than in any other major industrial country.[16] The growth of the United States economy was not especially dramatic in the 1950's either, but when the American economy picked up markedly after 1960 the English did not.

The balance of payments has been the critical point at which England's internal difficulties show up most clearly. Every time anything resembling a sustained expansion of investment gets under way, imports rise rapidly and exports become less competitive, the balance of payments turns sharply negative, and reserves disappear at a rapid rate. This has led repeatedly to deflationary monetary-fiscal measures, which save the balance-of-payments situation temporarily at the cost of slowing down investment and impeding improvements in efficiency.

One of the clearest analyses of this situation, written ten years ago but still convincing, emphasized the need to increase investment and exports relative to consumption.[17] Efforts have been made to move in this direc-

[16] Comparisons of growth rates on various criteria, for the economy as a whole and for individual sectors, are given for this period in Evsey Domar, Scott Eddie, and others, "Economic Growth and Productivity in the United States, Canada, United Kingdom, Germany and Japan in the Post-War Period," *Review of Economics and Statistics,* Vol. 46 (February 1964), pp. 33-40.

[17] Ragnar Nurkse, "The Relation Between Home Investment and External Balance in the Light of British Experience 1945-1955," *Review of Economics and Statistics,* Vol. 38 (May 1956), pp. 121-54.

tion, but they have not yet been succcessful. Two of the main culprits singled out as causes of this failure have been the rate of increase in wages, acting to impede exports and hold up consumption, and the policy of maintaining high employment which has both supported rising wages and conceivably had the effect of weakening efficiency.[18]

Wages and salaries in the United Kingdom have not risen at any extraordinary rate compared to those in most other European countries or Japan, though faster than in the United States. The trouble is rather that output per man has risen more slowly than in any other industrialized country, so the impact of rising wages on unit costs has not been sufficiently moderated. Average wages and salaries went up at a rate of 6.4 percent from 1946-47 to 1959-60, while output per man increased only 2.3 percent per year.[19]

Productivity and Employment

The relatively slow growth of labor productivity might in part be explained by a structural characteristic of the British economy. In most countries, a significant share of the growth in output per capita comes from a shift of labor from those occupations in which value of output per hour is below average, as it usually is in agriculture, toward sectors in which the value of output per hour is above average. But the United Kingdom reached a position long ago in which there was little reservoir of low-productivity labor in agriculture on which to draw. As compared to France and Italy in particular, and also to the United States, there was not as much scope for raising productivity through such reallocation.[20]

As compared to Germany and the Netherlands, the United Kingdom may have been held back by the absence of any significant inflow of foreign workers. That is a matter of national choice; immigration policy is not an inescapable structural characteristic. But the fact that the labor

[18] Cf. Milton Gilbert and Warren McClam, "Domestic and External Equilibrium: European Objectives and Policies," *American Economic Review,* Vol. 55 (May 1965), p. 197, and practically every issue of the *Economist* during 1966.

[19] J. C. R. Dow, *The Management of the British Economy, 1945-60* (National Institute of Economic and Social Research, 1964), p. 347, Table 13.2.

[20] Between 1961 and 1964, the French industrial sector added 356,000 workers; the agricultural sector released 334,000. In the same period, the industrial sector in the United Kingdom lost 141,000 workers (to services and construction, not to agriculture). United Nations, *Economic Survey of Europe in 1964* (Geneva, 1965), p. 28, Table 12.

force grew relatively slowly may, by lessening flexibility in adapting to changes in demand, have been a key factor holding down the rate of growth of productivity. It would not have been particularly important in a context of general unemployment, but must have become so under conditions of nearly continuous full employment.

Adjusted to American definitions, the rate of unemployment in the United Kingdom has not gone over 3 percent of the labor force more than once in the last decade. It averaged only 2.6 percent for 1960-65.[21] Forecasts of production growth and requirements for the next five years have helped spread the expectation of a continuing, acute, shortage of labor. It is clear that such a situation makes it difficult to restrain wages, but the really troublesome thought is that it may hamper efficiency too.

Security of employment, and plentiful alternative offers, should make it possible for workers to stop worrying about the possibility that greater efficiency will put anyone out of a job. It should promote mobility and clarify the point that rising real income can only be achieved through increases in efficiency. It probably does have these positive effects in many instances, but can also work in directions harmful for efficiency. Employers who fear that they may lose almost irreplaceable workers if they exert pressure for changes in traditional worn habits may keep quiet and pass on higher-than-necessary costs. Moreover, with continuously good demand conditions (for consumer goods on the domestic market at least, if not for exports), management itself may not be sufficiently concerned with reduction of costs.

It is not only labor productivity which has shown relatively slow improvement. The productivity of capital also seems to have deteriorated as compared to that in other industrial countries. Further, the residual rate of technological improvement (the gains in output not accounted for by capital or labor inputs) has also lagged.[22] Issues of wage-price policy have an aspect not encountered in the Netherlands, and not in the forefront in the United States: it seems to be at least as necessary to improve the rate of gain in efficiency as to slow down the pace of money wages.

[21] George P. Shultz and Robert Z. Aliber, eds., *Guidelines, Informal Controls and the Market Place* (University of Chicago Press, 1966), p. 131, for adjusted data from 1960 through 1965. On United Kingdom definitions, the rate of unemployment never got as high in any year of the 1950's as it did in 1962, a year for which the adjusted rate on American definitions was 2.9 percent.

[22] Domar, Eddie and others, *op. cit.* The United Kingdom registered the least improvement of the five countries studied on all three measures of efficiency, except for Canada with respect to capital productivity.

In the absence of any compelling explanation of how the many factors affecting long-run trends in productivity work out to determine the net result, it is treacherous to draw any firm conclusions about the effect of high employment per se. In the United Kingdom, the results look suspicious. But most of the other countries that did much better on productivity growth also had equally low or even lower unemployment rates, which at the least casts doubt on the dominance of this factor.

Whatever the more fundamental underlying causes may be, the very imbalance between wage gains and productivity improvement has become a serious handicap for productivity itself. The increase in the price level made it nearly impossible to maintain a satisfactory balance-of-payments position with a high level of investment, the government repeatedly turned to high interest rates and mild deflation to protect the balance of payments, and these interruptions of investment in turn dragged down the pace of improvement in efficiency. This might be corrected either by tax policies reducing consumption relative to income, or by a change in the exchange rate. But both of these lines of action would exert upward pressure on wage claims and prices, and would not work if prices rose rapidly. In such a situation, income policies might become a key ally of more fundamental corrective techniques, by restraining their secondary effects on prices.

Attempts at Wage and Price Restraint

The initial postwar effort to curb the rate of increase in wages, under the recovery program of Sir Stafford Cripps in 1948-49, worked but at considerable cost. The cooperation of the Trades Union Congress with the wage freeze had the side effect of undermining the ability of the national leadership to achieve coordination of wage determination or work practices at the local level.

Throughout the whole experience there was a progressive weakening of TUC authority over affiliated unions, which culminated (in September 1950) in the defeat of the General Council's proposals for a renewal of wage restraint.

A close analysis of the wage restraint episode reveals that wages cannot be restrained for any length of time without serious stresses developing within the affiliated unions, eventually driving union leaders into the abandonment of restraint rather than see their own authority undermined. The lesson is that in a favourable market unions have to engage in bargaining over money wages because it is their central function and the foundation of their existence.[23]

When the lid was taken off the restraints imposed in 1948, wages jumped immediately. Under the Conservative Governments in office from 1951 to 1964, the unions settled down into a position of antagonism toward any cooperation. This rejection rendered fairly useless the government's attempts to exert pressure for greater stabilization. The first, the Council on Prices, Productivity, and Incomes, was established in 1957 to provide purely advisory recommendations. The unions paid no noticeable attention to its advice.

In 1961 and 1962, the government tried more directly to limit wage pressures, first with a temporary "wage pause" intended to delay all increases, then with the creation of a new set of institutions for consultation and policy recommendation. The "pause" of 1961-62 was not pushed with the rigor of the freeze imposed in 1949, but the statistical test noted below indicates that the rate of increase of money wages slowed down temporarily, by about one percentage point.

In 1962, the newly created National Economic Development Council succeeded in getting TUC participation in discussion of ways to link questions of stabilization policy with a wider program to speed up economic growth. But the participation was based on the explicit understanding that specific wage restraints would not be recommended. That question was left up to another new agency, the National Incomes Commission. The Commission recommended an approach similar to the American guidelines, first stipulating a range of permissible wage increases between 2 and 2.5 percent, then moving this up one percentage point in line with new growth targets found to be feasible by the NEDC.[24] The unions never recognized the Commission as having any real authority.[25]

The Labour Government which took office in 1964 started differently by getting prior agreement on general lines of policy from both the TUC and the main employers' federations. A policy statement was signed by all

[23] John Corina, *The Labour Market* (London: Institute of Personnel Management, 1966), p. 13.

[24] Edelman and Fleming, *op. cit.*, pp. 187-97; International Monetary Fund, *Annual Report, 1964*, p. 118.

[25] E. H. Phelps Brown, "Guidelines for Growth and for Incomes in the United Kingdom: Some Possible Lessons for the United States," in Shultz and Aliber, *op. cit.*, pp. 154-57; Andrew Shonfield, *Modern Capitalism* (Oxford University Press, 1965), pp. 154-55.

sides, emphasizing agreement "to encourage and lead a sustained attack on obstacles to efficiency, whether on the part of management or of workers." It stipulated that each group would examine price or wage behavior by its own members to advise on whether they were in the national interest.[26] The TUC promptly set up a system for reviewing wage claims, though the employers' federations decided that price decisions by individual firms were outside their jurisdiction. On the other hand, the employers' groups took the potentially important step of forming a new central organization, the Confederation of British Industries, specifically for the purpose of coordinating policy with the government in this field.

The main question about the willingness of the TUC to cooperate with efforts to reduce restrictive practices and restrain cost increases is that the central union leadership has little power of decision over agreements at a local level. It is not just that particular unions are less eager to cooperate than others. It is rather that British trade union practices leave final decisions on work methods and even on pay to bargaining within the plant conducted by the shop stewards. The situation is somewhat similar to that of construction in the United States, except that in England it is general for manufacturing. It is possible for national agreements to be ignored in practice at the plant level, and there is not much that the national leadership can do about it even if they wish. Moreover, the more they try to force restraint, the more their present low degree of authority is likely to disappear completely.[27]

A number of unions have moved toward mergers to reduce conflicts among bargaining units, and toward centralization of internal decisions. The national leadership would, naturally, like to control events at the plant level more effectively. But this struggle between coordination and decentralized local decision, so familiar in the United States in both economic and political spheres, would seem likely to go on for a long time indeed. In the Netherlands, even the most successful examples of coordination and negotiated restraint might be dismissed as inapplicable to the

---

[26] "Joint Statement of Intent on Productivity, Prices and Income," December 1964. See also "Machinery of Prices and Incomes Policy," Cmnd 2577 (1965), and "Prices and Incomes Policy," Cmnd 2639 (1965).

[27] Cf. Corina, *op. cit.;* B. C. Roberts, "Trade Union Behavior and Wage Determination in Great Britain," in John T. Dunlop, ed., *The Theory of Wage Determination* (Macmillan, 1957); Edelman and Fleming, *op. cit.,* pp. 152-69; Allan Flanders, *Industrial Relations: What Is Wrong With the System?* (London: Institute of Personnel Management, 1965), Chap. 5.

United States because Dutch bargaining is so centralized and traditions of cooperation so strong; in the United Kingdom, weak results might equally well be considered inapplicable to the United States, because organizational forms in this field are so ill-adapted to cooperative restraint.

The Labour Government created yet another agency for price-wage matters, the National Board of Prices and Incomes, this time after obtaining general agreement from both the unions and the employers' federations. The Board was directed to consider standards for prices as well as wages. The first case it examined was one involving prices. About half of the eighteen references examined from its start in May 1965 up to its first general review of progress published in August 1966 were concerned with prices.[28] Four of these studies were concerned with wages in the government sector. The rest were split almost evenly between private and nationalized industries.

The role of the National Board for Prices and Incomes, and in particular its relationship to other agencies of government, has been left so loosely defined that almost anything could develop in practice. The Board was not intended to, and has not, leaned toward analyses of national criteria or any close identification with overall economic planning. Rather, it has emphasized investigation of organization and practice within particular industries and branches of government.

The cases which the Board studies are chosen by the government primarily with a view to developing analysis of issues likely to have general relevance, rather than to recommend solutions for cases under immediate pressure. The politically charged seamen's strike of 1966 was not referred to the Board, but to a special commission. The cases that the Board does get are sometimes grouped around a particular issue, such as the degree to which special pay awards ought to be used to induce unions to drop particular restrictive practices, but most of those studied so far have been investigated one-by-one in terms of the particular problems of the field. The Board tries to work with the unions and management groups concerned to examine possibilities for more rational organization, methods of setting prices, or wage structures.

[28] "National Board for Prices and Incomes, General Report April 1965 to July 1966," Cmnd 3087 (1966). The issues brought out and positions taken in these cases are systematically examined by Anne Romanis in "Towards an Incomes Policy: A Survey of Recent Institutional Developments in the United Kingdom," July 1966 (Mimeo.).

From the point of view of staving off balance-of-payments problems in the near future, or achieving any significant reduction in the general pace of increase in prices and wages, the operation of the National Board for Prices and Incomes must be recognized to be slow indeed. Its significance probably does not lie in any short-run gains on those matters. It is rather that its approach points government officials, people with experience in business and in labor, and economists as well, toward questions of efficiency in particular fields in which problems keep arising. Perhaps a consulting firm of efficiency experts could do much of the same job, and some of it better. There is no reason such experts could not be used along with everyone else. But the process as it is evolving seems to combine in a most healthy way a respect for the difficulties of the individual case along with concern for the national welfare. It is this microeconomic search, bringing together problems of restrictive practices and just plain inefficiency, joining elements of policy on competition and on regulation along with questions of organizational methods, which makes this new approach so very much worth developing.

Statistical tests of the possible effects of wage-price restraints under recent incomes policies suggest that they had some effect, even prior to the freeze imposed in 1966. Frank Brechling concludes that there have been three periods in which the pace of wage increases was reduced: by about 2 percentage points per year during the freeze applied by Sir Stafford Cripps in 1948-49, by about 1 point during the "wage pause" of 1961-62, and again by about 2 points per year in 1964-65.[29] These tests resulted in fairly accurate wage predictions, and statistically significant regression coefficients in most cases. Contrariwise, similar attempts to measure possible changes in price behavior did not give conclusive results.

The indications that wage restraints did have some effects in these three periods are of considerable interest with respect to arguments about interpretation of experience in the United States. Investigations showing changes in wage-price behavior for 1962-65 may be explained in terms of special characteristics of the period, and these factors may indeed have counted for more than the guideposts did. But any general suspicion that administrative restraints cannot work should be tempered by the indications from the United Kingdom experience that wage behavior changed in

[29] "Some Empirical Evidence on the Effectiveness of Price and Income Policies," paper presented to the Canadian Political Science Association, June 1966 (Mimeo.), pp. 6-10.

all three periods in which trials were made. On the other hand, the inconclusive results for tests on prices may add some weight to the position of the unions that more needs to be done to restrain prices if wages are to be held back. Simply working on wages, while high demand is operating to favor prices and profit margins, may mean that no net gain is achieved on the fundamental target of holding down price increases.

Continuing balance-of-payments difficulties and rising prices led the Labour Government to take the drastic step of ordering a complete stop on wage increases in the latter part of 1966, expected to go through the first half of 1967.[30] At the same time, measures were taken to reduce domestic demand and increase unemployment. In a way, the method might serve as a useful warning in other countries trying to induce cooperative restraint in order to avoid deflation. But a complete freeze must be regarded as an inefficient and undesirable solution in any case; when relaxed, the present one may run into an extremely rough situation if productivity gains are not fast enough to allow for some wage increases without raising prices. The country seems to need higher investment and faster productivity increases to make the system workable. With them, negotiated restraints might provide the additional help necessary to avoid falling back into the trap of the last two decades.

France

The French economy has advanced more successfully than the English in the last decade. This success, which has included some reduction of previously extreme inflationary pressures, does not owe much if anything to incomes policies. Still, the French have some elaborate theories in this field, and some unrelated but practical experience with direct controls bearing on these problems.

The French are accustomed to a higher degree of government intervention and more extensive use of direct controls than have been considered acceptable in England or the United States. From 1946 on, a national plan has been used to guide investment through a dual process of government-industry consultation and directed allocation of credit. This worked

[30] "Prices and Incomes Policy: Period of Severe Restraint," Cmd 3150, November 1966; *Economist,* July 16, Aug. 6, and Nov. 26, 1966.

out well in the sense of helping to stimulate a much higher rate of investment and more rapid economic growth through the 1950's than the
French economy had achieved in a long time, if ever. A seemingly mori-
bund economic system woke up and proved able to move fast.

French economic growth continued to be handicapped by difficulties in
exporting until the end of 1958, but a dramatic change in policy at that
time altered the situation fundamentally. The French simultaneously de-
valued the currency, joined the Common Market, eliminated quantitative
restrictions on imports from other countries in this group, and began to
move away from a nearly prohibitive set of tariffs. The modernization
process of the preceding twelve years paid off as soon as these measures
restored France's link to the world economy, applying simultaneously
both new incentives to export and new pressures for domestic efficiency.[31]

In the period from 1945 to 1959, extensive protective barriers against
import competition made it very difficult to restrain prices. Wartime authority to regulate individual prices was never abandoned, though attempts to use it varied greatly in intensity and consequences. The government tried hard to use controls to check inflation in conditions of aggregate excess demand from 1945 through 1948, and failed completely. The
next period of active control, combined with efforts to negotiate price decreases with major trade associations and retail chains, was made in
March 1952. The situation was one in which recovery from prior recession was slowing down, and signs of a possible new recession were developing, but retail prices kept on going up without slackening. The direct
intervention, backed by an agreement from the unions to halt wage claims
temporarily, achieved a slight reduction of consumer prices and the more
important effect of stopping the arbitrary upward trend. The interruption
proved more than temporary; prices held surprisingly stable through a period of rapid expansion and low unemployment from 1954 through 1956.
By 1957, with outright excess demand indicated by all measures of available capacity, controls again broke down completely.[32]

The 1954-56 experience had some interesting similarities to that in the
United States from 1962 to 1965. Unemployment was somewhat lower in

[31] Jacques Rueff, "The Rehabilitation of the Franc," *Lloyds Bank Review*
(April 1959); Shonfield, *op. cit.*, Chaps. V, VII, and VIII; John Sheahan, *Promotion and Control of Industry in Postwar France* (Harvard University Press, 1963).

[32] *Ibid.*, pp. 211-17; J. Benard, "Economic Policy in France, 1949 to 1961,"
in E. S. Kirschen and associates, *Economic Policy in Our Time*, Vol. 3 (Amster-
dam: North-Holland, 1964), pp. 323-43.

France in those years than during the later expansion in the United States, and wages rose faster in France, but aggregate demand and supply rose in close balance at a rapid rate. In both cases, productivity went up unusually fast, taking the sting out of wage increases. A high degree of price stability was maintained for several years in conditions that could easily, if once tilted upward, have become inflationary. The moving balance in France broke down in 1957 when rising expenditures associated with the Algerian War impinged on an economy with little slack, much as Vietnam War expenditures helped destroy stability in the United States from 1965, and controls proved useless from that point. A new French Government reversed policies and got out of Algeria two years later. Few mistakes, however unpleasant, go on forever.

The new government which carried out the successful devaluation at the end of 1958 was opposed to extensive use of price controls and temporarily abandoned them. But the rapid rate of expansion and strong balance-of-payments surplus which followed in the next few years, accompanied by levels of unemployment steadily around 2.5 percent of the labor force, generated persistent upward pressure on wages and prices. Unit labor costs in manufacturing increased about 7 percent in 1962 and in 1963.[33] In September 1963, the government decided that its opposition in principle to price and wage controls was a luxury that had to be suspended. A general freeze was included along with aggregate deflationary measures in an emergency stabilization program. In 1964, the unit cost of labor in manufacturing was held at the level of 1963, while output continued to rise rapidly. The following year, the stabilization program began to result in a severe drag on production. Unit labor costs in manufacturing started up again, not because wages rose faster but because the deflation slowed down the growth of productivity.[34]

The stabilization program was formulated by the Ministry of Finance in rather pointed independence of the national plan. It was not part of any long-term approach to incomes policy, simply a safety-first deflationary move putting price stability and the balance-of-payments ahead of everything else. It proved unsatisfactory in practice by 1965, and unsatisfactory in principle from the beginning.

Effort toward a more integrated policy was stimulated by a particularly

[33] Shultz and Aliber, *op. cit.*, p. 132.
[34] *Ibid.*; Organization for European Cooperation and Development, *Main Economic Indicators* (June 1967), p. 72.

dramatic strike in the nationalized coal industry in March 1963. The government had been trying to hold down its own budget, and to restrain the average pace of wage increases, by keeping the rate of increase of wages in the public sector below that in private industry. Government workers, both those directly employed in government agencies and those in the nationalized industries, focused their claims specifically on the "catching up" principle. The coal strike was called when supplies were low and inflationary difficulties serious. The government announced its firm determination not to get pushed around, and then turned the problem over to an independent group of experts to solve. The experts reached the conclusion that a wage increase of 8 percent was necessary to catch up, but then went much further to spell out the weaknesses of the collective race upward. As long as the nation failed to formulate any more coherent system, the government would surely have to live with the comparability principle. But why not formulate an overall plan for incomes, within which to set wage standards consistent with output growth, changes in the allocation of labor, and improved price stability?[35]

The experts' report settling the coal miners' strike led directly to a conference bringing together government officials concerned with economic planning and representatives of the country's principal economic and social interest groups.[36] Even the labor unions, which had consistently refused to have anything to do with incomes policies or with national planning, participated on the understanding that this was an exploratory general discussion and not a commitment to future cooperation.

One of the major proposals made at this conference by Pierre Massé, then director of the Planning Commission, was that the next five-year plan should develop a full set of projections for income flows in actual prices. This proposal was subsequently embodied in the Fifth Plan, covering 1966-70. Projections in physical terms for sector outputs and resource use are accompanied by a consistent set of estimates for income and expenditure flows in terms of forecast prices. This involves predictions of changes in the aggregate price level and in relative prices, as well as indications of the rates at which profits, wages, and other forms of income are expected to grow.[37] Unlike the practice in the United States and the United King-

[35] Jean Boissonnat, *La politique des revenus* (Seuil, 1966), pp. 87-88.

[36] "Rapport sur la politique des revenus établi à la suite de la conference des revenus," presented by Pierre Massé (La Documentation Française, 1964), cited hereafter as Massé, "Report."

[37] *Cinquième plan du développement économique et social, 1966-1970* (Paris, 1965), Vol. 1, pp. 177-91. Cf. J. Delors, "Politique des revenus et strategie du

dom of setting wage and other standards such that they might be consistent with stable prices, the French projections build in the assumption that prices will rise at an average annual rate of 1.5 percent.

Perhaps the key contrast to American guidepost policies, apart from the complexity of detail and the presentation of a complete set of accounts, is that the French approach involves explicit decision on how different forms of income should change relative to each other. The annual rate of increase in real wages per worker was projected at 3.3 percent, and of agricultural incomes per capita at 4.8 percent. The growth of total wage payments was projected as falling from 7.3 percent per year for 1960-65 to 5.0 percent for 1965-70, while the rate of increase in corporate saving was to go in the opposite direction, from 4.4 to 6.4 percent. The underlying pattern of choice was oriented toward holding back salaries and private consumption, which had been rising faster than national product, in order to permit more rapid relative growth of government services, corporate self-financing, and fixed capital formation in the industrial sector.[38]

Considering the problems raised for all attempts at incomes policies by the universal conflict between those who believe they are behind at the start and need to catch up, and those who regard historical differentials as minimum approximations to their just due, there is one particularly touching note in the fifth plan. It states, with that peculiarly Latin capacity for conjuring away the unresolved problem by declaring its nonexistence, that the "norm for each category will be considered in itself, and not by reference to other categories. More precisely, no category will draw from the actual progress of other categories any argument to be considered as justification for passing its own norm."[39]

It must be emphasized that the preceding projections are not accompanied by measures of control which can confidently be expected to make things turn out as intended.[40] The government's own expenditures and

---

développement, *Revue d'Économie Politique,* Vol. 75 (1965), pp. 559-92, and "L'Experience française de politique des revenus" (Fiuggi Conference, May 1966), mimeo.

[38] *Cinquième plan,* pp. 46-58, 182-91.

[39] *Ibid.,* p. 19.

[40] Except for incomes paid by the government. One interesting form of income in this category is that of doctors, practically all paid through the national medical program. The fifth plan envisages that doctors' incomes will be "aligned with the rate of growth forseen for wages" (Delors, "L'Experience française de politique des revenus, *op. cit.,* p. 21, note 1).

influence over the allocation of credit may be directed to fit the program, but the main point in the present context is that the system indicates a possible route for wage-price guidance if it is taken seriously as a part of macroeconomic policy. It aims at using income policy to reduce the need for periodic deflations, and thereby to raise the long-term rate of growth.[41]

Little has been accomplished so far in developing new operating techniques to implement guidance of wages or prices. A study commission was established in 1966, the "Centre d'Etude des Revenus et des Couts." The idea is sometimes discussed as if it were similar to the British National Board for Prices and Incomes, but the group is composed of important personalities with many other things to do, and it was not given staff or impetus corresponding to those of the National Board.

Two new institutional devices, the "stabilization contract" and the "program contract," have been devised as possible steps toward more active policy. They have been presented to industrial trade associations in the form of an offer to release associated firms from official price control in exchange for negotiated commitments. The stabilization contracts aimed at an agreement that any increases in product prices would be offset by decreases on other goods sold by members of the group. A number of such contracts are in effect, though apparently it has not been easy to enforce them. The program contract does not require any specific price behavior. It requests the firms to agree to cooperate with the government by giving access to information on costs, and to discuss the relationships among pricing decisions, wage practices, and investment. Several of these contracts have been negotiated in 1966, although no one seems to be sure what they are expected to accomplish.

French experience thus combines some practical results of detailed controls in earlier postwar years, innocent of any systematic program, with elaborate but untested schemes for integration of incomes guidance and overall economic policy. These newer ideas have at least two special merits. They attempt to reconcile open discussion of objectives with professionally integrated forecasts of income and product flows, and they go beyond the simple notion of parallel evolution of wages and output toward explicit consideration of desirable changes in income shares.

[41] Massé, "Report"; Jacques Lecaillon, "La politique des revenus," *Revue d'Economie Politique,* Vol. 75 (1965), pp. 517-58.

Observations on Experience Abroad

One of the benefits of reviewing price behavior and policies in other countries is the sense it conveys that local problems are by no means unique. If one were to characterize the American results with guideposts by the arbitrary statement that they have accomplished about 10 percent of the job intended, then by comparison most other countries would be strung out from about 2 to 10 percent. No country has scored any great success, if success is measured by maintenance of price stability for long periods at very low levels of unemployment.

Restraints on prices and wages have served at times to provide helpful breathing spells for short periods, and to break upward spirals that had continued from conditions of excess demand into a situation in which market forces should have stopped them but did not. They have also helped foster several years of fair stability while aggregate demand and supply were rising fast in close balance. It is also true that negotiated restraints and norms have proven futile everywhere under continuing conditions of excessive aggregate demand, but it should be noted that the breakdowns typically occurred at levels of unemployment well below those encountered in the United States in the last decade.

European countries have in general been less successful in holding down domestic inflation than the United States. Comparing year-to-year changes in consumer prices from 1950 to 1963, the median increase for thirteen European countries was greater than the American in ten of the thirteen years. The last time that the increase in the United States exceeded the European median was 1957-58.[42] As shown in Table 4, the net increase for the period 1958-66 was markedly below those in the other major industrial countries.

The greater degree of price stability achieved in the United States in the first half of the 1960's helped somewhat toward the crucial objective of maintaining competitive export prices, though not as much as might be suggested by differences in the behavior of domestic consumer prices. The results are summarized in Table 5, which may be compared to the poorer showing from 1953 to 1960 given in Table 1, page 6.

[42] H. A. Turner and H. Zoeteweij, *Prices, Wages and Incomes Policies* (International Labour Office, 1966), p. 12, Table 3.

TABLE 4

Comparative Changes in Cost of Living: United States,
West European Countries, and Japan, 1958–66

(December 1958 = 100)

Country	December 1960	December 1965	December 1966
United States	103	110	114
France	110	133	137
Germany	103	120	123
Italy	103	132	135
Japan	104	140	148
The Netherlands	103	124	128
United Kingdom	102	122	128

Source: International Monetary Fund, *International Financial Statistics* (June 1967), p. 33.

Italy and Japan continued to bring their export prices down relative to the United States, just as they had for 1953-60, but otherwise the relative showing of the United States improved. This time American export prices were reduced slightly compared to those of France and Germany, as well as to the United Kingdom.

Reviewing such data suggests that differences in national patterns of cost and price change may be too great to be handled successfully over long periods with fixed exchange rates. The United Kingdom can hardly hope to operate effective economic policy with indefinitely rising relative prices for its exports, nor the rest of the world to meet Japanese competition openly if their export prices keep on falling relative to those of all

TABLE 5

Indexes of Unit Values of Exports of Manufactured Goods, 1960–66

(1960 = 100)

Country	1963	1965	1966 Second Quarter
United States	101	105	104
Belgium	99	101	100[a]
France	101	106	108
Germany	105	108	110
Italy	98	98	96
Japan	92	90	88[a]
United Kingdom	105	110	115

Source: United Nations, *Monthly Bulletin of Statistics* (December 1966), p. xvi.
[a] Refers to first quarter of 1966.

other countries. It would be surprising if wage-price policies could iron out enough of these differences to reconcile high investment with external equilibrium in all these competing countries. Unless the countries suffering greater degrees of pressure on prices give up and accept slower growth, either by deflation or by trade restrictions hampering efficiency, they will have to change their exchange rates. But this in turn can make inflationary pressures more difficult to handle if the underlying causes are not corrected. Insofar as those causes include a significant element of discretionary, even conventional, wage-price upward interaction, governmentally guided wage-price restraints must take their part among the measures used to permit faster growth without repeated balance-of-payments difficulties.

The summaries given for some aspects of experience in three European countries should at least make clear that a variety of approaches is possible and that there is some degree of reality to the effort, but that actual accomplishments so far have been modest. Standing alone, these summaries are a poor reflection of the true range of policy devices being considered and tried. The account leaves out completely the different and highly interesting efforts in Sweden to use central norms more for increasing equality and lessening work stoppages than for short-run stabilization, as well as the fairly active policies in several other European countries.[43]

Outside Europe, where problems of serious inflation in conditions of high unemployment are often far worse, an extraordinary experiment in using eclectic wage-price and specific tax techniques to break extreme inflation is under way in Brazil. A fascinating econometric study of the factors involved in propagating rapid inflation, and the interacting effects of various possible changes in the key coefficients, has been prepared on the basis of Argentine experience.[44] Anne Romanis of the International Monetary Fund, in studies not yet published, has been building up a multicountry set of comparisons distinguishing consequences for wage-price policy of such aspects of the national economy as its degree of participation in world trade, degree of unionization, and behavioral characteristics of union and employer federations.[45]

[43] Cf. Fellner and others, *op. cit.*, and Turner and Zoeteweij, *op. cit.*, Chap. 5.

[44] Geoffrey Maynard and Willy Van Rijckeghem, "Stabilization Policy in an Inflationary Economy: Argentina" (Harvard Development Advisory Service, Bellagio Conference, June 1966).

[45] *Cost Inflation and Incomes Policy in Industrial Countries,* International Monetary Fund, *Staff Papers,* Vol. 14, No. 1 (March 1967), pp. 169-209.

Nobody has a clean analytical system or neat package of firmly established conclusions. Still, it would be a pity if preoccupation with more traditional monetary-fiscal techniques, or easy satisfaction with the evidence that wage-price policies used by themselves have had limited effects, led either governments or economists to decide that the issues involved are not worth continuing exploration. It would be a pity because the problems are real and nearly universal, and because there are grounds for believing that they might be handled more effectively if carefully developed wage-price policies are added to an appropriate mixture of more conventional techniques.

PART THREE

ISSUES OF ANALYSIS AND POLICY

IX

Causes and Varieties of Inflation

HUMAN INGENUITY CAN DISPLAY its unlimited resilience in manufacturing economic principles nearly as well as in any other area of existence. Theories of inflation are legion. Explanations of why there can be only one kind and one cure are popular too, both with those who think that the one kind is a matter of arbitrary exploitation by selfish interests and with those who think that the only question is the supply of money. For present purposes, the goal is not a survey of all possible positions but rather an analysis of arguments as to whether or not there is any logical role for a scheme similar to the guideposts.

Aggregate Demand and Supply

By analogy with an individual market, it has become standard practice to explain rising prices chiefly in terms of an excess of aggregate demand over aggregate supply. On the hypothesis that it is better to get one truth straight than a dozen confused, this is usually the main explanation given in the introductory textbooks. It makes a great deal of sense. During and immediately after World War II, and again during the Korean War, most industries operated close to capacity most of the time, food and raw material supplies and skilled labor became very tight, and it was difficult to conceive that further increases in demand could be met by corresponding increases in supply. Prices went up in many individual markets because

123

sellers could charge more without reducing sales below their capacity to supply, and because buyers were willing to pay more to get what they wanted in the face of scarcity. An adequate explanation of what was going on could be presented without referring to any occult forces or elaborate theories.

Although this concept of the relationship between aggregate demand and supply is useful, it gives some trouble in conditions such as those prevailing since the Korean War. In 1955 and again in 1965-66, there were many signs of pressure on capacity in particular industries, and some labor skills were in short supply; but there were also many directions in which output could have been raised by putting existing resources more fully to use. From 1956 to 1964, there was little question that the economy was operating well below its outer limits, but still there were some specific shortages. If physical resources and labor skills were completely interchangeable, so that excess demand in any one direction could promptly be met by bringing in productive resources from fields with excess capacity, the idea of a point of balance between aggregate demand and supply would be more meaningful. As it is, the question is one of identifying the degree of demand pressure considered troublesome, rather than ascertaining whether excess demand in some conclusive sense is really here.

One way to simplify the question might be to decide that demand should be considered excessive if prices begin to increase. This could provide an objective signal, but one which might do more harm than good. It could be a poor signal either because of failure to operate under conditions in which demand really outruns productive capacity, or because of premature operation when it does not.

Price signals could fail to operate under conditions of excess demand if increased imports or reduced exports were used to dampen domestic inflationary pressures at the cost of external stability. This was not the case in the United States during the early years of the guideposts. On the contrary, exports increased so much faster than imports that the current account surplus, which had fallen close to zero in 1959, reached $8 billion for 1964. But in the next two years imports did rise faster than exports, and the current surplus dropped by $3 billion. The increase in imports certainly played a role in holding down pressure on domestic prices in 1966. This was not necessarily a harmful process—the surplus remained extraordinary in historical terms, and strikingly so for a year of such strong demand pressure—but in some degree the change acted to short-circuit price indications of limits on capacity.

Price indicators could also fail to identify conditions requiring aggregative deflation if controls were used to block increases despite genuine supply shortages. "Genuine" here means shortages that are not consequences of deliberate impediments to supply, nor purely transitory accidents, but that derive from inability to obtain the productive resources necessary for expanding output at current prices. When the marginal cost of increased production exceeds a controlled price, maintaining the control is harmful. When this happens in many markets, there is no way of knowing that those supplies which are available are being allocated to their most valuable uses; prices do not guide the decisions of producers efficiently, and real welfare may be persistently undermined. Such a situation might be called an inflation, even though price indexes remain stable. Or it might be described as a condition of suppressed inflationary pressure, but whatever it is called it is something to be avoided.

Much of the criticism directed against the guideposts reflects the suspicion that they might be used to block price signals when there are genuine shortages. Official statements of the guideposts have always declared that they were not to be applied in such conditions. In the cases of copper and hide prices discussed above, they were used in violation of the stated principle. Such departures might or might not be defended as desirable on other grounds; if generalized, they would be seriously harmful for economic efficiency. When they occur, they can be identified; when they are considered, they can be avoided. They are not inherent in the system.

The more common problem with reliance on rising average prices as a signal of excess demand is that they have often gone up despite objective evidence of significant unemployment and underutilized plant capacity. Prices went up in every year from 1934 to 1937, with unemployment on the order of one-fifth of the labor force. Measures of productive potential indicate a great deal of idle capacity from 1955 to 1965, but the wholesale price index went up in several of these years and the consumer price index in all of them. Using the consumer price index as an indicator would have called for deflation in every one of the last ten years. Had the government always followed this signal, the waste of productive potential would have been enormous.

Anyone may as a matter of preference argue for measures to reduce demand whenever prices rise, but it would be misleading to suggest that increases necessarily demonstrate inability to raise production further. Many factors other than excess demand may be involved. They should probably all be regarded as second-order considerations, operating to change the course of prices moderately as compared to the more powerful force coming from the relationship between aggregate demand and supply. But if they operate to make prices rise by even one or two percentage points more than would otherwise occur, that may be enough to weaken important exports, to push wage claims and other reactions more in the direction of causing serious cumulative difficulties, or to trip the signal that leads to aggregative deflation and rising unemployment.

Discretionary Wage and Price Changes

Both wages and prices can be raised in conditions of excess supply, and often are. Powers of organization and ability to exert influence on costs and prices have been demonstrated by professional groups, farmers, factory workers, and even corporations. It is not common to hear any seller explain why the price he is getting fully compensates his costs or the value of his services. Most are either resigned to waiting for the next feasible chance to move up, or are actively trying to move. The miracle is not that prices and wages often rise in conditions of unemployment and idle capacity, but that they do not go up faster.

In most other countries they go up faster than in the United States. Most of the credit for the differences should go to the forces of competition which still work so powerfully in many fields. It is easy to show evidence of concentration in manufacturing, restrictions on entry in labor markets, and government regulations blocking access to alternatives in transportation and in agriculture. Such obstacles are widespread, but it remains true that buyers usually have alternatives. This is less evident in labor than in product markets, but it must be recognized that unions do not set wages. They have to negotiate them with employers who can sometimes turn to machinery, to purchased components, to alternative products or regions, or even to alternative workers, and who must consider the effects of increased prices on sales. The arbitrary power which remains is real enough in many cases, but may easily be overestimated.

Wages

Wage rates do not exhibit much downward flexibility; neither employers nor completely unorganized workers would regard reductions as within the bounds of civilized behavior except in the most extreme circumstances. But the rate at which wages increase is a variable subject to constraints. Wage increases should not be regarded as an inexorable pressure before which everything else must give way. Rather, the tendency to go up operates more strongly when the constraints lessen and slows down when they tighten.

The Phillips curve idea of a schedule of possible rates of wage increase depending on certain conditions would be a good picture, provided it were recognized that several different factors may move the schedule to the right or left. Empirical studies of American data suggest that the most powerful of such factors, other than the level of unemployment, are the rate of profit (or perhaps the level of value productivity acting on profit), and possibly the rates of change in unemployment and in the cost of living.[1]

The relative weights of the factors cited change from period to period. The general interpretive point to which they lead does not depend on any idea that wage changes may be accurately predicted from past relationships. It is simply that wages are responsive simultaneously to two streams of influence: to varying degrees of tightness in labor markets and therefore of competitive pressure as firms try to get or to hold the workers they need, and to a host of considerations involving judgment by the two sides with respect to the multiple goals with which they are concerned. What determines the numerical relationship observed in particular statistical tests, and what causes the coefficients to change among periods, is the complex web of expectations and judgments of proper standards, acting within the loose constraint imposed by imperfect markets. The bal-

---

[1] Otto Eckstein and Thomas A. Wilson, "The Determination of Money Wages in American Industry," *Quarterly Journal of Economics,* Vol. 76 (1962), pp. 379-414; Frank C. Ripley, "An Analysis of the Eckstein-Wilson Wage Determination Model," *Quarterly Journal of Economics,* Vol. 80 (1966), pp. 121-36; Edwin Kuh, "A Productivity Theory of Wage Levels—An Alternative to the Phillips Curve," *Review of Economic Studies* (forthcoming); George L. Perry, *Unemployment, Money Wage Rates, and Inflation* (Massachusetts Institute of Technology Press, 1966).

ance of judgment in regard to proper practice in the United States yields rising wage rates even with employment falling, or stable wage rates at fairly high rates of unemployment. New standards of what is acceptable may change the way the scope for discretion is exercised, and apparently did do so from 1962 through 1965.

Prices

Prices move more diversely among industries than wages do, partly because cost trends may differ widely. Some industries are able to hold or to raise profit margins even with falling prices, while others may be suffering pressure on profit margins despite rising prices. But diversity of cost trends does not explain all the differences in behavior in pricing. Chart 1 in Chapter 4 shows many cases of decreasing prices associated with rising productivity between 1959 and 1964, but in the automobile industry in the same period prices stayed up and falling unit costs yielded rising profits.

Taking a cross section at any one time, profit rates differ widely among industries. One of the most important factors explaining such differences is the scope for new competition through new entry.[2] Another is the degree of cooperation among existing firms, which tends to be high in fields in which there are few sellers. Competition is strong in many fields, but it does not by any means eliminate all scope for choice in setting prices.

Where such scope does exist, economic principles provide a solution to how it may be exercised. The logic of profit maximization suggests that the margin above costs will be determined by the way in which sales respond to price changes. A low elasticity of demand, meaning that buyers do not have good competitive alternatives and will not decrease purchases significantly at higher prices, leads to high markups.[3] This apparently reasonable proposition constitutes an intellectual block for some people. It seems to say that firms will set their most profitable prices in a deter-

[2] Joe S. Bain, *Barriers to New Competition* (Harvard University Press, 1956). and *Industrial Organization* (University of California Press, 1959), Chap. 10.

[3] One way of expressing the relationship is the following formula, in which p stands for price, mc for marginal cost, and e for elasticity: $p = mc \left(1 + \dfrac{1}{e-1}\right)$.

Cf. Tibor Scitovsky, *Welfare and Competition* (Allen and Unwin, 1952), Chap. 13.

minate pattern within which there is no place for discretionary variation. The implication is that monopoly power can explain high profit margins, or high prices, but not *rising* margins or prices: market power cannot explain inflation.

The proposition leads to difficulty if it is taken to be an exact description of what is the case at any given time, and still more so if it is considered as indicating a definite solution to which the firm may be expected to adhere for prolonged periods. In the first place, the idea that elasticity is known in any precise sense must be recognized as a myth. Elasticity may be fairly well ascertained by the seller if the firm is in a monopoly position and is only concerned about the buyer's ultimate preferences for the product. But nearly all firms are engaged in competition with at least a few close rivals, and it is no help to know that sales of the product will be little affected by higher prices if some of these rivals are in a position to take over all the sales by quoting lower prices. The whole concept of a determinate solution is a hangover of thinking in terms of a two-dimensional world of either pure monopoly or pure competition. It misses the critical role of potential undercutting when cooperation among sellers is, as it nearly always is, something less than perfect.

Because of uncertainty about reactions of buyers and of rival sellers firms must experiment to find out what prices are best. Since any change in price by a seller uncertain of the reactions of rivals may provoke costly repercussions, the firm is not free to move prices up and down with great frequency.[4] It must be the rare exception, rather than the general rule, when the firm is completely satisfied that the price set is the optimal one to which it would like to cling indefinitely.

Case studies of business behavior suggest that the firm is usually inclined to avoid change if the existing situation appears reasonably satisfactory, but likely to be more willing to risk a trial upward when rivals are believed to be dissatisfied with the current price or too fully occupied to be leaning toward competitive underbidding. The description of the steel industry in the 1950's by M. A. Adelman, showing their efforts to get to a higher rate of profit by a series of individually modest upward steps

[4] Two fundamental articles explaining the tendency of prices to stay put in oligopolistic markets are: Paul M. Sweezy, "Demand Under Conditions of Oligopoly," *Journal of Political Economy*, Vol. 47 (1939), pp. 568-73, and George J. Stigler, "The Kinky Oligopoly Demand Curve and Rigid Prices," *ibid.*, Vol. 55 (1947), pp. 432-49.

spread over many years, is a more illuminating picture of reality than any concept of a known target to which the firm goes directly and stays.[5]

In addition to the variability introduced by uncertainty about rivals' reactions, the firm must usually be concerned with the problem of change in the nature of the alternatives open to potential buyers. Changes in tastes, in technical characteristics and availabilities of possible substitutes, in prices of substitutes, and in all the factors that make the elasticity of demand what it is, must be expected to occur all the time. In highly competitive markets, prices change frequently also, reflecting both cost and demand variations. In less intensely competitive markets, prices change less readily, but there is no reason to expect that the factors bearing on demand and costs are any more rigidly set. The logic of profit maximization implies that a particular price will be optimal at any given time, but it does not mean that the firm just finds it and stays there. In the usual situation, the management of the firm must be uncertain, considering possible change, and continuously alert to the behavior of rivals for indications of when and in which direction it may be advisable to make the next move.

If the preceding description is accurate, or at least more nearly accurate than the idea of firms sitting comfortably with their prices fixed at optimal levels, the existence of market power may contribute to an explanation of rising prices. In conditions of moderately strong demand, with some costs rising and others falling, market power may alter the average trend of prices by preventing decreases that might have been possible in cases of falling unit costs. In conditions approaching full employment, with wages and competitively set prices moving upward, firms which are not in highly competitive industries find it easier to move up toward the levels they would prefer because each can be more confident that the others' costs are increasing, and that business is not so poor as to provoke price shading to capture market shares from each other.

Descriptions of behavior by firms with some degree of market power suggest that semiautomatic rules of pricing are followed by many companies, but that price leaders and more actively managed companies give a lot of thought to decisions and weigh a good many short- and long-run factors in the process. It may be a generally valid description to say that they aim at maximum profits, other things equal, but some may so aim by trying to hold down prices and raise their market shares, some by mini-

[5] "Steel, Administered Prices and Inflation," *Quarterly Journal of Economics,* Vol. 75 (1961), pp. 16-40.

mizing any possible provocation through changes in relative prices, others by sacrificing some current profits in order to minimize a real or imaginary threat of regulation, some by focusing on sales volume to ensure long-range growth, and so on almost indefinitely according to the judgment of the management involved.[6] Discretionary judgment is exercised in variable ways within the sometimes wide boundaries imposed by external constraints. Any marked change in the climate of understanding of what is or what is not acceptable pricing behavior may conceivably affect decisions.

It is not easy to measure the independent effect of discretionary decisions on prices because they are so intimately linked with changes in costs. Adelman's article on pricing in the steel industry during the 1950's brings out particularly well the interactions between the industry's power to raise prices and the union's power to insist on sharing gains by faster wage increases. Prices rose out of line with increases in most other industries, but wages did too and eroded profits, providing excuse and stimulus for further price increases. In such a process, each side virtuously blames the other. It is equally true that if the union were weaker and unable to get such fast wage increases, prices would increase less, and that if firms had less market control and did not try to increase prices, wages would increase less. It is also true that such interaction between mutually offsetting claims results in a faster rate of increase in the price level than would occur if both sides could jointly be induced to moderate the ways in which they use their discretionary power.

The empirical relationships established by George Perry for manufacturing industries in the period 1947-60 make it possible to measure the approximate consequences for employment and wages of different rates of profit. Perhaps the most revealing comparison is one which estimates the level of unemployment that would be necessary to hold the rate of increase in wages down to 3 percent per year, taking the cost of living as fixed. Assuming that the rate of profit after taxes was held at the 1947-60 average of 11.8 percent, the relationships prevailing in this period were such that it would be necessary to hold the rate of unemployment as high as 6.4 percent. If the rate of profit were reduced one point, to 10.8 per-

[6] Cf. W. J. Baumol, *Business Behavior, Value and Growth* (Macmillan, 1959); R. M. Cyert and J. G. March, *A Behavioral Theory of the Firm* (Prentice-Hall, 1963); Robin Marris, *The Economic Theory of "Managerial" Capitalism* (Free Press, 1964).

cent, unemployment could be brought down to 5.4 percent consistent with the same rate of increase in wages.[7]

Negotiated increases in wages, short of full employment, can push up costs and lead to higher prices. Discretionary increases in prices can occur in conditions under which the firms concerned would have been willing and able to expand production at prior prices, if the opportunity to do still better by raising prices were somehow excluded. Discretionary price increases can stimulate higher wage claims, or be added to a wage increase that ran higher in the first place because both sides knew that prices could readily be raised as an offset. The relationship of aggregate demand to potential supply always affects the trends of wages and prices, but it does not determine a unique result immune to changes in judgment.

Cyclical and Trend Behavior of Controlled Prices

While there is little question that large firms in concentrated industries often have room for discretion in setting prices, it does not follow that they are usually the ones who initiate inflationary pressures. The contrary is often nearer the truth: "Wage rates and competitively determined prices are the dynamic elements which drag along in their wake, but sluggishly and slowly, the prices of products produced in highly concentrated industrial markets."[8]

The preceding quotation refers to experience in the late 1940's, under conditions of general excess demand. It would fit 1965-66 fairly well. It does not describe the 1950's nearly as accurately. Cyclical behavior may vary considerably according to the degree to which the economy pushes toward the limits of its capacity; and the net result through several cycles may look different from that during an individual upswing.

Prices in highly competitive industries respond more rapidly than those of concentrated industries in the initial stages of an upturn. Competitive producers do not normally operate with excess capacity. Increases in demand have to be met with rising production at higher marginal cost, or with rising prices if output cannot be increased quickly. The extreme illustration used to be the agricultural sector, and it still is for those agricultural products not under administrative controls. Competitive manufacturing industries behave in much the same way, though usually with more scope

[7] Perry, op. cit., p. 59.
[8] Edward S. Mason, Economic Concentration and the Monopoly Problem (Harvard University Press, 1957), p. 170.

for increasing production in the short run and therefore with somewhat more stable prices.

Manufacturing firms in highly concentrated industries are more likely to take long-run objectives into account, to place a premium on avoiding frequent price changes because they may upset existing market shares, and to react to rising demand at first by putting idle capacity into operation rather than by increasing prices. Their interest in minimizing frequency of changes has also led toward longer-term wage contracts, providing more predictable wage costs regardless of changes in labor market conditions during the life of the contract. If aggregate demand rises rapidly, their initial price behavior provides an element of stability; if aggregate demand falls off they are likely to stay put while more competitive prices come back down, in which case their behavior looks less like stability and more like a trouble-creating inflexibility.

This general pattern of behavior during a cyclical upswing does not mean that prices in the more concentrated industries stay put indefinitely. Quite the contrary. The "annual round" of price increases in the steel industry during the 1950's, or the once-a-year price changes for automobiles, can add up to more of a net increase in the course of a decade than hundreds of back-and-forth swings in more competitive industries. From the 1947-49 average to 1958, wholesale prices for all manufacturing went up 30 percent, those for primary metals 82 percent, automobiles 53, and apparel products 1 percent.[9] In such a process, the fact that apparel prices swing up earlier than those of metals and autos in cyclical recoveries becomes of secondary importance.

In the 1950's, unlike the late 1940's, aggregate demand was rarely strong enough to bring the economy close to the outer limits of capacity. Prices of the more competitive industries moved up when demand improved, but came back down again when aggregate growth faltered. In industries less vulnerable to restraining pressures from weak demand prices moved upward when conditions seemed opportune, or remained stable when they did not. Because of the lack of overall inflationary pressure, their periodic increases stood out as a source of general upward bias. The steel firms, the aluminum companies and the automobile producers in particular were the industries that provoked the guideposts.

The rationale of the guideposts is more appropriate to the 1950 type

[9] Harold M. Levinson, "Postwar Movement of Prices and Wages in Manufacturing Industries," Study Paper No. 21, Joint Economic Committee, *Employment, Growth and Price Levels,* 86 Cong. 2 sess. (1960), p. 14, Table 8.

situation than to one of generally strong and rising demand pressure. With rising demand, the competitive industries lead the way upward, as they should. It would not help if their market-determined increases were restricted by administrative intervention. It would be equally unhelpful if they were accompanied by arbitrary, if slower, steps upward in more concentrated industries still operating with excess capacity. If the latter industries also moved up to capacity too, and demand continued to grow, the scope for useful application of the guideposts would diminish and the need for aggregative deflationary brakes would be clear.

If the brakes were too severe, and demand began to fall seriously short of capacity, prices would come down in many competitive fields. They would be much less likely to come down in the more concentrated industries. Some of the experience in the 1950's suggested that they might even go on upward, in an attempt to maintain profits despite falling volume. At that point, the guidepost-type restraints would regain their full relevance, not as a cure for general inflation but as a means to avoid distortion and to make clear the desirability of renewed increases in demand.

The Pace and Balance of Expansion

The potential output of the American economy grows at a rate of about 4 percent per year. From an initial position close to the ceiling, actual output could not increase faster than that without provoking inflationary difficulties. If the initial position were one-tenth below potential, actual output could be increased faster than 4 percent per year without causing inflationary pressure, but any attempt to bring it up to the ceiling in a short period would send prices up. The existence of idle capacity would not be a sufficient dampening factor if demand increased very rapidly, because supply reactions take time to carry out. The speed of change is a separate factor which can give rise to signs of inflation even with substantial unemployment.

The independent relevance of the rate of change of output may be of special significance in explaining the course of prices in the 1960's. The expansion from 1961 through 1964 gradually reduced the gap between actual and potential output, at a pace which did not give rise to any serious strains of adjustment. In the second quarter of 1965, when a major increase in defense spending coincided with an acceleration of business investment, the rate of growth of GNP speeded up from 5.5 to 7.2 percent per year.[10] Both wholesale and retail prices began to move up fast almost immediately. Monetary and fiscal restraints began to take hold in the following year: the increase in GNP between the first and the fourth quarters of 1966 was one-fifth less than in the preceding three calendar quarters. Even though the average level of unemployment stayed lower in the last half of 1966 than it had been in the last half of 1965, the rates of increase in both wholesale and consumer prices slowed down markedly.[11]

The independent importance of the rate of change of output has not been determined in any sense commanding general agreement, but the principle is clearly relevant and is supported by empirical studies of wage behavior. Even in the original Phillips curve investigation, deviations of wage changes from those which would be indicated by the level of unemployment were explained primarily by reference to differences in the rate of change of unemployment. In more precise statistical tests, the rate of change of unemployment was shown to be at least as dependable as the level of unemployment, and for long-run tests superior, as a basis for prediction of wage changes in the United States.[12] This does not mean that the level of unemployment is irrelevant, but it may mean that the inflationary signals in evidence in 1965 and the first half of 1966 were not due as much to the fact that unemployment fell below 4 percent as they were to the speed with which the economy was moving at that point.

The idea that the degree of difference in rates of growth of output or employment among sectors may affect the price level has been presented logically and backed by empirical evidence for both the United States and the United Kingdom. One of the more convincing expositions is that of Charles Schultze.[13] He suggested that wages will go up faster in a particu-

[10] *Economic Report of the President, 1967*, pp. 45-47.

[11] *Ibid.*, p. 47.

[12] William G. Bowen and R. Albert Berry, "Unemployment Conditions and Movements of the Money Wage Level," *Review of Economics and Statistics*, Vol. 45 (1963), pp. 163-72.

[13] "Recent Inflation in the United States," Study Paper No. 1, Joint Economic Committee, *Employment, Growth and Price Levels*, 86 Cong. 1 sess. (1959). See also Richard G. Lipsey, "The Relation Between Unemployment and the Rate of Change in Money Wage Rates in the United Kingdom, 1862-1957," *Economica*, Vol. 27 (1960), pp. 17-23; W. G. Bowen and S. H. Masters, "Shifts in Demand and the Inflation Problem," *American Economic Review*, Vol. 54 (1964), pp. 975-84; Keith Hancock, "Shifts in Demand and the Inflation Problem: Comment," *ibid.*, Vol. 56 (June 1955), pp. 517-22.

lar field the faster that employment rises in it, and also that powerful factors operate to keep wages in all industries approximately in line with each other. For a given increase in aggregate demand, the leading rates of wage increase will be lower if all industries expand employment at approximately equal rates than they would be if the demand and employment growth were concentrated on a few fields. When it is sharply concentrated, as it was on the capital goods industries in 1955-56, wages in those fields go up rapidly, and these rates are quickly followed as standards in other fields.

During the expansion of 1961-65, the growth of output and employment was more evenly balanced among industries than it was in 1955-56.[14] This may have accounted in some degree for the fact that wage rates rose less rapidly than predicted on the basis of prior relationships to levels of unemployment and profits. Attempts to test the quantitative significance for prices of varying degrees of imbalance among expansion rates have not as yet proven highly successful, but there is no reason to doubt that this may be a contributing factor of some importance in particular cycles. In 1965, the surge of investment demand and defense expenditures concentrated on industries already running close to capacity brought the 1955-56 type of problem back into play.

Money Supply and Budget Deficits

The three preceding sets of factors bearing on price changes are not meant to be considered as mutually exclusive explanations. They all act together, with varying relative importance in particular periods, and they do not by any means exhaust the list of significant considerations.[15] Given the wide range of factors shown by so many careful investigators to bear on the course of prices, it is strange that some observers still insist on finding a single cause that will rule out all the others. Practically every possible explanatory factor has its champions who insist that their particular solution is the sole answer, but perhaps the most determinedly exclusive are those who focus on the money supply or on governmental budget deficits.

[14] *Economic Report of the President, 1966*, pp. 67-72; *ibid., 1967*, pp. 72-79.

[15] Cf. Martin Bronfenbrenner and Franklyn D. Holzman, "Survey of Inflation Theory," *American Economic Review*, Vol. 52 (1963), pp. 593-661, and the 183 references cited there.

A recent study published by the International Labour Office starts its explanation of inflation in the following way: "Strictly speaking, the term 'inflation' means an increase in the supply of money in relation to that for commodities."[16] It is not clear what is so strict about it. And this particular approach invites confusion. An increase in the supply of money relative to goods can be a great benefit if the economy is able to respond by increasing production and employment. Any precautionary movement toward holding larger cash balances on the part of the public could be costly unless it is offset by a deliberate increase in the supply of money relative to goods. Changes in the money supply can be good or bad, depending on many things. The definition quoted tends to confuse technical mechanisms with real goals of policy.

"Inflation is always and everywhere a monetary phenomenon, resulting from and accompanied by a rise in the quantity of money relative to output. . . . It follows that the only effective way to stop inflation is to restrain the rate of growth of the quantity of money."[17] The context quickly explains that inflation refers to "substantial changes in prices," of which the examples cited are the aftermath of the Russian Revolution in 1917, the American Revolution and Civil War, and the two world wars. All of these experiences involved rates of increase in prices far beyond any experienced in the United States in peacetime, and all were associated with extraordinary increases in the money supply. It might be doubted that curtailment of the money supply to reduce inflationary pressures would have been an ideal policy prescription in the middle of either world war, but the general logic of the possibility cannot be denied. The question is whether this casts any light on the relevance of guidepost-type constraints to reduce the upward bias of prices in more usual peacetime conditions.

Those who believe that there is a possible role for the guideposts do so because they think that discretionary decisions by some firms and unions can exert variable degrees of pressure on the price level in any given monetary situation. If the airline machinists win a wage increase of 5 percent instead of settling for 3 percent, airline fares, air freight charges, and costs for numerous fields will be higher than they would otherwise have been,

---

[16] H. A. Turner and H. Zoeteweij, *Prices, Wages, and Incomes Policies* (International Labor Office, 1966), p. 28.

[17] Milton Friedman, "What Price Guideposts," in George P. Shultz and Robert Z. Aliber, eds., *Guidelines, Informal Controls, and the Market Place* (University of Chicago Press, 1966), p. 18.

whatever the path of the money supply. Secondary repercussions may decrease expenditures and lower prices in other directions, or they may not. The net consequence with a given money supply may be a decrease in real national income accompanied by a higher price level. Those who do not think that discretionary settlements can affect the general price level may reply that, if monetary restraints were tightened, this would drive down expenditures and reduce prices somewhere in the system. No matter what happens in individual markets, monetary deflation could always hold down the level of prices. This is an important proposition, but it is one of the possible techniques for stopping motion, not an exclusive explanation of what causes the motion in the first place.

The reason that argument on the point becomes so intense is that those advocating monetary restraint intend that it be used to ensure stabilization of prices even if the result is to cause substantial unemployment and waste of potential productive capacity. No one on the other side is opposed to the use of monetary policy to restrain aggregate demand when it is clearly excessive in the sense of outrunning capacity to produce. The essential difference of opinion is not over the efficiency of monetary restraint as a means of holding down prices, or the desirability of doing so when they rise very rapidly, but over the merit of applying deflationary restraints in conditions of substantial unemployment.

What "substantial" unemployment amounts to is a matter of judgment. The Council of Economic Advisers operated for several years on the premise that an unemployment level of 4 percent or more was too high; the Chairman of the Federal Reserve Board argued for monetary deflation in 1961 when the unemployment rate was nearly 7 percent. The Council was more concerned about production and employment, and the Board more about price stability. Both sides cared about the other objectives too, which is the reason the Council proposed the guideposts to promote greater price stability with given levels of employment, and why the proponents of monetary restraint like to suggest that any sign of rising prices is an indication that there is little scope left for increases in production and employment.

It happened that the policy of expansion chosen in 1961 proved that there was then a great deal of scope left for raising production and employment. The system is tilted upward, in the sense that prices begin to rise for many reasons when output is still well short of capacity. If expansion stops at this point, many people will still be looking for work and unable to find it, and billions of dollars worth of potential capacity to produce will still be idle.

A deficit in the national budget means that the government is adding more to aggregate demand by its own spending than it is canceling out by taxing away private purchasing power. Such additions to demand need not, and normally do not, have inflationary effects. They will have such effects only when aggregate demand is either pressing against the limits of productive capacity at full employment, or is already in the process of rising so fast that any additional boost strains the economy's adaptive capacity.

Deficits may be deliberately planned and implemented by tax reductions or increases in government spending, or may develop as the passive result of a fall in national income and a consequent decrease in tax receipts. When a deficit develops because of falling national income, it serves to cushion the effects of the decline in output and employment. If the government were to cut its own spending or to raise taxes to avoid a deficit in such conditions, it would drive output down still further. A passive deficit does not have any inflationary effect: it simply lessens the waste of idle productive capacity by lessening the impact of any initial downturn.

A deficit that is deliberately planned and implemented by either reductions in tax rates or increases in spending, under conditions of substantial unemployment, will raise demand and production. Insofar as it raises employment, it contributes an upward pressure to the rate of increase in wages. Insofar as capacity is underutilized, it also contributes to a better use of employed labor and other factors of production, helping to raise productivity and reduce average costs. The balance between stimulation of wages and stimulation of productivity could work out either way as far as the net effect on unit costs is concerned: from 1961 through 1965, it happened to work out with practically unchanged labor costs in manufacturing. But as full employment comes closer, or the rate of growth of demand speeds up, the positive effect on wages is increasingly likely to outweigh that on productivity. Further deficits under such conditions are likely to have inflationary effects, both because they create shortages, and because they will speed up the pace of wage increases.

Deficits, like changes in the money supply, are best understood as working through the basic relationships of aggregate demand and supply. They are special factors which help determine the course of demand, among many other things. Since they can have inflationary implications under some conditions, and do not under others, it would seem more useful to concentrate attention on those fundamental conditions rather than on these separate, if important, parts of the picture.

Causation and the Guideposts

It is easy to explain inflation without reference to discretionary wage and price increases. Pressures of aggregate demand on supply, overly rapid expansion even with considerable unemployment, overly concentrated expansion creating bottlenecks, or rapid increases in the money supply when unemployment is very low, all could give rise to inflation in the most perfectly competitive economy. But discretionary wage and price increases can occur, and can raise the general price level, even when aggregate demand is stagnant, unemployment is fairly high, and the money supply is held constant. They do not constitute the whole story, just one more valid concern. They would be no concern if the economy were perfectly competitive in labor and product markets, but it is not. They would be of overwhelming importance if competition were next to nonexistent, but it is not. Guidepost restraints have a limited, but genuine, role to play as a supplement to aggregative techniques which can do most, but not all, of the stabilization job.

The American economy is not so well organized by sellers that prices can be expected to race upward by more than 5 percent a year or so unless demand is exerting strong pressure on capacity in many fields. Steeply rising prices are best treated as a manifestation of excess demand, properly answered by monetary and fiscal restraints. But the economy is well-enough organized to yield price increases of 2 to 4 percent per year at the consumer level even in the presence of considerable unemployment and idle capacity. In this range, discretionary wage and price increases in individual industries can add up to enough upward pressure to constitute a "cause" in their own right. They do not constitute an independent determinant. Market conditions can be made so bad by aggregative deflation that this source of upward pressure may be drowned out, or at least seriously weakened. They do constitute an aggravating additional consideration, and may be the main component of the upward creep observed in conditions of moderate unemployment here and everywhere else.

The rationale of the guideposts is the thought that such upward pressure may be moderated in some degree for any given level of unemployment, by bringing a new factor into consideration when discretionary decisions on prices and wages are formulated. The logical and empirical bases of the idea are not such as to suggest any revolutionary accomplishment. They do provide grounds for hope that fewer people need be denied the opportunity for employment, and higher real incomes may be made possible, consistent with whatever rate of increase in prices the society may decide to accept.

X

Effects on Efficiency and Growth

EFFECTS OF THE GUIDEPOSTS on economic efficiency should be considered on two levels: what the consequences would be if the policy were pursued in all sectors of the economy as originally suggested, and what the consequences may be of the differential incidence it has actually had. For the price guidepost, the main departures from the original intent have been the inability to obtain reductions (that would not otherwise have occurred) in cases of falling unit costs, and the selective rather than general success in holding down prices in industries with discretionary market power. With respect to wages, restraining pressure has been somewhat greater on the better organized unions in basic industries and in the government than on less organized groups, though it is possible that the forces operating to resist changes in differentials may have made the effects of the effort toward wage restraint somewhat more general than that for prices.

Allocation of Resources in the Short Run

As originally formulated, the guideposts were completely consistent with basic concepts of efficiency in resource allocation. The key saving clause, for both prices and wages, is the stipulation that increases should be permissible in conditions of shortage. This would mean that the restraints would not be applied in those situations in which purely competitive markets would be expected to yield increasing prices or wages.

If this crucial exemption clause were left inoperative, the system would give highly undesirable results. One particularly severe denunciation of the approach apparently assumes it to be inoperative:

The trouble fundamentally is that the articulation of the guidelines principles largely ignores the role of changes in demand in our system. Our economy depends for its efficient operation on extremely complex and sensitively adjusting pricing relationships that serve as the communications system for promptly reflecting the ever-changing pattern of demands. . . . An economy whose pricing system operates according to the guidelines as enunciated would certainly find its capability for progress weakened.[1]

The point at issue would be extremely important if the central guideline for prices were interpreted literally and the exception stated for conditions of demand pressure were ignored. This could seriously weaken the response of the economic system to changes in consumer preferences. On one side, this danger is at best abstract. Nothing in the system acts to hold up prices if demand falls off and competitive pressure operates to force decreases. The danger is rather on the other side, that demand pressure calling for increases in prices as a signal for expansion of capacity might not lead to the proper response if short-circuited by rigid interpretation of the central guideline. A rise in price should not be blocked in conditions of excess demand and would not if the clause allowing for increases when shortages occur were strictly followed. The problem is not in the nature of the system, but in the possibility that it may be oversimplified in practice.

The cases described earlier include several in which restraints were applied that went contrary to efficiency. These involved two different market situations. One, exemplified by copper and by hides, is that of industries in which there is normally a high degree of price competition. The other, exemplified by molybdenum, is that of industries so well organized it would be ridiculous to call them competitive, but in which demand exceeded supply in conditions of production at full capacity.

Application of pressure to block price increases in either of these situations lowers efficiency. A rising price in a competitive market may indicate a mistaken temporary flurry of demand, but the price cannot stay up unless the value to the firms that want to use the product is equal to or greater than the cost of increasing its production. To prevent an increase in price in such conditions is to force rationing and to deny supplies of the

[1] Paul McCracken, "Price-Cost Behavior and Employment Act Objectives," *Twentieth Anniversary of the Employment Act of 1946,* Hearing before the Joint Economic Committee, 89 Cong. 2 sess. (February 1966), p. 71.

product to some users who may be able to produce more valuable goods with it than do others who get it because they are familiar customers. The existence of the secondary market with a free price took much of the sting out of this problem in the case of copper, but the general point remains. Holding down a price that a competitive market is trying to bid up may raise costs elsewhere and make the general price level go higher than it would have if the price of the competitive commodity had not been blocked in the first place.

In the case of molybdenum in 1966, there was not much competition, but there was a severe shortage. Blocking the price in such conditions holds down costs for those firms which get the input they need more cheaply, but raises costs for others which must either get the commodity by some subterfuge or find a more costly alternative. Some potential users must be denied the commodity if there is not enough to go around; but there is a sound basis for the presumption that the net costs to the economic system and the final effect on prices are higher when rationing is practiced on an arbitrary basis than when supplies are allocated by the price system to those users for whom the value of additional productions made possible by the supplies is highest.[2]

Similar distortions might conceivably occur in labor markets, but there is not much evidence that they have. Underemployment was too pronounced up to 1966 to suggest that restraint on wages in general was contrary to principles of allocative efficiency. Where particular skills were in short supply—as in medical services and some branches of construction—the guideposts did not do much to limit increases. The differential impact suggested by somewhat greater rates of increase in the less well-organized sectors between 1961 and 1966, and by Perry's data for manufacturing showing relatively greater restraint in the more "visible" industries, probably worked in the direction of establishing a wage structure more nearly in line with relative scarcities than would otherwise have occurred.

If labor in general were in short supply, in the unambiguous sense that it was during World War II in the United States or has been in the last few

---

[2] For an impressive exposition of the general logic of market pricing, directed specifically against intervention of the type practiced in connection with the guideposts, see Milton Friedman, "What Price Guideposts?," in George P. Shultz and Robert Z. Aliber, eds., *Guidelines, Informal Controls, and the Market Place* (University of Chicago Press, 1966), pp. 17-39. This exposition is valid for the special cases of competitive markets, or shortages in noncompetitive markets. It fails to make clear that it does not fit the case principally intended by the guideposts.

years in the Netherlands, administrative pressures for restraint on wages could lower efficiency by making it difficult to attract and hold labor in the fields subject to effective control. The original formulation of the guideposts would argue for relaxing them in such conditions and using monetary-fiscal restraints instead. It is possible that efforts at wage restraint in 1966 were on the borderline of creating such distortions, but hardly likely that they went beyond it. The overall percentage of unemployment was still twice as high as that reached during World War II, unemployment rates for negro workers remained excessive by any defensible standard, and the Bureau of Labor Statistics identified only a small number of specific skills as being in short supply.[3] It seems fair to conclude that attempts to use the guideposts to restrain wage increases in basic industries were still consistent with principles of allocative efficiency. When the economy moves into this zone of low but not absolutely minimal unemployment, the grounds for doubt that efforts to get restraints will have any effect strengthen faster than the basis for belief that efficiency in allocating labor will be undermined.

At the opposite pole from McCracken's argument that the guideposts ignore the role of changes in demand, Allen Wallis suggests that the "fine print" about exceptions to the central norms makes the approach "nearly equivalent to a statement that each particular wage rate or price should be set in accordance with demand and supply."[4] This is nearer to the truth than the idea that they neglect demand and supply, but it is a way of approaching the truth that could easily mislead. The guideposts would allow for price increases when demand exceeds a competitively determined supply. They aim at preventing price increases under conditions in which a competitive market would prevent them. They were devised because prices did go up on numerous occasions in the preceding decade, in important industries, under conditions in which a competitive market would have held them steady or brought them down.

It begs the central question to talk about demand and supply in terms suggesting that they are objective phenomena given to the firm from the outside. In the oligopolistic markets characteristic of most of American industry, prices are set by firms taking into consideration both objective

[3] Arthur M. Ross, "Theory and Measurement of Labor Shortages," in F. H. Harbison and J. D. Mooney, *Critical Issues in Employment Policy*, Princeton Manpower Symposium (May 1966), pp. 13-38.

[4] "Guidelines as Instruments of Economic Policy," in *A Symposium on Business-Government Relations* (American Bankers' Association, 1966), p. 90.

cost factors and estimates of possible behavior by rivals. They may, and sometimes do, raise prices because they think that they can make more money by doing so, even though demand does not exceed the amount that could profitably be supplied at existing prices. The guideposts were aimed at limiting the scope for such arbitrary increases. To the extent that they do so, they do not interfere with economic efficiency but on the contrary act to improve it.

Considering the economy as a collection of activities ranging from highly competitive at one extreme, through moderately but meaningfully competitive in the majority of instances, to fairly high degrees of market control in a number of important fields, the differences have the general effect of pushing resources toward the more competitive sectors and holding down employment and production at the other extreme. In the competitive areas, prices reflect the value of the resources used in production. In the others, they overstate to varying degrees the value of the resources used. If the situations in which prices overstate the opportunity costs of providing goods and services could be corrected, the level of real income and the rate of economic growth possible for any given level of employment could be higher. This is one of the many considerations underlying the effort to enforce greater competition through the antitrust laws. To the extent that the latter do not solve everything, economic efficiency may be improved by limiting profit margins in noncompetitive industries. Such limitations could make the structure of relative prices closer to what it would be in a more thoroughly competitive system. They could make the price system more accurate, in the sense of making relative prices better reflect relative costs.

The fact that an industry attempts a general price increase cannot be taken as evidence that increased production would not cover added costs at existing prices. When the aluminum industry raised prices in 1954, and when the steel industry tried to so in 1962, most or all of the firms concerned had considerable idle capacity. The price per unit of output was almost surely above the marginal cost of added production. In such situations, it may be true both that the producers would make more profits at higher prices, and that they would be able and glad to sell more at the existing price if an increase were for some reason ruled out. Competition should block an increase in such conditions. In some industries, it does. Where it does not, the guideposts may provide a useful complement.

Since the rate and trend of profits affect wage decisions in the pattern-setting industries, guidepost restraints on price increases may, by holding down unusually high profits, slow down money wage rates in these fields. Such cases as that of the primary metals industries in the 1950's, in which unusually rapid wage increases went hand-in-hand with market control and unusually rapid price increases, act simultaneously to raise the general price level, to favor protected groups at the expense of the rest of the community, and to lower economic efficiency.[5] This sector provided a natural target for attention under the guideposts because of the distortions resulting from its behavior in the absence of external restraint. It seems highly probable that application of external restraint has raised efficiency by making both relative wages and relative prices more accurate indicators of opportunity costs.

Some of the same characteristics which give rise to market power and collusion in the first place are such as to make the application of external restraint more desirable and more likely to be effective. In fields in which there are hundreds of concerns producing varied products, it is difficult for any governmental agency to exert meaningful restraint. For the same reasons, it is difficult for the firms to control prices. Where the commodity is standardized, the number of firms not very great, and the pace of technological change moderate, it is at once easier for the firms to cooperate on pricing and easier to see from outside what is happening. There is a high degree of natural coincidence between market power and guidepost pressure.

The fact that in practice the guideposts must be applied selectively is an advantage, not a weakness. They should not be applied in competitive industries. When they were used in such fields, they probably lowered the efficiency of the economic system. They seem to bear unfairly on a few fields, particularly basic metals, but the selectivity reflects the fact that some of these industries are particularly well placed to exercise market power to the detriment of the economy. The selectivity practiced has not been ideal, but the proper target of guidepost restraint is a differential one. If applied only to well-organized industries with significant market control, the guideposts could supplement efforts to make the economy more competitive, avoid interference with competitive solutions, and raise efficiency.

---

[5] Charles L. Schultze and Joseph L. Tryon, "Prices and Costs in Manufacturing Industries," Study paper no. 17, Joint Economic Committee, *Employment, Growth, and Price Levels,* 86 Cong. 1 sess. (1966), pp. 42-45.

Effects of Guideposts on Wage Costs

The pressure of high wages in the United States is a powerful factor driving industry forward in its search for labor-saving techniques of production. The expectation that wages in real terms will continue to rise relative to the costs of machinery and equipment provides a continuing incentive for research on ways of raising labor productivity. The dynamic process involved is vitally important for long-run improvement of living standards at home or ability to help raise living standards in poorer countries. If the guideposts weakened the forces operating to raise labor productivity in the long run, this would be a most serious objection.

The intent of the guideposts was that wage rates in all fields should rise at rates parallel to the overall trend of productivity improvement, and that prices should be reduced in those industries in which above-average gains in productivity resulted in falling unit costs. This might seem to take away any advantage to an industry arising from a successful effort to raise productivity, or any loss from failure to do. Considered collectively, the relation of wage costs to prices would be constant for all industries whether they succeeded in raising labor productivity rapidly or failed to do so.

To consider the question in such collective terms is a logical error. Research and innovation are not carried out by industry in general but by firms. Any firm that reduces its labor costs per unit relative to its competitors gains greater profit now and would continue to do so even under a literal application of the guideposts. Any firm which lags behind its industry is likely to run into trouble now, and would still if unit costs in the industry were used systematically to guide prices.

If costs moved in parallel for all firms within an industry (which they normally do not), success in obtaining above-average rates of gain in productivity would lead to lower relative prices. It would do so either under competition or under the guideposts. Falling relative prices should in turn facilitate faster growth, greater volume, and possibly greater profits for the group as a whole. It would mean greater profits if demand for the product grew rapidly, or lower profits if preferences were such that the community wished to redirect resources out of the field.

In practice, one of the most pronounced departures from the original intent has been the failure to reduce prices in cases in which above-average gains in efficiency resulted in falling unit labor costs and rising profits. Market forces took care of many of these instances, as noted in Chapter 4. Where market forces did not succeed, as in the automobile industry and in airlines, the firms at first kept most of the gain through higher profits, and then unions broke through the wage guidepost to share with them. This process contributed to making the rate of price increase higher than it would have been with stricter application of the guideposts, but also had the effect of leaving a greater share of the gains from productivity improvement in the hands of the firms and workers who achieved it. This type of departure from the original intent would not seem necessary to ensure incentives for labor-saving innovations, but insofar as it occurs it may act to strengthen such incentives.

This issue is a subject of intense debate in England in particular, and would be likely to become so in the United States if guidepost-type restraints were applied more intensively. On the one hand, the case for giving a high share of the gain made possible by added productivity to the firm and workers who implement it adds to their incentives. On the other hand, differential income gains for particular firms and workers penalize the rest of the community and move prices out of line with opportunity costs. Since many forms of productivity improvement come out of general gains in education, higher volume arising out of aggregate growth, and scientific advance in the community at large, it is not true that all gains in productivity in a particular field are properly to be attributed to the people in the industry.

Competitive industries yield high rewards for efficiency gains to the individual firms making them first and staying ahead, not to all the participants in the industry. This solution allows for possibly differential rewards for superior achievement, but erodes the gains of any innovating firm which does not keep moving ahead of the rest. The pressures to improve efficiency are intense. They are believed by some to be excessive in the sense that they do not allow any secure forecast of the gains from innovation, since the gains will disappear when other firms catch up with the change that gave rise to them. The patent system represents a compromise answer, blocking competition to some degree for specified periods in order to raise the profits from invention. Few economists are happy with it, and no one is sure of the net advantage to the economy of this departure from competitive solutions.

The guideposts were designed to approximate the results that would follow from more intensive general competition, and thus fall heir to traditional debates about the ways in which competition might not be optimal. If they resulted in bringing down prices for all those industries in which labor-saving innovation reduced unit costs, they would, just as competition does, lower the differential profits deriving from superior rates of innovation. They would not eliminate differential profits for the individual leading firm, and they would push on the laggards, which is all to the good. But it is not possible to be sure of the degree to which it would be helpful to bring down prices as fast as unit labor costs fall, assuming that this could be done. If power to enforce the guideposts were increased, it would be highly desirable to face this issue explicitly and attempt to reach a collective decision on whether or not it is preferable to follow the competitive model all the way and insist on price reductions to the full degree that unit costs are reduced.

The compromise on patents points to a possible intermediate position: differential productivity gains might be allowed to yield higher profits for some short period, such as a year, by a general rule of reducing prices in line with falling unit costs (for the industry), at some stated time after the fact of reduced unit costs has been demonstrated. This would, of course, apply only to industries with discretion in setting prices. In competitive industries, the price would be driven down just as fast as competitors caught up with the innovation.

Effects of Guideposts on Profits and Investment

One of the important determinants of the rate of investment is the level of profits. How much a rise in profits tends to raise investment may vary widely with other factors, such as the degree of utilization of capacity, expectations in regard to long-run growth, the liquidity of the firms involved, or current monetary conditions in the general economy.[6] But if such additional factors are taken as given, it may confidently be expected

---

[6] James S. Duesenberry, *Business Cycles and Economic Growth* (McGraw-Hill, 1958), Chaps. 4-6; John Meyer and Edwin Kuh, *The Investment Decision* (Harvard University Press, 1957); Frank de Leeuw, "The Demand for Capital Goods by Manufacturers: A Study of Quarterly Time Series," *Econometrics*, Vol. 30 (July 1962), pp. 407-23.

that rising profits will lead to higher investment, and thereby to greater efficiency. The guideposts as intended would allow for persistently increasing profits and would thus work powerfully to keep investment rising and real income growing.

The central idea of matching the rate of increase in wage rates to the rate of gain in output per man-hour would allow both total wages and total profits to rise at the same rate as national product. Wages and profits would each remain a constant percentage of a growing national income. The most reasonable first approximation of how this might affect investment would seem to be that it should go up at the rate at which profits rise. This would mean that the proportions of investment and of consumption to national product could stay approximately constant, reflecting the fixed proportions of profits and wages. But too many complicating factors would enter to allow any great confidence that such a process would work out smoothly. The most important of these complicating factors are the rates of growth of the labor force and the productivities of capital and labor.

If the rate of growth of the capital stock is very high relative to that of the labor force, this pulls up real wages and encourages substitution of capital for labor. This could involve severe downward pressure on returns to capital, but such pressure is lessened by labor-saving innovation acting to reduce the demand for workers associated with any given rate of growth of the capital stock. This whole process could work out to permit relatively constant wage and property shares in national income, with real wages per worker increasing, rates of return on capital remaining stable, and the capital stock increasing faster than the labor force. Or it could lead to serious difficulties if the net result were to pull up requirements for labor too fast to permit maintenance of returns on capital sufficient to induce continuing investment, or if the capital stock grew too slowly to provide sufficient equipment with which to keep the labor force employed.[7]

Historically, the relative shares of wages and property income have not been constant. Employee compensation averaged 55 percent of national income in the 1900-09 decade, 61 percent in the 1920's, and 67 percent in the period 1949-57.[8] Among the factors underlying this trend, two of

[7] Cf. John Power, "The Economic Framework of a Theory of Growth," *Economic Journal*, Vol. 68 (1959), pp. 34-52, and "Laborsaving in Economic Growth," *American Economic Review*, Vol. 52 (1962), pp. 39-45.

[8] Irving B. Kravis, "Relative Income Shares in Fact and Theory," *American Economic Review*, Vol. 49 (1959), p. 919.

the more important were the long-run shift out of agriculture and the rise of government employment. For purposes of assessing the implications of the guideposts, it is more relevant to abstract from these changes by considering the distribution of income within the corporate sector separately. Comparing employee compensation to total income originating in corporate business, there was also a significant rise in the employee share between the average for 1946-49 and that for 1955-59, though there was practically no further change between the two high-employment periods of 1955-56 and 1965-66.[9]

Changes in income shares have been slow, and the guidepost notion is not so strict as to rule out the gradual adjustments that might be needed to promote efficient combinations of the factors of production.[10] But this does not mean that the question is irrelevant. No one can know how fast the optimal balance might change in the future. In particular, the periodic interruptions to capital formation which have occurred in past depressions may be less likely to recur, which may mean that the capital stock will rise more rapidly relative to the labor force than has been the case historically. It might also mean a faster pace of labor-saving innovation, or it might not. The likelihood that unchanging income shares would work out just right must be regarded as low, and any attempt to force constancy could turn out to be costly.

Exports, the Balance of Payments, and Utilization of Potential

The most direct way that implementation of the guideposts could act on efficiency and growth would be to raise them both by reducing the rate of price increase associated with any given level of unemployment. Monetary and fiscal policy can be used to set the level of unemployment, but the choice made will be higher if the associated rate of increase of prices is lower. It will be higher because the two main preferences which come into

[9] U.S. Office of Business Economics, *National Income and Product Accounts in the United States, Statistical Tables* (1966), p. 22, Table 1.14; *Survey of Current Business* (March 1967), p. 5, Table 5.

[10] Robert M. Solow, "The Wage-Price Issue and the Guideposts," in Harbison and Mooney, *Critical Issues in Employment Policy*, Princeton Manpower Symposium (May 1966), p. 68.

play to limit the use of monetary-fiscal policy for expansion, those favoring stable prices and protection of the balance of payments, could both be satisfied at higher levels of employment.

If community preferences were not strongly oriented toward preservation of price stability, the goals of export promotion and protection of the balance of payments could be pursued by devaluation of the currency. Such a policy would be essential if the currency were seriously overvalued in the first place.

In the late 1950's, it looked as if the United States would not be able to combine rapid growth and a satisfactory balance of payments. From 1961 through 1965, the actual result was to combine rapid growth with an improved surplus on current account. By 1966, with prices moving up faster and military expenditures abroad increasing rapidly, the situation again became more questionable. But it is hardly one that requires or would clearly be aided by devaluation. One of the reasons that devaluation seems less likely is that the guideposts helped to restrain the rate at which prices increased in the meantime.

The guideposts and exchange rate variation should not be considered mutually exclusive alternatives. Greater restraint on price increases helps to avoid the necessity of depreciating the currency, if it is not seriously overvalued to begin with, or to lessen the rate of depreciation that may be necessary if it ever becomes so. If devaluation becomes desirable at some point, guidepost-type policies could add to the chances of making it effective by distributing the burdens of adjustment systematically and reducing the danger of a scramble for defensive price and wage increases.

Given a stable exchange rate, restraints on prices induced by guidepost-type policies could encourage exports and favor sales of domestic goods as against competing imports. In particular, the markets for imported manufactures within the major industrialized countries are highly responsive to changes in relative prices.[11] These are the countries which matter most from the viewpoint of the United States balance of payments. They are the principal countries which accumulate reserves and convert significant fractions of such increases from dollars into gold, at the expense of international liquidity. A modest decrease in the prices of American manufactured goods relative to those of Germany, France, Italy, and

[11] Helen B. Junz and Rudolf R. Rhomberg, "Price and Export Performance of Industrial Countries," International Monetary Fund, *Staff Papers* (July 1965), pp. 224-69.

Japan could have a pronounced effect on American exports to these countries, and indeed on the whole world monetary situation.

Greater restraint on wage rates is not an end to be sought in itself; it serves a positive function only if it permits a faster rate of growth in real earnings. If wages rise faster than output per man-hour, they tend to push up costs and prices and thereby to brake exports and call forth more cautious monetary and fiscal policies slowing down production. Holding the rate of increase in money wages to that in productivity, if accompanied by success in holding down profit margins in those industries with market power, could favor exports and higher levels of current production. In turn, higher production and income encourage greater investment and faster gains in productivity. Greater restraint on wages and prices at low levels of employment can thus raise efficiency both by facilitating fuller use of the productive resources currently available and by raising the base of resources that will be available in the future.

XI

Questions of Equity

THE GUIDEPOSTS AIMED AT neutrality with respect to the balance between wages and other forms of income, in the sense of suggesting equal rates of growth for both. This type of neutrality might also be called preservation of the status quo. It sounds that way to labor, at any rate. A possible answer is that everyone should get progressively better off in real terms. But people care a great deal about relative positions too. Equity considerations are inescapably involved in any attempt to guide the evolution of incomes.

Three of the main questions concerned are the relationship of wages to profits, the structure of earnings within the labor force, and the possible impact of the guideposts on the relative positions of those groups—such as the independent professionals or the retired—which are neither among the wage earners nor direct participants in profits. An additional issue of a different type is that of discriminatory application of restraints to a few chronic victims, as opposed to general guidance of claims by all sellers.

Wages and National Income

If wage rates increased at the same rate as output per man-hour and consumer prices were stable, real wages in the aggregate would remain a constant proportion of a rising national product. This need not mean that they would keep up with corporate profits. Other forms of income, such as

155

interest, rent, and income of farm proprietors, may change in ways offsetting relative increases or decreases in profits, while employee compensation remains a stable share of national income. But labor spokesmen repeatedly emphasize comparisons of profits and wages to underline their dissatisfaction with the guideposts, and it is true that the former have risen faster than wages since 1961. It is also true, and a more relevant cause for complaint, that real wages have not risen as fast as the intended wage norm.

Cyclical Changes in Profits, Wages, and Productivity

Between 1961 and 1966, total compensation of employees increased 43 percent. Corporate profits after taxes increased 77 percent. The main reason for the difference was that this was a period of recovery from recession. Profits are always more volatile than other forms of income. They fall in absolute terms in recessions, as in 1960-61, while other forms of income continue to increase. In recovery periods, they swing up more rapidly than national income. This is chiefly because many elements of cost are relatively fixed. They stay up and undermine profits when volume falls, and stay put allowing profits to increase rapidly when volume rises.

The guideposts do not aim at making wages and profits rise in step each year. They relate wage earnings to the long-run trend of productivity improvement. This would permit steady wage increases through all phases of the cycle no matter how profits were moving. Any illusion on the part of labor unions that it might be a desirable target to match current changes in profits should be dispelled by considering what happens to profits in recessions.

Cyclical changes in productivity generally include rapid gains at the start of recovery from recession, continued above-average gains as long as expansion proceeds but does not hit bottlenecks, then slower or no gains when a recession develops. To link the norm for wages to the long-term trend of productivity implies a lag of wages behind productivity on the upswing, and then continued increases exceeding productivity gains during recession. During a recovery period, such a pattern would restrain consumption and favor investment. Close to full employment, as in 1966, the balance might go either way. It could work out, though it did not in 1966, that wage and productivity increases would match each other. On the downswing, the system would imply rising unit costs.

Is the cyclical pattern implied by this system a desirable one? It sounds good on the upswing, when investment is typically recovering from unduly low levels and the danger of premature inflation is a real concern. It also sounds good for a situation close to full employment, provided that the pace of productivity gain at that stage falls close to the long-term trend. But it does not seem very appealing on the downswing. This is not a good time to raise unit costs either. And who is to require the firm for which profits are falling, and demand for labor decreasing, to raise wages at the rate indicated by long-term productivity trends?

Myron Joseph has suggested that the guidepost approach should be modified to fit a different cyclical pattern: that productivity gains expected for the year ahead should be stated each January and used as the wage guide for that year.[1] This would make unit labor costs more nearly stable through the course of business cycles. It would not match wages with profits each year—the latter would still move up relative to national income in periods of recovery and down in recession—though it should hold the two forms of income somewhat closer in line. It would weaken to some degree the originally intended restraint on costs and consumption in the upswing, and gain more stable unit costs on the downswing.

For equity considerations, the pattern suggested by Joseph is particularly relevant on the downturn. With unemployment rising, the market forces pulling up wages in the less organized industries weaken rapidly. This is the stage in which more arbitrarily set wages pull ahead: the major unions push for, and the less competitive industries accept, conventionally familiar rates of wage increase regardless of falling employment. This might be a period in which a guidepost limit on wage increases could be especially useful, because increases per se have little or no short-term economic function, and those which do occur generally act to widen inequalities. A lower ceiling in such a situation, a limit geared to currently low gains in productivity rather than the long-term average, would be practically irrelevant for those wages determined by market factors and would reduce the likely spread in favor of those set more conventionally.

The best way to reconcile all these objectives would be to keep the economy on a stable growth path, without cycles, so that current and long-run productivity gains would come close to matching each other. Wages could then go up at the same rate as both of them, without any periods of rising unit costs or any necessary contradictions between the wage

[1] "Requiem for a Lightweight," University of Pennsylvania Conference on Pricing Theories, Practices, and Policies, October 1966 (Mimeo.), pp. 20-21.

norm and the direction of current market forces. But what has man done to merit a world of neat solutions? This particular conflict—the question of what to do about a wage norm in the period in which productivity gains slow down because of recession—will probably have to be lived with. When it comes, the system of using a stable long-term norm for wage gains is not going to look ideal.

The Lag in Real Wages, 1961-66

In the long run, increases in real compensation per man-hour come very close to matching increases in output per man-hour. For the whole period 1947-62, the trend increase in compensation in the private economy was 3.1 percent per year, and that in output per man-hour was 3.2 percent. During the first four years of the guideposts, from 1961 to 1965, real compensation fell behind. It increased only 3.0 percent per year, while the average rate of gain of output per man-hour rose to 3.5 percent.[2]

As noted above, there were normal cyclical factors operating in the period 1961-65 to raise profits faster, and wages more slowly, than national income. Employee compensation usually catches up when the economy slows down, as it did in the second half of the 1950's. In 1966, as the rate of growth of output decreased, real hourly compensation rose 3.6 percent and overshot the gain in productivity.

Comparing employee compensation in the corporate sector to total income originating in corporate business, it fell from 80.7 percent in 1960-61 to 78.5 percent for 1965-66.[3] This was a reflection of the improvement of economic activity between the two periods: profits were subnormal in the recession years of 1960 and 1961, and above trend because of unusually strong prosperity in 1965 and 1966. In fact, the average employee share of corporate income in 1965-66 slightly exceeded (by 0.5 percentage points) that for similarly prosperous conditions in 1955-56.

[2] Jerome A. Mark and Martin Ziegler, "Recent Developments in Productivity and Unit Labor Costs," U.S. Bureau of Labor Statistics, *Monthly Labor Review*, Vol. 90 (May 1967), p. 29. Real wages were estimated by applying the implicit price deflator for the consumption component of GNP, instead of the consumer price index. All growth rates from this source were computed from least squares trends of the logarithms of index numbers; they differ from calculations such as those underlying Table 2 above, where the growth rates given are simple percentage changes between terminal years.

[3] U.S. Office of Business Economics, *National Income and Product Accounts in the United States, Statistical Tables* (1966), p. 22, Table 1.14; *Survey of Current Business* (March 1967), p. 5, Table 5.

Neither the data on employee compensation as a share of corporate income, nor those on real hourly wages and productivity, prove any exceptional wage lag beyond that to be expected in a period of recovery from recession. But it remains true that real hourly compensation did not keep up with the norm indicated by the guideposts. This applies to the private economy as a whole, and much more strongly to manufacturing, for which the rate of increase in hourly compensation was approximately one-third less than that for all employees in the private sector.[4]

From 1961 to 1966, hourly compensation in money terms came close to matching the rate of growth of productivity, slightly exceeding it for the whole private economy but not for manufacturing separately. In manufacturing, unit labor costs remained stable. But the consumer price index kept right on increasing. Two of the main reasons that the original guidepost expectation did not work out were that prices went up in some sectors for which unit labor costs are a secondary consideration, and that prices failed to come down in some industries in which productivity gains were above average.

As noted in Chapter 3, the price increases coming from sectors outside manufacturing raised a difficult issue about the guidepost concept as applied to wages. If the norm for wage increases in a given year were calculated by adding the rate of gain in consumer prices to that in productivity, unit costs of labor would be increased and the price rise accentuated; if anything less than the cost of living were added, the real rate of gain in earnings would remain below that in productivity.

A compromise as suggested in the 1967 *Economic Report* could conceivably succeed if consumer prices could be stabilized quickly, and held stable in the future. But this must be regarded as a most dubious vision of the possible outcome. To allow money wages to overshoot the productivity target would be to add to the likely price increase in the following year, not to approach stability. It is possible to cite temporary shortages of particular commodities in 1965-66 to support the idea that prices could quickly be stabilized, and this might happen, but most economists would ask heavy odds before betting on stable prices at low levels of unemployment as a general rule for the future. Nothing significant has been accomplished or even put into motion to slow up costs of medical services or construction, let alone to change the trend for prices of dairy products and beef. This is not to say that nothing can be done—the scope for corrective programs is enormous—but rather that some of the upward bias in con-

[4] *Economic Report of the President, 1967,* p. 83, table 12.

sumer prices at high levels of employment is going to be difficult to eliminate in a short span of time. The problem is too difficult to solve by a compromise on industrial wages.

Any idea of matching real wages to the rate of increase in productivity probably has to be modified. It is at least highly possible that the shift of demand toward professional services will add a persistent upward factor to the consumer price index for a long time to come. If price stability is the target, unit wage costs would need to be reduced gradually, not kept stable. In another direction, it is also likely that rising preferences for public services will continue a trend toward rising local taxes, which also appear in the cost-of-living index. In real terms, this means that part of the increase in the price index matches a gain in income received in a form other than wages and salaries. Again, a wage target consistent with price stability would require that they rise by less than the rate of gain in productivity.

The problem of adjusting a norm for real wages to a situation of increasing prices comes close to a more familiar set of arguments about the advisability of cost-of-living escalator clauses. The Council of Economic Advisers has consistently opposed the use of automatic escalators in wage contracts, on the ground that they contribute to inflation. This has always been an uncertain point. It may be that the escalator component in an agreement substitutes for a higher wage settlement in the first place. If the price index then turned out to be relatively stable, the escalator clause would have contributed an additional stabilizing influence. If, on the contrary, the price index rose very fast, an escalator system would make things much worse, both for aggregative inflation and for the distribution of income. It is particularly objectionable when a few strong unions, in industries readily able to defend their profit margins, protect themselves by escalators at everyone else's expense.

Within the context of a guidepost policy, cost-of-living escalators could be completely destructive. The most that could be hoped for in wage negotiations involving strong unions in favorable bargaining situations would be that settlements might be held close to the upper limit indicated by the wage norm. Escalator clauses would then be purely additional, accentuating any initial price increases by pulling wage rates above the norm consistent with stable unit costs.

Unions in positions to insist successfully on cost-of-living escalators might well wish to reply that opposition to such clauses is a confession that guideposts are not really expected to work: if the norms are properly established and everyone follows them, prices should be stable so the escalation provisions would not take effect. This is a genuine question. For the reasons suggested above, it does not seem likely that the consumer price index would remain stable under conditions of high employment even if unit costs in manufacturing were completely constant. The trends of demand and supply in services, and perhaps also in agriculture, suggest that manufacturing prices would have to fall to keep consumer prices steady at the employment levels reached in 1965 and 1966. This may not always be true, but the possibility should be considered explicitly. It means either that the norm for money wages must be set below the rate of gain in output per hour, or that the consequences for real wages of a probable increase in prices must be worked out and made specific. To use a target in terms of real wages, in a situation in which prices are expected to change, requires conscious use of an escalator principle applied to the norm itself.

The preceding is not meant to imply that it is necessary to take the price trend for sectors outside manufacturing as given by inexorable factors immune to corrective action. There are many elements of discretion involved. They include government controls limiting supply in agriculture, barriers to entry established by professional and labor groups, and options on the use of selective monetary and fiscal techniques. Improvement on all these matters would probably still leave an upward bias associated with resource limits and public preferences, but it could make the difficulty with the norm for wages much easier to handle.

If any concept similar to the guideposts is to survive, it probably must be extended to include policies bearing on agricultural prices, on entry into professions, and probably even on the organization of production and the provision of services in such fields as construction and medical care. It would require a significant step toward coordination of present government activities bearing on costs and prices. The Departments of Agriculture, Labor, Transportation, and Health, Education, and Welfare have extensive authority and active programs that might be pointed more explicitly toward the objective of long-run price stability. To make the guideposts work, it would be necessary to add stress to this particular policy goal. Such an attempt would force attention toward cost-reducing methods, and run head-on into established traditions of protecting farmers and others from strong market forces. Many of those traditions are rooted in failure of aggregative policies to maintain high employment; they need to be altered toward a more positive stress on increasing supply and improving efficiency if high employment is to be more consistently achieved.

Income Shares in the Long Run

As discussed in the preceding chapter, there are a variety of conditions under which considerations of economic efficiency would make it desirable for wages to rise at different rates than profits. It is sometimes tempting to make a distinction between such considerations and those concerned with equity; a higher share of wages relative to profits would imply a more equal distribution of income, and this is a worthwhile goal in its own right. But attempting to divorce the two sets of goals is an invitation to confusion.

A pace of wage increase that is intended to move ahead of that of national income might work out well. It would do so if it proved consistent with the rate of capital formation needed for the type and total of output demanded at rising incomes. Alternatively, it could make inequality much greater by gradually raising unemployment if it proved to be inconsistent with the rates of change in efficiency of capital and labor. If the objective is truly that of greater equality of incomes, this can be accomplished with greater precision and with much less possibility of negative effects on real incomes through more active use of differential taxation and social welfare expenditures. Deliberately raising wages more rapidly than productivity gains by administrative techniques would be an atavistic policy, a blunt instrument at least as likely to worsen inequality as to improve it.

The guidelines dodge the issue by implying equal rates of growth and constant proportions between wages and profits. Labor spokesmen are correct that there is nothing sacred about the initial distribution that argues in favor of its continuation. They are wrong only in assuming that establishing differential rates of growth more favorable to wages is a good way either to improve the distribution of income or to raise real wages more rapidly.

For questions concerning alleviation of poverty or achievement of more equal income distribution, the broad categories of profits and wages are not very meaningful. Many a small businessman would be delighted to trade his profits for the average wage of an airline pilot. The hard core of poverty that continues to be so important despite general prosperity is not closely identified with low wages but rather with inability to work regularly. Few industrial workers with full-time employment can be considered to be in any danger of serious poverty. The really high incomes that distort the distribution at the upper end are at least as likely to be associated with special tax privileges (as in oil or ownership of tax-exempt securities), or with outsize bonus payments or expense privileges to executives, as with profits in general. Better medical care regardless of income, and more equitable opportunities for education, plus a tax system with a more effective bite at special privileges, would be more promising than attempts to raise wages relative to profits as ways to reduce poverty and improve the distribution of income.

Differential Earnings Within the Labor Force

Attempts to use guidepost type policies inevitably run into a quandary with respect to wage differentials. In the United States, the guideposts specifically allowed for above-average wage increases for groups with subnormal earnings. In the Netherlands and the United Kingdom, governments and national unions have consistently advocated differential restraints, allowing the lower-paid groups to catch up. But it never seems to work. The initial differentials prove terribly sticky, because the groups that are relatively better placed regard themselves as injured when lower-paid workers begin to gain on them. In the Netherlands, the unions eventually joined the employers in insisting on a return to a greater degree of decentralized decision at the industry level. In the United Kingdom, relatively favorable treatment of low-paid groups has repeatedly been followed by effective use of the precedent as a reason for raising wages of the better paid.

The issue is discussed above in Chapter 5, in connection with wages of government employees. As noted there, Charles Schultze argued that the guidepost exception applied only to cases of extreme need, not simply to wages that are below average. The notion of an average or norm to which any given group is entitled to catch up is almost infinitely troublesome; every group in the society can readily identify others ahead of them with whom they ought to catch up. The standard is movable, and attempts to even out earnings seem more likely to raise the average rate of increase than to reduce disparities.

For the reasons suggested, it does not seem desirable to give much weight to the original exception in the guideposts for above-average wage increases for lagging groups. But this does not mean that the existing structure of differentials need remain untouched. It has been altered slightly in the last few years, by a combination of guidepost restraints and market forces. The restraints worked to some degree to hold down the rate of increase in wages in manufacturing, without preventing faster increases in extremely low-paid fields such as retail trade and agriculture. The differential movements in this sense were particularly notable in the year to June 1966, when the level of unemployment first came down below 4 percent.

Table 6 indicates that the lower-paid groups gained on manufacturing between 1960 and 1966. Through 1965, manufacturing wages lost some ground relative to the still higher-paid field of contract construction, and just held even with railroad wages. This picture is not one of enormous progress toward equalization. It might have been more so if a more effective effort had been made to restrain wage increases in construction and railroads.

It would be a serious mistake to hold down wage increases automati-

TABLE 6

Relative Hourly Wages and Rates of Change,
by Major Sectors, 1955–66

Sector	Average Gross Hourly Wage in 1960 as Percent of Average for Manufacturing	Percentage Increases in Gross Hourly Earnings		
		1955–60	1960–65	1965–66
Manufacturing	100	22	15	4
Contract construction	136	25	19	5
Retail trade	72	21	20[a]	5
Wholesale trade	99	23	16	5
Coal mining	140	28	11	4
Railroads	115	30	15	[b]
Telephones	100	24	19	3
Agriculture	36	21	16	8

Source: *Economic Report of the President, 1967*, Table B-27.
[a] Series for retail trade changed in 1964 to include eating and drinking places, which reduced average from that reported on former basis. Comparable wage of 1965 estimated at $1.94 per hour, applying percentage increase in new series to officially stated comparable figure of $1.87 for 1964.
[b] Not available.

cally in every field in which earnings are above average. Where demand trends require an increase in particular skills, and the people available with them are persistently in short supply before general full employment is reached, their earnings should increase at above-average rates. But when an industry is reducing its labor force for an extended period, and wages are already well above average—as in the steel industry from the mid-1950's on—continuing high rates of wage increase become almost purely arbitrary. In such situations, slowing them down from the outside is consistent with improvement of both efficiency and equity. In railroads, where the number of employees decreased nearly 50 percent between 1950 and 1965, any presumption that above-average wage increases reflect market forces is subject to question. In construction, many skills have repeatedly been in short supply, but this in turn has been related in some areas to restrictions on entry, racial discrimination, and arbitrary limits on technological substitution for labor.

The guidepost approach could serve to moderate profit differentials based on market power, and wage differentials related to this factor, so they might slow down some of the increases for groups already at the higher end of the range. But they cannot hope to accomplish this without bitter struggle unless they act on all, or nearly all, of the groups in such favored positions. Again, their scope would need to be extended in practice to cover more of the areas in which discretionary power is important.

The most nearly workable approach would probably be to keep the level of unemployment down, while restraining arbitrary increases at the upper end of the range. This should work toward gradual reduction of differentials. In the cases in which it did not—in which wages still moved ahead unusually fast—there would be a better basis than there is now for the presumption that such changes signaled real scarcities and helped guide the allocation of labor more efficiently.

Professional and Other Non-Wage Incomes

The guideposts did not make any explicit reference to incomes of such groups as independent professionals, managers, farmers, or the retired. As noted above, demand trends at higher income levels indicate that professional and technical employment should be expected to increase faster than that of industrial labor, which could easily lead to a change in relative earnings adverse to industrial wages. Since supply adjusts continuously too, it is not necessarily the case that the change in relative earnings will go in any particular direction, but it is likely that some groups will have to accept income gains below the productivity indicator because demand trends and skill differences are bound to move others ahead of it.

Two questions are involved here. One is that of consistency of the system. It must allow for some differential rates of increase, and probably for a specific bias toward above-average increases for many professional and technical categories. The second is the issue whether there may be extra-market factors, such as restriction on entry or other barriers to competition, pulling up some of these earnings faster than would be necessary to induce people to move toward those professions which the community wants to encourage. Both are delicate questions, and both should be faced if guidepost-type policies are to be followed.

The question of extra-market influence on earnings trends has been particularly important in the medical field. Competitive practices are not encouraged by the professional associations, standards for the establishment and expansion of training facilities may have been at times more rigorous than necessary, use of foreign-trained doctors and nurses is blocked in some hospital systems, and fees considered to be standard are clearly formulated on a group basis in each community.

A weaker version of a somewhat similar approach has acted in college teaching. The American Association of University Professors established a specific goal of raising salaries and compensation at the rate of 7.2 percent per year. It reports annually on the pace of progress toward this norm, with a system of grading for individual institutions according to the acceptability of their salary standards. Between the 1963-64 and 1965-66 academic years, salaries and other compensation of professors in public universities went up at a rate of 7.0 percent, and those in public technical institutes at 9.7 percent.[5]

It may be that the association's pressure has no great effect on the rate of earnings in the field, but it would be surprising if it had none. Universities care a great deal about their quality ratings. To get a specific grade, formulated on a measurable basis by the main professional association and published along with names of rival schools, can hardly be irrelevant

[5] American Association of University Professors, *Bulletin* 52, No. 2 (June 1966), p. 159.

to considerations affecting the scale of increases to be granted next year. The costs of education have been rising very fast. Who knows how fast they need to rise to equate the flow of new people to the rise in demand, and whether it is necessary that the profession's target be more than twice the national guidepost for wages?

To make the guideposts work out well, it would probably be necessary to consider such questions more explicitly, and in some cases to exert pressure to change either governmental regulations bearing on entry or the goals and practices of some of the professional associations.

With respect to the incomes of the retired or disabled, they too must fit the system somehow. The general effect of the guideposts on them must be favorable. Given the inflexibilities of the legislative process, social welfare payments tend to be fixed in the short run. This means that the real welfare of the retired and disabled can be eroded by faster rates of increases in prices, even if they catch up again when new legislation is enacted. Insofar as the guideposts slow down wage and price increases, they help protect the people outside the labor force.

As a matter of smooth long-run adjustment, it would be desirable to link the guidepost target for wages to the pace of improvement in welfare payments. If it is decided to raise the latter faster than output per man, it would be necessary to compensate by holding wage increases below the pace of gain in productivity. This could be, and should be, an integrated process of legislative decision on the distribution of real income between the active labor force and the retired.

Discriminatory Application of Restraints

If guidepost-type policies are to have any chance of working effectively, they must be accepted as reasonably fair in their application. This is not to say that each industry or union affected need agree that restraint in its own case is proper. That would be a near impossibility; no one attempts to get a price or wage increase which is not fully justified. The essential consideration is that any firm or union put under pressure to compromise on its objectives believe that it is being treated according to standards equally applicable to others.

Anyone tuning in on the comments of spokesmen for the steel or automobile workers, or for producers in the basic metals industries, must be impressed by the vehemence with which they insist that they have been singled out for pressure not applied to others. They are correct that they have been subject to special attention. The question is whether this is unfair.

The guideposts sound general, but they can be applied with serious pressure only in a small number of cases. They must rely on example and indirect influence if they are to have a general effect. Like the antitrust laws, they have to combine selective enforcement with hope that the examples given will condition choices by others.

Discrimination in application is not only inescapable, it is also desirable. Identical restraint on claims of the powerful and the weak is not equal treatment; the latter are not likely to be getting away with anything, and the former are. In terms of economic efficiency, there is a reasonable expectation that extra-market restraints on firms or labor in competitive markets will be harmful. There is an equally reasonable expectation that such restraints in conditions of significant market power can be helpful. What is needed is selective restraint, discrimination against those with market power, rather than equal degrees of pressure everywhere.

The genuine issue is that of selecting the best areas for restraint. It is argued above that the selections made so far have included some mistakes. Restraints were applied to some competitive industries and to some noncompetitive ones in conditions of shortages at existing prices. On the other hand, there have been many fields in which arbitrary elements have entered price or wage decisions, but in which the guideposts were not applied. Some better mechanism for selection, preferably guided by a few explicitly formulated rules of choice, would be desirable. The presumption should probably be that only a small minority of industries and unions are proper targets for such extra-market pressure, but it should also be that a few areas of restraint are better than none at all.

If only one industry in the United States could be subject to external restraint on its pricing, it would probably be better to select one for such treatment even though all the rest were untouched. In fact there is a good, widely accepted candidate: local electric utilities. They are not absolute monopolies—they face marginal competition from other energy sources —but they come quite close. If they were left completely alone to set their prices, the odds are good that electricity would be more expensive than it is, without any likely compensation in terms of better quality or service. The case is so clear that they are not left to themselves. And the discrimination against them, along with closely similar fields such as telephones and local transport services, is generally regarded as fair because they have more power than most other industries to abuse their position if left alone to do so. But just *more* power. They are not absolutely alone.

It might be conceivable to establish something like a list of industries in descending order of market power, even if only roughly grouped from "a great deal" down to "very little." The problem would be made more manageable by thinking in terms of thirty or forty (narrowly defined) industries, perhaps a dozen unions, and a small number of professional groups. If only a few of these problem cases could be effectively limited by guidepost-type restraints, the economy would probably work better than it does now. If the limitations could be extended to most of the important cases, there would be some additional gain. But extending the list indefinitely would yield decreasing gains, and then increasing losses. It would be wrong to think of a large number of targets. It would be better to err on the side of too few than to go on aggressively into more and more areas.

The suggestion that some such list of cases be considered is not meant to imply an eternally fixed group of victims. Rather, the emphasis should be on the process of defining explicitly the market characteristics that warrant direct restraint. Ideally, restraint should be accompanied by effort to promote changes that would allow the market itself to function better, so that the list might be reduced at least as fast as new sources of trouble emerged. On most criteria of market power, the railroad industry required regulation for a long period, but might better have been released from it since. Changing technology often works wonders to undermine market power. Another hope would be that the antitrust laws might be called in to change the market characteristics giving rise to difficulties, so that the field concerned could be dropped from attention by the guideposts. It might be possible to envisage a coalition of the two sets of policies, with antitrust action given preference every time it seemed to have any hope of success, and with guidepost-type restraints filling in where market characteristics giving rise to private interferences with pricing or innovation did not prove susceptible to correction by antitrust action.

In the nature of the process, attention must be concentrated on the cases where it can make a significant contribution. Fairness requires that the general criteria of selection be reasonably objective and known to all. But selection itself is a good principle, which could make the economy more efficient than either total or nonexistent restraint, and could make the course of prices and wages more equitable at the same time.

XII

Government Intervention and Private Markets

IT IS A RARE YEAR IN WHICH technological change, new business decisions, farm problems, judicial interpretations, new legislation, or revised
administrative rulings do not call into question the existing boundaries
between government and the private sectors of the economy. The economy
would not be as strong as it is if these boundaries were not kept fluid and
responsive to a continuously changing world.

The responses ought to go both ways. Many changes make economic
decisions more interdependent, more complex, more in need of guidance
to make the parts fit together. But many others are such as to open up new
possibilities for gain from greater freedom for private decisions. Many of
the forms of government interference with markets at any given time are
likely to be out of date or poorly designed. It was a desirable move to initiate control of the railroads in the nineteenth century, but probably not to
extend similar regulations to trucking in the twentieth. Airlines needed
extensive guidance and control in the early years, but government restrictions on new entry are probably no net advantage to the country now. It
was never a very good idea for the government to interfere with oil imports, and it was helpful to reduce this interference in 1965. Probably
most of the restrictions on business choice at any one time make some
positive contribution to welfare, but surely not all. Equally surely, any set
of boundaries and rules that might have been optimal in 1947 would not
be optimal in 1967.

The guideposts were not a move in a wholly new direction, but they constituted an effort to induce major changes in the relationships among business, organized labor, and the government. They asserted a more general interest of the government in price and wage decisions than had been considered normal in peacetime. The assertion was mild, and was properly regarded by most people as well within a now familiar range of debate. But if kept alive it does, it must, lead to a continuing series of questions about many relationships previously taken for granted.

Possibilities of Conflict Between Government and Labor Unions

With the guideposts, the more frequently debated issues of balance between the authorities of government and of business widen out to a triangle. The conflicts with business over pricing have become inextricably entangled with questions of union power to influence costs. It is difficult, to say the least, for any administration to take the guideposts seriously and to avoid sharp clashes with unions. Guideposts could easily turn into a conservative, antiunion, force. In the opinion of many labor leaders, that is what they are.

The intensity of denunciations of the guideposts by labor spokesmen, discussed above in Chapter 5, greatly resembles the attitude of industry officials confronted with the possibility of new regulation restricting their choices. On both sides, moral principles get mixed with fears of material loss. In the case of the unions, the fears go deep. To many of their leaders, the reason for the existence of the union is chiefly to make sure that workers get as rapid an advance in their standard of living as possible. If the government determines how fast that advance can be, the role of the union becomes doubtful. The loyalties of the workers could conceivably shift to the political leadership that determines the result. Unions might simply wither away.

While it is impossible to foresee how the role of unions might evolve in the long run, it seems probable that such fears are exaggerated. In a great range of service industries, in trade and in less-organized branches of manufacturing, the problem in wage negotiations is usually that of improving gains that will at best remain below the ceiling suggested by the guideposts. Employers do not simply offer the guidepost limit. They offer less when they can get plenty of labor, and retreat to a weaker bargaining position when labor is scarce. Even if a guidepost ceiling were applied strictly, there would normally remain a lot of room for bargaining.

For the better-organized unions, and particularly those in fields in which the characteristics of the market are such as to make the impact of price increases on sales relatively mild, an effective guidepost constraint would take away part of the ability of the union to justify itself to its members. The part taken away would be the possibility of raising wages faster than productivity; that part which acts to raise the price level. It seems doubtful that this loss would make the union itself pointless.

It might be suggested rather that the essential role of the union is that of providing a means by which the individual worker can find a powerful organization to represent him in conflicts with the firm. Unions do not simply raise wages. They make it possible to complain effectively about unfair treatment of the individual, to transform arbitrary decisions about working conditions into mutually acceptable compromises, to get equal treatment for equal effort, to change what would be a humiliatingly one-sided relationship into something resembling a balance. They can enhance human dignity. Some of them have done so. They will probably continue to do so even if an upper limit is placed on how much they can raise wages each year.

The reason for trying to place a ceiling on the rate at which wages can be raised is that the rise normally impinges on the price level. To the union, the increase is a matter of redistributing the income of the firm toward well-earned wages at the expense of profit. This can be the result in exceptional circumstances, but the usual consequence is that higher wages are paid by the purchasers of the product concerned.

There is no economic or moral principle which dictates either that buyers in general should pay for higher wages, or that workers in general should take lower wages to aid buyers. In real terms, the result could come out the same, if and only if a higher price level did not have negative consequences for employment and growth. It is precisely this possibility, that a higher price level would have negative effects for real income, either by provoking monetary-fiscal deflation or by worsening the trade balance, that gives weight to the guidepost rule for splitting the decision: for giving workers an annual gain up to that rate which might be consistent with stable average prices, and not asking the community at large to pay for any higher gain. This proposal has no claim to ultimate justice. It is merely a workable rule which would make possible greater price stability and a higher average level of employment.

To enforce any such rule, in the face of the unions' conviction that higher wages need not mean higher prices, would imply a heightened degree of conflict between the government and some unions. It would probably make strikes more frequent. The airline strike of summer 1966 is a perfect example. The companies would have settled quickly on a high rate of increase if the government had not urged resistance to get a settlement less violently contradictory to the guideposts.

If unions refuse to accept the principle of mutual restraint, either the guideposts will have to be scrapped, or the risk of more strikes will have to be accepted, or new legislation limiting the right to strike would seem to be necessary. The airline episode again provides a good example. Legislation to end the strike, or to curtail the possibility of similar strikes in the future, seemed a possible outcome in the period immediately preceding the settlement. The government faced the precise option suggested, that of sticking with the guideposts by moving toward more explicit limitation of union autonomy, or giving up for the time being on the guideposts. The choice for the latter was understandable, but the cost was high.

It is clear that unions play a positive role in American society, but not that their present degree of freedom to maneuver in wage negotiations need be considered untouchable. The guideposts did touch it, just barely, in a few cases. Some of the results, in terms of domestic price stability and a better export position through a period of rising employment, were highly valuable. If the elements of inequity in the process could be corrected—the lack of restraint on wages in some privileged fields, the lack of any attention to professional and managerial earnings, and the unnecessarily rapid pace of gain of profits leading to temporarily excessive investment—it is hardly conceivable that unions would refuse flatly to cooperate. It is probably not a matter of choosing between the guideposts and outright warfare between the government and unions. It is more a matter of negotiation, compromise, education, and slow reshaping of established positions to make the economy as a whole work better.

Questions of Legality

Under our form of government the use of property and the making of contracts are normally matters of private and not of public concern. The normal rule is that both shall be free of governmental interference. But neither property rights nor contract rights are absolute; for government cannot exist if the citizen may at will use his property to the detriment of his fellows, or exercise his freedom of contract to work them harm. Equally fundamental with the private right is that of the public to regulate it in the common interest. . . .[1]

The quotation is from the majority decision of the Supreme Court in a landmark ruling of 1934. It has been strengthened subsequently by consistent rulings in the same sense, destroying piece by piece the barrier built up during the preceding half century to deny the authority of the government in questions affecting business decisions.[2]

There is no question that the government has the constitutional right to enact legislation to control prices and wages. But this is not a sufficient answer to the issues involved in the guideposts. In the first place, the guideposts have never been enacted into law by Congress. In the second place, judicial rulings upholding the right of the government to regulate prices and wages have always insisted on avoidance of arbitrary or discriminatory action, and such action may be charged to the guideposts.

The absence of congressional authorization may be considered irrelevant, on the ground that the guideposts do not really constitute regulations, that they simply provide guidance for private decisions. Good lawyers disagree on this. To Philip Kurland, reviewing their legal position, they involve strong compulsion. "Compliance resulting from the threat of withdrawal of government contracts, or from the threat of depressing the market through the sale of stockpiled goods . . . can hardly be said to be

[1] Justice Roberts, in *Nebbia v. New York*, 291 U.S. 502 (1934), quoted from Robert E. Cushman, *Leading Constitutional Decisions* (F. S. Crofts, 8 ed., 1946), p. 156.

[2] Cf. Philip B. Kurland, "Guidelines and the Constitution: Some Random Observations on Presidential Power to Control Prices and Wages," in George P. Shultz and Robert Z. Aliber, eds., *Guidelines, Informal Controls and the Market Place* (University of Chicago Press, 1966), pp. 109-41, and Clair Wilcox, *Public Policies Toward Business* (Irwin, 3d ed., 1966), Chap. 2.

voluntary. These sanctions—if not that of threat of public infamy—must be said to amount to compulsion."[3] To another legal analyst, Benjamin Aaron, the forms of pressure involved have not been significantly different from the economic inducements and penalties operating in private markets. "The compulsion is primarily economic, and to me at least, it is similar to that exerted by unions and employers against each other in collective bargaining. Many an employer and many a union has had to comply with the dictates of its adversary—to yield to compulsion, if you will—simply because the latter had superior economic power."[4]

The government has exercised economic pressure to induce compliance with the guideposts, but similar pressures of economic advantage or disadvantage enter into everyone's decisions in the normal course of business. The issue is whether there is anything improper about the forms in which economic pressures are applied. Selling materials from the government's stockpile to restrain prices would hardly seem to be a great deal less proper than the decision to buy them to support earnings in the first place. The government should in the interests of efficiency and equity be constantly on the alert to place contracts where prices are lowest, and to minimize the inflationary consequences of its actions. It takes quite a bit of straining to make the economic moves of the government in its efforts to implement the guideposts sound sinister.

It is rather the noneconomic forms of compulsion used in the steel case of 1962 that would seem best qualified as improper. The facts are not easy to verify, but there was a great deal of publicity in the newspapers about antitrust violations and possible investigations of income tax returns. Such forms of harassment can cost a lot in terms of money and reputation, no matter how ill-founded. They have apparently not been used since 1962, and should not be, but the possibility of their use returns to Mr. Kurland's point. There are issues of the proper use of governmental power involved, not just questions of well-reasoned advice.

Since some forms of pressure are much less desirable than others, the guideposts ought to be constrained by formal decisions on what techniques should not be used. It would be possible for the President's Labor-Management Advisory Committee to consider such a question and provide suggestions. It is likely that reasonable people representing business, labor, and the executive branch could work out a set of rules for normal

[3] Kurland, *op. cit.,* p. 237.
[4] "Comments," in Shultz and Aliber, *op. cit.,* p. 249.

practice. If conflicts developed that proved too deep to reconcile in such discussions, the case would be strong for taking the question to Congress. It is not necessary to see the end of human liberty in every action of the executive branch in order to appreciate the preference for explicit limitations on the ways in which it may act.

Discussions of the legal status of the guideposts often stress the absence of explicit standards for selection of cases for direct pressure, and the lack of clear-cut channels of appeal and debate. These are questions of degree. The Council of Economic Advisers has repeatedly asked that firms considering important changes in prices advise the Council and discuss the matter beforehand. If taken literally by hundreds of firms every day, they could not really carry out the offer. As it is, they have not been swamped.

Neither the Council nor the President sets prices or wages. They put on pressure to get settlements on lines specified in terms of general norms. The pressure takes the form of argument, not decree. It can hardly be said that either business or labor is denied the right to argue and appeal. Still, it can be said that they were not able to participate in setting up the general rules, or in deciding on the weights to be attached to particular exceptions. More participation representing all interests would make the process more equitable.

The guideposts involve the use of presidential power in ways never authorized by Congress. American history is rich in demonstrations that Presidential courage and initiative to act without prior congressional direction can often be a great service to the country.[5] Congressional authority can be asserted at any time by passing legislation to restrict or eliminate the guideposts. They have been in existence for five years, and hearings have been held on the subject of possible legislation. The fact of inaction speaks rather plainly. It does not absolve the executive from responsibility to establish and follow reasonable standards, but it supports a strong presumption of legality until a contrary intention is stated by Congress.

[5] Cf. James M. Burns, *Presidential Government* (Houghton Mifflin, 1966); Louis W. Koenig, *The Chief Executive* (Harcourt, Brace and World, 1964), Chap. 11; Grant McConnell, *Steel and the Presidency* (Norton, 1963), Chap. 6.

The Entering Wedge

What bothers many people about the guideposts is less the conviction that they have somehow been harmful than the belief that they might easily lead to a great deal more direct intervention in price and wage decisions. And if in prices and wages, in what other spheres? Robert Solow made a pertinent comment in reply to this line of argument in the Chicago Conference on Guidelines in April 1966: "Great oaks from tiny acorns grow, but they don't just go *swoosh!*"

The guideposts are slightly past the acorn stage, but the society will have many chances to change or reject them before they can grow into a powerful new obstacle to the free exercise of private choice. They can be reshaped, and certainly will be. Still, it is true that they add a dynamic factor to the relationships between the government and the private sector, working to undermine arrangements previously in force. They should not be dismissed as innocuous.

Many of the ways in which the guideposts tend to set change in motion have been noted throughout preceding chapters. They focus attention on the ways in which particular markets behave, and bring into new relief institutional arrangements which make prices higher than necessary. They helped to reduce restrictions on oil imports, and to stimulate a new plan for government-sponsored efforts to reduce costs in construction. They may well reenforce efforts to do something about training requirements and conditions for qualification in the medical profession. They may impinge on the role of the Civil Aeronautics Board in determining airline fares. They came close to stimulating new legislation on the right to strike in connection with the airline dispute. They force the government to choose strategic points of action to restrain prices, and thereby foster continuous questioning of a series of relationships that might otherwise have been taken for granted. Insofar as they succeed in preventing false signals of inflation in conditions of underemployment, they even put pressure on the government to pursue the fiscal and monetary policies appropriate to keep demand in pace with potential supply.

Serious effort to implement the guideposts makes them a dynamic force

because they must be supported by evidence of reasonably equitable application. This means that it must be possible to demonstrate to labor, if
labor is to give them any consideration, that professional and managerial
incomes are not being raised arbitrarily. Similarly, it means that pressure
is set up to find new ways of exercising restraint within the labor force, if
some group is clearly faring much better than others because of a superior
bargaining position. Labor unions in construction have felt the hot breath
of pursuit in the last few years, so far without being caught. The system
cannot stand still. It does not have to grow in the sense of putting pressure
on a greater number of points, but it must keep moving in the sense of
identifying new areas of difficulty and finding ways to deal with them.

Continuous movement and readiness to open up new relationships offer
the promise of a healthier, more equitable, society. They also offer a
threat of unpredictable change. No one can be sure how the process will
turn out. If it moved toward thorough regulation of prices and wages in
nearly all sectors of the economy, that would be an intolerable price. If it
moved toward more systematic limitation of abuse of market power in the
most important cases, the gains could be substantial. The question is not
one of forecasting the future. It is one of determining it by arguing or acting against mistakes now so that the oak will grow in a healthy way.

Denial of an effort that promises the possibility of important gain, on
the ground that it might work out badly if allowed to develop, is never a
fruitful position. It is not much help to argue one way or the other about
the width of that part of the wedge which is yet to be unveiled. The other
end of the wedge will be a result of what Congress, the President, labor,
and business, collectively decide it ought to be. The future shape of the
guideposts (or their descendants) is open to determination.

PART FOUR

ALTERNATIVES

XIII

Major Options

THE FRIENDS OF THE GUIDEPOSTS are notable for their prudence. "The case for the guidepost policy does not rest on the contention that it is without serious imperfections. The case for the guidepost policy rests, rather, on the proposition that any alternative strategy for dealing with the grand dilemma would be more objectionable—that there is no better way to seek to resolve the apparent conflict among full employment, price stability, and the preservation of free economic institutions."[1]

Four basic alternatives to the guidepost approach were cited by Kermit Gordon: (1) to accept whatever inflation results from pursuit of full employment, (2) to keep unemployment high enough to stabilize the price level, (3) to use mandatory controls to stabilize prices at full employment, or (4) to use antitrust policies to break up concentrations of market power in business and labor. A fifth alternative, envisaging much more active governmental effort to forecast and help solve bottlenecks in supply, has been emphasized by John Dunlop.[2]

These five lines of policy are "alternatives" only in a rather special sense. They all interact with each other, and any or all of them might be combined with some degree of reliance on guidepost-type policies. It is a

[1] Kermit Gordon, "Price-Cost Behavior and Employment Act Objectives," *Twentieth Anniversary of the Employment Act of 1946: An Economic Symposium,* Hearing before the Joint Economic Committee, 89 Cong. 2 sess. (February 1966), p. 66.

[2] "Guideposts, Wages, and Collective Bargaining," in George P. Shultz and Robert Z. Aliber, eds., *Guidelines, Informal Controls, and the Market Place* (University of Chicago Press, 1966), pp. 92-96.

question of emphasis, not of selection among exclusive options. And the choices are not restricted to these lines of policy as against a fully specified set of guideposts. There are many conceivable variants of the latter which might serve, with different kinds of costs, to help achieve greater price stability under conditions of high employment.

Alternative Policies and Their Relations to the Guideposts

The first two of the suggested alternatives, either accepting whatever inflation that may come with full employment, or whatever unemployment may be necessary to prevent inflation, amount to settling for the system as it was before the guideposts. The other three point toward changing the way the economy previously operated by using techniques stronger than the guideposts. The rules for price and wage behavior represent something of a compromise between acceptance of the status quo and an option in favor of more vigorous intervention.

Inflation and Unemployment

The alternatives of accepting inflation at full employment, or that level of unemployment needed to keep prices stable, cannot usefully be separated. The problem is that full employment is an ambiguous notion. What most people mean by it is a level of unemployment that is as low as can be maintained without too much inflation. The judgment of what is acceptable in terms of inflation and of unemployment has to be made jointly in terms of a schedule of possible combinations.

An unemployment level of 1 percent or below might conceivably be achieved, but the associated rate of increase in prices would be very high.[3] It is not easy to say how high it might be, because the United States has not in peacetime come anywhere near this degree of intensity in use of

[3] Cf. George Perry, *Unemployment, Money Wage Rates, and Inflation* (Massachusetts Institute of Technology Press, 1966), especially p. 64, figure 3.8c. The chart indicates rates of price increase around 4 percent per year at an unemployment level of 3 percent, with the rate of price increase rising very steeply for small further decreases in unemployment. (The assumed rate of gain in productivity is 3.3 percent per year.)

labor, but the speed of price increases would surely be greater than the society would accept.

At the other extreme, the experience of the 1950's indicated that wholesale industrial prices could be kept stable, without guideposts, at an unemployment rate of about 6.5 percent.[4] In between, George Perry suggests that the rate of exchange between unemployment and price increases gradually alters. A drop of 1 percent in the unemployment ratio is associated with a rise of slightly over 1 percent in the rate of price increase when the level of unemployment moves between 4 and 5 percent; a steeper rate of price increase is associated with falling unemployment below 4 percent.

What one chooses to define as full employment is thus a function of the weight attached to the penalty of rising prices. The Council of Economic Advisers suggested in 1961 an intermediate target of bringing the unemployment ratio down to 4 percent, on the expectation that this might possibly, with the help of the guideposts, be consistent with approximate price stability. This level has no more claim to being called "full employment" than any other, but it provides a point of reference for consideration of the costs in terms of inflation of operating at high employment without the guideposts.

The quantitative tests discussed in Chapter 7 suggest that the difference in the speed of increase of wholesale industrial prices made by the guideposts may be estimated at about 1.0 percentage point per year, through 1965.[5] For consumer prices, the difference between the increases with or without the guideposts would be less because other sectors affecting consumer prices were less subject to restraint.

If the preceding is the approximate order of magnitude to consider, the cost in terms of inflation of dropping the guideposts would not seem to be high. A conscious decision to keep the level of unemployment from rising above 4 percent would not blow the lid off the economy with or without them. But this is perhaps a backward way to consider the question. If higher employment is limited chiefly by resistance to the degree of inflation it would bring, it would be more useful to consider the problem in terms of the differences in level of unemployment that might be achieved for a given degree of price increase.

[4] This is the approximate level indicated from 1954-60 results in Federal Reserve Bank of Cleveland, *Economic Review* (April 1966), p. 4. (See Figure 2, p. 81.) Perry suggests 6.4 percent, from 1947-60 experience; *op. cit.*, p. 59.

[5] See especially pp. 90-92.

The rate of exchange between employment and price increases is a variable, as noted above. Perry's estimates suggest that, when considering the range between 4 and 5 percent unemployment, the cost of reducing unemployment by 1 percent would be a rise in the speed of price increases by slightly over 1 percentage point. If the guideposts make a difference of about 1 percentage point in the rate of increase of wholesale industrial prices, at an unemployment level of 4 percent, they make approximately the same difference, on the order of 1 percent, in the level of unemployment to be associated with a given rate of increase in prices.

A difference of 1 percentage point in the unemployment rate can have a more than proportional effect on GNP when unemployment is falling. It could make a difference of about 0.8 percent in total output as a continuing result of a persistently higher level of employment.[6] Considering a continuously lower level of unemployment, a difference of 1 percentage point would mean a gain of about $5 billion in total output per year, rising each year in line with the growth of potential production.

Such numerical measures can be no more than broad indications, subject to a wide margin of error. They may still give a rough idea of what the country could gain from a policy that permits higher employment. Greater current output is not the only gain. When labor becomes relatively scarce, employers take a more active role in seeking out people who might otherwise be considered incapable of work, in training them, and in enabling them to become better integrated members of the society. This is particularly important for the minority groups who are always left on the margin of the labor force, whatever their real potential, and are likely to be the greatest gainers in a situation that makes employers seek workers more actively. Insofar as the guideposts make a higher level of employment possible for a given limit in terms of price increases, they help improve the opportunities for everyone to find preferred types of work and to worry less about possible personal hardship. The costs of going back to a system without guidepost-type restraints could be substantial in terms of both productive efficiency and personal welfare.

Mandatory Controls

If the guideposts have some helpful effect on behavior, why not increase the gain and systematize the method by establishing mandatory controls?

[6] Edwin Kuh, "Measurements of Potential Output," *American Economic Review*, Vol. 56 (September 1966), p. 762.

One answer might be that this would constitute rejection of another goal that is highly valuable in its own right: freedom of private decision in economic matters. This would not be a good answer as applied to a distinction between the guideposts and mandatory controls; the guideposts themselves attempt to reduce the range of discretion open to business and labor. The difference between the two is in degree and method rather than in direction. But degree and method can be extremely important.

Absolute freedom for financial institutions, utilities, powerful unions, or manufacturing corporations with a high degree of market control, is not consistent with a well-functioning economy. Banks are not allowed by the Federal Reserve to behave as freely as they did in the nineteenth century, and the banking system works much better than it did before these regulations were imposed. Electric and gas utilities are subject to many restraints, and are among the more convincingly efficient branches of the economy. Violence and aggressively unfair methods of bargaining in labor markets have been greatly reduced by governmental agencies, and this has surely increased the efficiency of the collective bargaining process. Antitrust actions prove repeatedly to be necessary to break up restrictive arrangements among the most respectable of manufacturing corporations. And such regulations as those protecting customer health and worker safety help make the economic system function more satisfactorily than it otherwise would. None of these types of intervention was invented to forestall an imaginary difficulty. All of them were responses to actual problems.

The question is not one of restraint as against total freedom, but of finding restraints that will limit damage while allowing as much freedom of choice for constructive action as possible. The guideposts represent a mild restraint, which may be considered to be an advantage as compared to mandatory controls, but they also lack some of the clarity and force which might be expected from the latter. While mandatory controls sound far worse than informal restraints, this can hardly be a matter of black and white; they are accepted as desirable in a few fields with particular characteristics, and some of these characteristics are shared in varying degree in many sectors.

The intensity with which economists normally react against any idea of price or wage regulation, outside the areas in which it has long been customary, may be due in part to a tendency to think that mandatory controls mean controls on *all* markets. Comprehensive and detailed regulation of a productive system with as strong a competitive element as that of the

United States would be wholly undesirable. But if the problem is considered rather to be the specification of limits on behavior in a small number of cases with evident market power, there are valid considerations on both sides.

A major consideration in favor of explicit legal regulation of price and wage setting is that such a step would require more exact specification of what is and what is not permitted. It would necessarily specify the exceptions in such a way that legality could be predicted and would undoubtedly provide for systematic methods of appeal. It would work toward the construction of case precedents and reduce the arbitrary element in choice of actions by the government. It would make it less likely that those who refused to accept the discipline intended would get away with anything at the expense of those who did.

The disadvantages of mandatory regulation include the creation of more complex machinery, an almost inevitable tendency toward more rigid interpretations and rules of behavior, and the increased possibility of momentum toward ever-widening specifications of limits on choice. It might mean more freedom for some of the industries that have recently been under closest check, but would certainly mean less for some others relatively untouched by the guideposts. It would lessen any sense of responsibility to follow the spirit of the effort for price and wage restraint and return more to the traditional rationale in economic matters that anything one can get away with legally is by definition acceptable.

Congressional hearings on the issues involved in moving toward more formal regulation were held in September 1966. In the course of the hearings, the Chairman of the Council of Economic Advisers took a strong position against any change toward mandatory controls. While arguing in favor of persuasion and mobilization of public opinion as legitimate restraints, he insisted that "firms and unions must be able in the end to violate the guideposts with impunity."[7] The process of restraint "must—in order to be successful in the long run—remain a matter of understanding and freely volunteered cooperation."[8]

In the event, the hearings did not lead to new legislation. But it is not clear why the advantages of informal restraint are so overwhelming. If they are, why not rely on them for electric utilities also? The case against

[7] Statement by Gardner Ackley in *A Bill to Amend the Employment Act of 1946*, Hearings before the Executive and Legislative Reorganization Subcommittee, House Committee on Government Operations, 89 Cong. 2 sess. (1966), p. 34.

[8] *Ibid.*, p. 37.

mandatory controls would be convincing if the option were between informal guideposts applied to a few extreme cases and detailed regulation of most sectors of the economy. If formal regulation were considered for the same number of cases as those to which the guideposts are actively applied, the traditional advantages of rule by specified law as against administrative discretion would make a defensible counterweight to the flexibility offered by the more informal alternative.

Intensive Antitrust Enforcement

There is no necessary conflict between antitrust policy and the use of guidepost-type techniques of restraint. In the ways they have both been used, they are complementary. Insofar as antitrust enforcement keeps markets more competitive, it gets the results intended more accurately than the guideposts could. Insofar as some forms of market control prove difficult to handle through antitrust action, the guideposts provide a possible way to deal with them that does not require pushing antitrust remedies to extremes likely to provoke negative reactions.

The two directions of policy may represent alternatives if either of them is pushed greatly beyond the intensity of application which has been the case so far. On the one hand, antitrust policy might, conceivably, destroy all the market power that the guideposts were intended to restrain. This has been a policy option open to the country, but not chosen, for more than half a century.

Antitrust laws have been applied vigorously to prevent formal agreements to raise prices or to restrict sales, but enforcement has only rarely proceeded to the point of breaking up large firms or forcing radical changes in the organization of particular markets.[9] Arguments that existing corporate arrangements permit high efficiency, or provide essential defense production, or support valuable research, have often been accepted as reasons to preclude the really drastic antitrust remedies that might be necessary to create highly competitive markets. Remedies including dissolution of large firms might often be consistent with continued or even improved efficiency, but the courts have been understandably reluctant to impose remedies requiring dissolution or other extreme changes in organization for fear there might be important losses. This reluctance makes it difficult to do anything about behavior in the more concen-

[9] Clair Wilcox, *Public Policies Toward Business* (Irwin, 3d ed., 1966), Chap. 11.

trated industries, in which informal leadership by one or a few firms sometimes permits a high degree of control of the market.

"A public policy which attempted to eliminate all positions of monopoly would confront a problem of impossible scope and complexity. It is, furthermore, by no means clear that the preservation of all the competitive elements and the suppression of all the monopolistic elements would be in the public interest, however conceived."[10] These doubts do not mean that more intensive antitrust enforcement would be harmful. It could do a great deal of good. But no one is sure where the ultimate limits of gain by this route may be, and history suggests a considerable reluctance to go very far toward a radical solution on these lines. If the choice continues to be made as it has up to now, islands of important discretion are likely to remain.

At the other extreme, it is conceivable that the guideposts or similar types of administrative restraint might be pushed to the point at which they would interfere with otherwise feasible antitrust measures. For example, it could be that officials administering the guideposts might lend their support to measures limiting competitive pressures, or even discourage antitrust action, for a particular industry offering price stability in exchange for such support. The arrangements made in the copper industry leaned in the direction of siding with producers to reduce market flexibility. Such arrangements are not implicit in the guidepost system. They are possible, and might become more tempting if primary reliance for price stability were placed on administrative restraints rather than market forces.

Direct Action to Raise Efficiency

Under one form or another, many governmental agencies are actively concerned with efforts to improve the organization of markets in the interest of greater efficiency. Many governmental programs in agriculture are aimed at reducing costs or guiding producers toward more valuable lines of producion. Educational and labor training programs are also important examples of governmental activities which help raise productive efficiency. There is nothing radically new in the idea of forecasting possible supply difficulties and providing direct help to ease them, but it is clear that

[10] Edward S. Mason, "Monopoly in Law and Economics," *Yale Law Journal,* Vol. 47 (1937), reprinted in *Economic Concentration and the Monopoly Problem* (Harvard University Press, 1957), p. 346.

some difficult issues of choice are involved in pushing the approach in new directions as part of an effort to facilitate rapid growth without inflation. It involves an intrusion of governmental agencies into an area that private firms regard as their own at least as intensely as they do pricing decisions, namely that of production and investment choices.

As proposed by Dunlop, the idea would be to abandon administrative restraints on prices and establish instead a "bottleneck-oriented program." The main reasons for preferring the latter were that it would focus on raising supply, making a direct contribution to welfare, and that rapid resolution of bottlenecks would do more to hold down inflationary pressures than a relatively weak system of wage-price restraints possibly could. "Structural changes in organizations, in ways of making decisions, and in criteria of internal success typically come about very slowly, and yet, these institutional changes are likely to be most decisive in achieving greater stability in wages and prices at high degrees of utilization."[11]

The particular methods to be used to forecast and prepare for solution of bottlenecks would have to be worked out in each field by joint consultation among the producers, workers, and governmental agencies concerned. As Dunlop emphasized, this could require specialized organizations to carry out detailed studies and corrective policies, new legislation, new effort to coordinate conflicting governmental policies, and strong leadership. The sectors which he suggested as most critical for early action were "some branches of transportation, medical and hospital services, construction, local government services, certain professional services, and perhaps automobile manufacturing."[12]

With the exception of automobile manufacturing, the suggested list aims at fields in which problems of relatively rising costs and of inadequately improving efficiency have been serious. Again with that exception, it does not aim at the large manufacturing corporation but rather at the more dispersed fields in which individual enterprises, professional associations, and smaller-scale operations are the rule. These are sectors that have escaped effective attention under the guideposts.

The suggested lines of action are not particularly competitive with the use of guidepost restraints on prices and wages. Progress on the lines suggested by Dunlop could do a great deal to make the guideposts more

[11] John T. Dunlop, "Guideposts, Wages, and Collective Bargaining," in George P. Shultz and Robert Z. Aliber, eds., *Guidelines, Informal Controls, and the Market Place* (University of Chicago Press, 1966), p. 95.

[12] *Ibid.*

workable, by reducing the difficulties caused by rising prices in construction and services, which have acted to raise the cost of living despite stability of unit labor costs in industry.

The bottleneck-breaking proposal offers significant possible gains. It also comes at higher cost than the guideposts, in terms of overt expenditure, administrative apparatus, and increased participation of the government in private decisions. The proposal thus poses some extraordinarily important choices in its own right. Its pursuit or rejection should not hinge on acceptance or abandonment of the guideposts. Such a program could work equally well with or without the guideposts, and the latter would work better than they have if supported by more systematic efforts to raise efficiency in those sectors toward which demand moves particularly rapidly at rising levels of income.

Alternative Forms of Guidepost-Type Techniques

The range of possible guidepost-type policies is enormous. In one dimension, they might run from generalized admonition to the opposite extreme of a large-scale administrative system keeping watch on and issuing specific advice to every industry and labor group. In another, the techniques used could run from pure advice to coordinated application of the government's many powers to make things unpleasant. They could be operated with great informality by the Council of Economic Advisers, as a sideline to the Council's primary concern with aggregative fiscal and monetary policies, or with more organized attention by an agency created for the particular purpose. They could be narrowly confined to price and wage decisions, or they could be extended toward questions well outside the original intent, such as barriers to entry, provision of information and of training to promote greater flexibility, and all the other lines of productivity improvement associated with Dunlop's bottleneck-oriented approach.

Guidepost-type policies could aim at keeping stable income shares, allowing drift toward changing shares, or planning a deliberate path of change. They could stress exact price stability or allow deviations adding up to a slow rate of increase in prices. They could aim at correcting distortions in a few corners of the economic system, or making the whole sys-

tem behave differently. They could be suspended in conditions of low unemployment or intensified at such times. They do not constitute a determinate package to be accepted or rejected, but rather an idea susceptible of almost infinite variation in practice.

The idea is that the assertion of the public interest in how wages and prices are set in those markets in which discretion exists can make the rate of price increase associated with any given level of unemployment lower than it would otherwise be. Since the objective is generally agreed to be worthwhile, and the possible ways of going about it are so many, it would seem more fruitful to argue or even experiment with different methods than to settle down to either defend or bury the present system.

Questions of Organization and Forms of Application

To ensure systematic choice of cases, avoiding either the appearance or the reality of obsession with particular victims, it would seem preferable to move toward a somewhat more formal organization with more clearly stated criteria. The advantage of keeping the system within the Council of Economic Advisers is that choices would be more likely to be informed by high-quality economic analysis coordinating microeconomic decisions with aggregative policies. The advantage of taking the system out of the Council and establishing a specialized agency is that the latter might be expected to operate with more explicit rules and to devote more time to the specific market issues concerned. If the system as a whole were to move toward one of productivity improvement or even investment guidance in addition to price and wage restraint, a separate and more specialized agency would seem more likely to be effective. The nature of the option is essentially between a smaller-scale informal approach with greater flexibility and a more predictable system that might have a tendency to move toward a greater degree of control.

In the absence of any more formal organization, it might be worthwhile to provide for an explicit system of consultation within the government on price-wage questions. Individual regulatory agencies, let alone the Department of Agriculture, often become too absorbed in the needs of the producers with which they are concerned to spend much time worrying about possibly excessive earnings or cost-raising implications of the ways in which earnings are obtained. The CAB, the ICC, and other agencies are likely to feel that each is the proper judge of rates and earnings in its own sphere. But they are all busy agencies focused on matters other than price stability. An office or joint consultative group concerned with generalized problems of cost and price implications of government decisions, and sufficiently well placed to be an effective irritant could perform a useful public service.

The areas of the economy to which guidepost-type policies might normally be applied should be carefully reconsidered. As originally stated, they seemed to aim at all possible cases of discretionary decision on wages and prices. In practice, they have been directed almost exclusively at the industrial sector. Since many of the problems of rising prices in 1965-66 developed in connection with construction, agriculture, and services, it may be that attention should be shifted more actively to such areas. Such a shift might be thought of either in terms of a greatly magnified system or alternatively as one of considering a wider area within which to select a small number of cases for emphasis. A wider area of concern need not result in more administrative apparatus or a greater number of cases of active pressure. It might well lead to more emphasis on supply improvement as distinct from price and wage restraint.

Questions of Objectives

One of the main assumptions in the preceding discussion is that the economy is mostly quite competitive; that the areas in which the exercise of discretion in prices and wages can make a significant difference are not numerous. If correct, this means that guideposts or any other type of administrative restraint need not imply extensive direct intervention. But it must be emphasized that this is a matter of judgment, which depends on the degree of perfectionism considered appropriate.

It is probable that most independent observers could agree on ranking industries by broad categories in regard to their relative degree of market power and the significance of that power. Where disagreement enters is on the question whether all but the one or two worst cases should be considered "reasonably competitive," or all but the worst ten, or practically none. This latter function of determining where the line ought to be drawn is a matter of fundamental public policy, not simply of professional knowledge of industry detail. Whether the question concerns antitrust action, guideposts, or direct regulation, the basic option concerns the degree of difficulty which is to be considered severe enough to warrant correction. If nearly all market imperfections were taken as invitations for corrective action, any one of these approaches would quickly become overextended and probably harmful. If only severe cases are to be tackled, they are not numerous.

Another important option is that between use of behavioral rules that would allow prices and incomes to move with some freedom subject to limits, versus more detailed planning and attempts to make all the parts add up to a specific program with a high degree of precision. For anyone who simply does not like planning or intervention in any form, the choice is easy. But if the case for some intervention is accepted, then it may be less equitable to let things work out freely than it would be to establish precisely defined targets. If the latter were the path chosen, the crucial question would be the process of bringing all interested parties together to establish the targets on some agreed criteria. Democratically established goals of some clarity may be preferable to an informal system that allows the more powerful to get away with more than the rest. But the precise goal comes at a high cost too: it leads toward freezing relationships that economic pressures of relative scarcity and changing preferences would contradict.

A specific wage norm is surely necessary. Pure preaching in favor of responsible use of discretionary power has little chance of effect in a society so strongly oriented toward the idea that one's earnings measure one's worth. A stated wage norm helps make clear that increases above the specified rate may be antisocial, just as the price guidepost helps make clear that some ways of raising profits are antisocial. But the wage norm need not be a single figure. If a more flexible system is preferred, even at the cost of some possible inconsistency, it might be better to state a range. For example, it might be specified that increases of 3 percent should be considered an upper limit in all industries in which employment is decreasing, while all others could bargain up to a ceiling of 4 percent. Or a limit of 3 percent could be stipulated for all wages already more than double the legal minimum (subject to exceptions for clearly demonstrated shortages), while all others were exempted entirely.

Another alternative with respect to the wage guide is the suggestive idea of Myron Joseph, discussed in Chapter 11, under which the central norm would be set according to expected productivity gains in the year ahead rather than according to the long-term trend. This would have both advantages and disadvantages. One of the gains is that it would permit faster increases on the upswing, when market forces are working in that direction, and would (if effective), curb increases in the more organized industries during a downswing in which the less well-organized may not be getting any increases at all.

Finally, guidepost-type policies might conceivably either be intensified or be suspended in conditions of high employment. Under such conditions, public concern with rising prices becomes more acute, and the government is likely to be more active in trying to exert pressure for restraint. This is what happened between 1964 and 1965, with the administration taking a fairly passive role in this field in the former year and stepping up its activity in the latter part of 1965. It may well be argued that this is the wrong way to move. With high unemployment and considerable idle capacity, restraints on price and wage increases are in many cases likely to serve the useful function that competitive markets would have fulfilled. Under conditions of high employment and strain on productive capacity, prices and wages should normally respond by more frequent increases related to genuine changes in scarcities. To step up the number of cases of administrative restraints in such conditions is in general an unhelpful response.

Although it would seem more desirable to use guidepost-type restraints vigorously in conditions of underemployment than when demand is pressing strongly on aggregate capacity, it is possible that the better way to look at the question might be to stay with constant criteria in all conditions. If one of the rules for the guideposts continues to be that of following the way competitive markets might be expected to behave, prices and wages would be allowed to increase in conditions of specific scarcity of the particular goods or skills concerned. This would mean that the great majority of price increases, or above-guidepost wage increases, would be properly subject to criticism in conditions of general unemployment, and that fewer cases would call for intervention in conditions approaching full employment. Fewer, but probably still some. It might be necessary to intensify resistance when arbitrarily high increases are proposed, at the same time as increases are accepted in many industries that would properly be subject to restraint in conditions of underemployment.

The option here is between restraint of price increases per se when public concern is intense, and willingness to continue stressing efficiency and equity even at the risk of a rising cost of living. If the increases truly signal scarcities in nearly all cases, then the efficient response would be aggregative deflation. If that is too slow, or not sufficient, there is a strong case for allowing the general price level to rise rather than trying to suppress it despite shortages. Stress on the evils of inflation can lead to antieconomic policies and excessive controls. The hope of the guidepost-type approach is not that it replace desirable aggregative restraints, but that it permit the economy to move to higher levels of employment and output before deflationary brakes need to be employed, by reducing the possibility that misleading signals of inflation may be generated by arbitrary price and wage decisions in the absence of excess demand.

XIV

Conclusions

THE AMERICAN ECONOMY WORKS WELL whenever aggregate demand rises sufficiently fast to activate its productive potential. It worked distinctly better than usual in the early 1960's when rising demand was combined with the guideposts. As compared to the 1950's, production increased faster, and the rate of increase in prices slowed down.

The restraint on prices and wages provided by the guideposts was a junior partner in this achievement. The impetus for improvement came from the choice of more expansionary aggregative policies, and the successful reaction to these policies was made possible by the extraordinary efficiency and flexibility of the productive system. The guideposts supplemented this more fundamental process, and helped make possible its continuance, by restraining nonfunctional price and wage increases.

Statistical Evidence and Its Interpretation

The statistical examinations discussed in Chapter 7 will undoubtedly be followed by new ones resulting in better understanding of the process, but they now make a fairly convincing case for the belief that price and wage behavior was more restrained after the introduction of the guideposts than it had been in the preceding decade. The evidence goes through 1965, and into 1966. The restraint being exercised in these last two years was clearly not sufficient, but it is probable that the rise in prices was less than it otherwise would have been.

The empirical tests considered do not all fit neatly with each other as measures of the magnitude of change. This is neither surprising nor indicative of such confusion as to warrant complete agnosticism. It is not surprising because the basic data are themselves imperfect estimates of the forces being measured, and because there is legitimate scope for a wide variety of hypotheses as to the real determinants of price and wage behavior. With some investigators stressing the level of unemployment and others its rate of change; with one considering the reserve of people outside the active labor force rather than official unemployment, and another leaving unemployment out entirely; with some adding profits or changes in them, or changes in the cost of the living or in primary materials prices; with one adjusting for the timing of multiyear wage rounds and the rest not—it would be a miracle if they all predicted the same set of wage and price relationships. Given all the open questions, it is impressive that the majority of the investigations come as close to agreement as they do.

For wholesale industrial prices, the change from what would be expected on the basis of prior behavior appears to have been about 0.8 percentage points per year on the lowest basis of estimation, and 1.6 percentage points on the highest, for the period from 1961 through 1965. Even on the lower basis, the actual increase in this period appears to have been less than half of what would have been expected from relationships in the 1950's. For manufacturing wages, the range of estimates for downward deflection varies from 0.3 percentage points per year to 0.9. For employee compensation in the whole private economy, the lower figures indicate no change and the higher ones a deflection downward averaging 0.5 percentage points. All measures show moderate or no downward deviations in 1962-63, and then rising degrees of shift up to 1965. For that year, the most conservative estimate shows downward wage deviations of about 1.0 percentage points for both manufacturing and the whole private sector, and the one indicator of restraint for the GNP deflator shows a reduction of 0.8 percentage points.

The change in wage behavior seems to have been concentrated in the better organized sectors of manufacturing, leaving other sectors of manufacturing and the service industries relatively untouched. Exceptions to this generalization are that the guideposts were used in successful efforts to limit wage increases for government employees and in the maritime industry.

The reasons for the greater stability of price and wage behavior go well beyond the guideposts. More intensive competition from imports almost surely helped, and a lessening of inflationary expectations probably did too. The successive recession of 1957 and 1959-60 undermined the conviction that inflation was here to stay, and thus established conditions favorable for price and wage stability. But there was some tendency to reignite expectations of inflation when the Kennedy Administration began to adopt more expansionary policies, and the guideposts may have played a crucial role at that point by providing evidence that the administration was sufficiently concerned about price stability to be willing to try new methods to achieve it. Stabilizing expectations can be helpful, and the guideposts probably did provide reassurance on this score.

They would not have made much impact on public thinking if they had been left as a general statement. The dramatic interventions of the President in the steel wage and price conflicts of 1962, coming just a few months after presentation of the principle, must have played a vital role in getting the guideposts taken seriously. One might easily credit the evidence of willingness to act, rather than the principle, as the important contribution. Perhaps it would be more accurate to think of them as necessary supports for each other.

Efficiency

One of the main fears of those who admit some relevance to the guideposts, but still wish that they would go away, is the possibility that they might block the flexible evolution of prices and wages as guides to efficient decision. If they did, they would not be worth it, no matter how much they helped to stabilize the price level. The productive capacity, potential for growth, and power to hold down costs of the American economy could be seriously undermined by any extensive system of wage and price controls.

The guideposts are sometimes defended as if they did not constitute controls, but the argument is dubious. They set up principles and call for actions that reduce the scope for discretion in the private sector. They are relatively mild, informal, and infrequently applied with serious pressures, but they aim at bringing governmental influence to bear in order to change private decisions.

If one thinks of the economy as a highly competitive system, such intervention seems certain to distort incentives and reduce efficiency. But although the United States economy probably is more competitive than that of any other country, it has imperfections. These include limitations on competition by firms, through both implicit and explicit understandings and in some cases through barriers to entry; entry restrictions and directly exercised control of supply by some unions; varied forms of market control and organized pressure exerted by some professional groups; and governmental restraints that are often ill-suited to promotion of efficiency. If administrative restraints were prescribed for all departures from strictly competitive norms, the result would be a nightmare because there are countless departures. But most of them are of minor importance and intrinsically transitory. If attention is limited to significant cases, there are probably not an overwhelming number. Either the guideposts or more formal restrictions might be thought of as highly useful for a small number of cases; doubtful if extended widely; dangerous if allowed to intrude on the great majority of reasonably competitive market solutions.

As exercised, the guidepost policy has led to a few intrusions that shifted markets away from competitive solutions. The three principal cases discussed here were copper, hides, and molybdenum. In these instances, the original proviso for allowing prices to rise in conditions of shortage was violated. These doubtful cases argue for more clearly stated criteria and more careful selection, not giving up on the problem.

Where significant market power does exist, there is a good basis for the belief that placing limits on private discretion will improve efficiency. If restrictions are placed on price increases in the absence of shortages, or on wage increases that are greater than productivity in the presence of unemployment, behavior can be brought closer to that which would result from a more completely competitive system. The guideposts can perform an important supplementary role, preventing the distortions which arise from the coexistence of a few areas of market control within a generally competitive economy.

Distortions adverse to efficiency and equity are not limited to those conventionally discussed in terms of the logic of profit maximization. Unions tend to race each other upward, with the faster increases serving as targets by which the success of other unions is judged. If the leading increases are associated with genuine skill shortages, there is little the guideposts can or should do to limit them. But if they are associated rather with the exercise of bargaining power in the presence of unemployment, as they seemed to be much of the time during the 1950's, then administrative restraints on the more aggressive groups will serve to lower the pace of settlements for money wage increases in general.

The race in question is not limited to unions. Some corporations and professional groups act in similar ways. With corporations, the test for successful managment is often formulated in terms of the rate at which earnings can be increased. If the pace upward is not fast enough, one of the remedies is to reach for price increases. It is possible that economists brought up on traditional methods of abstract analysis, crediting firms with the knowledge and foresight necessary to choose the prices that will yield maximum profits at all times, underestimate the variability of behavior likely to occur in a world of uncertainty and constant change. Mechanistic explanatory systems seem to rule out any possibility that firms may choose higher or lower prices according to their estimates of what others are likely to be doing, of what the general trend of prices is likely to be, or of what public pressures may be brought to bear on them. This approach leaves a great deal of economic life out of account.

In particular, if longer-term wage contracts and year-long or seasonal price setting grow in importance relative to immediate market adjustments, it would seem that everyone's decisions would be altered considerably by expectations as to general price and wage trends. This could lead to extreme difficulties if everyone came to predict continuing inflation. It does lead to a real indeterminacy which may be significantly affected by changes in standards of what constitutes acceptable behavior.

Two alternatives have been proposed as superior methods of improving price stability under conditions of high employment. One of them suggests concentration on study of possible supply bottlenecks and preparation of measures to ease them in advance of serious difficulties. This approach would require larger and more active governmental agencies cooperating with management and labor. It could pay off enormously in terms of efficiency and improved price stability at high employment. It would seem to be a necessary line of action for a society trying to combine full employment and price stability. It might or might not lessen the scope for gain from guidepost-type restraints on prices and wages. It is difficult to see why there should be any conflict between the two.

The other major alternative envisions more aggressive use of antitrust policies to reduce undue concentration of market power. This, too, seems a desirable direction in which to move, but not any more likely to be a completely satisfactory solution in the future than it has been in the past. More vigorous antitrust action could make the economy function better than it has, but administrative restraints might still provide a useful supplement for the areas of important discretion which will remain.

Equity

The original formulation of the guideposts aimed at equal rates of increase for profits and wages, but did not go any further into the treacherous terrain of income distribution among groups. It sounds as if the details could be left to be determined freely in individual markets. But this would mean that any departures from the central norms—either because of specified exceptions or because of failures to accept the norms—could make the total result deviate from the intended target. The system cannot be expected both to leave decisions free in individual markets and to make the totals come out right.

A sustainable system probably requires more attention to questions of income distribution. Profits can be too low for adequate investment or too high for aggregative balance. Exceptionally low-paid workers ought to be entitled to above-average rates of wage increase, but this implies a specific offset in terms of below-average increases for others. The desirability of rising relative prices and incomes in cases of particular shortages was recognized, but general logic is not a sufficient guide. If market-determined factors can be expected to raise the price level despite stable labor costs in manufacturing, the central idea of matching money wages to the rate of gain of productivity has to be amended. How much? For which groups inside and which groups outside the labor force? How are the various totals expected to fit together, or who is to be left behind if they do not?

In practice, the guideposts seem to have borne down more heavily on the rates of wage increase in some of the better-organized manufacturing industries than they have on other forms of income. There is some rough justice to this, but rough is the correct word. The gains of the steel and automobile workers in the 1950's came partly out of the real income of less-organized and lower-paid workers, and had little or nothing to do with considerations of rational resource allocation. But to place some brakes on them, while higher-paid construction and railroad workers keep on moving ahead of the rest of the labor force, and while many forms of professional income move up even faster, is a crude form of correction.

Profits rose much faster than wages from 1961 to 1966, but this was not caused by the guidepost restraint on wages. It was a natural process, since the period was one of recovery from a recession in which profits had fallen much too low for adequate investment. They would have outpaced wages on the recovery had there been no guideposts, and should have. But by 1964-65, the rate of increase of profits probably did go beyond anything defensible in terms of investment requirements. Investment, accordingly, began to go up too fast for aggregate stability. The guideposts may have helped a little by blocking a few arbitrary price increases, but they worked unevenly and did not help enough. Fiscal techniques intended to restrain the increase in profits would probably have been in order.

To make the system viable, people must believe that it works with a high degree of fairness. It has fallen short on this score. To do better would require reaching out to exert pressure on some labor groups as yet untouched, and to some firms and professional groups as well. Again, the approach is one that points toward new questions about old relationships.

Possibilities

For anyone who would prefer to keep the economic system just as it is, the guidepost idea must be and remain wholly undesirable. Efforts to keep it alive almost inevitably lead toward new forms of action. Some people do not like change and for them there is not much to debate. For those who admit or even welcome the prospect of change, the guideposts may be given a hearing, but there is no necessity that the reaction be favorable. The system could easily go astray, and can hardly thrive on the basis on which it has operated so far. But the idea has a solid logical foundation. There is scope for discretionary decision in the private sector, and that discretion may be influenced for either the good or the harm of the society. There is a real problem that ought to be handled better in order to permit higher employment for any given level of tolerance of price increases. And the balance of results for 1962-65 seemed clearly to be on the positive side, however imperfect.

One of the more important results that has barely begun to show, and should be pursued relentlessly whatever is done in the private sector, is that more attention has been focused on the government's contributions to market imperfections. Who would have predicted in 1960 that the powerfully defended system of restrictions on oil imports would be undermined by concern over the role it played in raising prices? Great improvements have been introduced in the system of intervention in agriculture, which are probably not unrelated to concern for the overall price level. Having run into so much trouble because of the failure to use its authority to bring down airline fares when profits rushed up in 1965-66, is the government likely to be quite so negligent on this score again? The guideposts might be seen as one part of a wider tendency, to which they may have contributed an added sense of urgency, to examine the way particular markets can contribute to changes in the general price level, and to move the vast range of governmental administrative decisions toward greater attention to effects on efficiency and prices.

Concern with price stability can help push decisions in directions raising efficiency, or it can lead to fearful mistakes. Perhaps the worst mistake would be to drive up unemployment and waste potential production in order to gain a measure of added price stability that could have been achieved at much lower real cost by limiting arbitrary increases. But it is clear that administrative restraints can go wild if price stability becomes too much of an end in itself. Restraining prices in conditions of specific market shortages acts to reduce welfare. Aggregative deflation is infinitely preferable when shortages are general.

It has been suggested frequently that the guideposts have no real function in conditions of either large-scale unemployment or full employment; that their possible usefulness is confined to an intermediate band in between. This does not seem to be a good way to put the matter. Prices went up fast during the depression of the 1930's, and fast enough to be disturbing during the recessionary period of the late 1950's. These increases rarely had any positive function, and they served to help frighten the government into excessively deflationary aggregative policies. Something like the guideposts might have helped forestall the costly deflation of 1937, and eased the severity of, or even avoided, that of 1959.

If the guideposts were to be ruled out for any particular phase of the business cycle, it would be best to drop them in conditions of prosperity. In such a situation, there is greater danger that they may be used to block price or wage increases related to genuine shortages. But such a general presumption is an unnecessarily oversimplified basis for decision. Blocking the attempted increase in the price of aluminum under conditions of high employment during 1965 did not lead to shortages or stop the expansion of capacity in the industry. It simply kept the price level a shade lower than it would otherwise have been, or possibly more than a shade if the action had any effect on other price and subsequent wage decisions.

The economy is almost never likely to be in a condition of excess demand in all markets, except in wartime. There will probably be a few valid cases for the exercise of pressure even in strong prosperity and in serious depression. Another way to put it is that aggregative monetary-fiscal management can be expected to keep the economy practically always in the middle zone, above total disaster and below all-out inflation. The guideposts then become a part of the second line of economic policy, gaining in relative importance because of the very success of improved aggregative techniques.

The guideposts represent an intelligent gamble in an important direction. They have probably served at the very least to direct attention toward the issues involved in trying to link individual market problems to those of economic growth, to the efficiency of the productive system as a whole, and to the distribution of income. They might best be seen as a manifestation of the ancient impulse to be dissatisfied with something that is working well but imperfectly. It is no accident that they came on the heels of a major improvement in the ability to use monetary and fiscal policy more effectively to prevent major depressions. That improvement makes it possible to keep the economy at persistently higher levels of employment, and by the same token makes price stability harder to achieve. Every gain comes at some cost.

The healthy reaction is probably that of attacking the cost so that it may be reduced, even though this brings new difficulties in its wake. The guideposts were not a sufficient solution. They are not satisfactory as they stand. They were simply a promising move in a direction that yielded some gain and created some new problems. They may just possibly lead to a better understanding of the ways to reconcile a flexible price system with improved social control of the elements of discretion within it.

SELECTED BIBLIOGRAPHY

Selected Bibliography

Adelman, M. A., "Steel, Administered Prices and Inflation," *Quarterly Journal of Economics,* Vol. 75, 1961, pp. 16-40.

AFL-CIO Executive Council, "The Wage Guideline." Report of Economic Policy Committee. Bal Harbour, Florida, 1966. (Mimeo.)

American Assembly, *Wages, Prices, Profits and Productivity.* New York: Columbia University Press, 1959. 193 pp.

Bain, Joe S., *Barriers to New Competition.* Cambridge: Harvard University Press, 1956. 329 pp.

————. *Industrial Organization.* New York: J. Wiley & Sons, Inc., 1959. 632 pp.

Baumol, W. J., *Business Behavior, Value and Growth.* New York: Macmillan, 1959. 164 pp.

Bhatia, Rattan J., and Bouter, Arie C., "A System of Governmental Wage Control; Experience of the Netherlands, 1945-60," International Monetary Fund, *Staff Paper,* Vol. 8, 1961, pp. 353-79.

Boissonnat, Jean, *La politique des revenus.* Paris: Seuil, 1966. 125 pp.

Bowen, William G., *The Wage-Price Issue.* Princeton: Princeton University Press, 1960. 447 pp.

Bowen, William G., and Berry, R. Albert, "Unemployment Conditions and Movements of the Money Wage Level," *Review of Economics and Statistics,* Vol. 45, 1963, pp. 163-72.

Bowen, William G., and Masters, S. H., "Shifts in Demand and the Inflation Problem," *American Economic Review,* Vol. 54, 1964, pp. 975-84.

Brechling, Frank, "Some Empirical Evidence on the Effectiveness of Price and Income Policies," presented to Canadian Political Science Association, June 1966. (Mimeo.)

Bronfenbrenner, Martin, and Holzman, Franklyn D., "Survey of Inflation Theory," *American Economic Review,* Vol. 52, September 1963, pp. 593-661.

Brown, A. J., *The Great Inflation, 1939-51.* London, New York, Toronto: Oxford University Press, 1955. 321 pp.

Caves, Richard E., *Air Transport and Its Regulators.* Cambridge: Harvard University Press, 1962. 479 pp.

Clark, John M., *The Wage-Price Problem.* New York: American Bankers' Association, 1960. 68 pp.

Commissariat Général du Plan, *Cinquième Plan du développement économique et social, 1966-1970,* Vol. 1. Paris: Imprimerie des Journaux Officiels, 1965. 191 pp.

Corina, John, *The Labour Market.* London: Institute of Personnel Management, 1966.

Council of Economic Advisers, "Report to the President on Steel Prices." Washington, April 1965. (Mimeo.)

Dacy, Douglas C., "Productivity and Price Trends in Construction Since 1947," *Review of Economics and Statistics,* Vol. 47, November 1965, pp. 406-11.

Delors, J., "L'Expérience française de politique des revenus," Fiuggi Conference, May 1966. (Mimeo.)

———. "Politique des revenus et strategie du développement," *Revue d'Economie Politique,* Vol. 75, 1965, pp. 559-92.

Domar, Evsey D., and others, "Economic Growth and Productivity in the United States, Canada, United Kingdom, Germany and Japan in the Postwar Period," *Review of Economics and Statistics,* Vol. 46, February 1964, pp. 33-40.

Duesenberry, James S., *Business Cycles and Economic Growth.* New York: McGraw-Hill, 1958. 335 pp.

Dunlop, John T., *The Theory of Wage Determination.* London: Macmillan, 1957. 437 pp.

Eckstein, Otto, "Economic Conditions and the Success of United States Policies Against Inflation, 1961-1965," a paper prepared for the Expert Council on German Economic Development, November 1966. (Mimeo.)

Eckstein, Otto, and Fromm, Gary, "Steel and the Postwar Inflation," Study Paper No. 2, Joint Economic Committee, *Employment, Growth, and Price Levels.* Washington: Government Printing Office, 1959.

Eckstein, Otto, and Wilson, Thomas A., "The Determination of Money Wages in American Industry," *Quarterly Journal of Economics,* Vol. 76, 1962, pp. 379-414.

Edelman, Murray, and Fleming, R. W., *The Politics of Wage-Price Decisions, A Four Country Analysis.* Urbana: University of Illinois Press, 1965. 331 pp.

Federal Reserve Bank of Cleveland, "Prices: Patterns and Expectations," *Economic Review,* April 1966.

Flanders, Allan, *Industrial Relations: What Is Wrong with the System?* London: Institute of Personnel Management, 1965.

Gordon, Kermit, "Price-Cost Behavior and Employment Act Objectives," *Twentieth Anniversary of the Employment Act of 1946: An Economic Symposium,* Joint Economic Committee, Feb. 23, 1966, pp. 59-67.

Hancock, Keith, "Shifts in Demand and the Inflation Problem: Comment," *American Economic Review*, Vol. 56, June 1966, pp. 517-22.

Harbison, Frederick H., and Mooney, Joseph D., eds., *Critical Issues in Employment Policy*. Princeton Manpower Symposium, May 1966. 162 pp.

Heller, Walter W., *New Dimensions of Political Economy*. Cambridge: Harvard University Press, 1966. 203 pp.

Hessel, Willem, "Quantitative Planning of Economic Policy in The Netherlands," pp. 163-78 in Hickman, Bert G., ed., *Quantitative Planning of Economic Policy*. Washington: Brookings Institution, 1965. 279 pp.

Hoopes, Roy, *The Steel Crisis*. New York: John Day Company, 1963. 314 pp.

Joseph, Myron L., "Requiem for a Lightweight," presented at University of Pennsylvania Conference on Pricing Theories, Practices, and Policies, October 1966. (Mimeo.)

Junz, Helen B., and Rhomberg, Rudolf R., "Price and Export Performance of Industrial Countries," International Monetary Fund, *Staff Papers*, Vol. 18, July 1965, pp. 224-69.

Kervyn, A., "Politique des Revenus: L'Expérience Hollandaise," *Revue d'Economie Politique*, Vol. 75, 1965, pp. 608-37.

Kravis, Irving B., "Relative Income Shares in Fact and Theory," *American Economic Review*, Vol. 49, 1959, pp. 917-49.

Kuh, Edwin, "Measurements of Potential Output," *American Economic Review*, Vol. 56, September 1966, pp. 758-76.

———. "A Productivity Theory of Wage Levels—An Alternative to the Phillips Curve," *Review of Economic Studies*, forthcoming.

Lawrence, Samuel A., *United States Merchant Shipping Policies and Politics*. Washington: Brookings Institution, 1966. 405 pp.

Lecaillon, Jacques, "La politique des revenus," *Revue d'Economie Politique*, Vol. 75, 1965, pp. 517-58.

Levinson, Harold M., "Postwar Movement of Prices and Wages in Manufacturing Industries," Study Paper No. 21, Joint Economic Committee, *Employment, Growth, and Price Levels*. Washington: Government Printing Office, 1960.

Lipsey, Richard, "The Relation Between Unemployment and the Rate of Change of Money Wage Rates in the United Kingdom, 1862-1957: A Further Analysis," *Economica*, Vol. 27, 1960, pp. 1-31.

Mark, Jerome A., and Kahn, Elizabeth, "Unit Labor Costs in Nine Countries," *Monthly Labor Review*, Vol. 88, September 1965, pp. 1056-68.

Mark, Jerome A., and Ziegler, Martin, "Recent Developments in Productivity and Unit Labor Costs," *Monthly Labor Review*, Vol. 90, May 1967, pp. 26-29.

Mason, Edward S., *Economic Concentration and the Monopoly Problem*. Cambridge: Harvard University Press, 1957. 411 pp.

Massé, Pierre, "Rapport sur la polìtique des revenus établi à la suite de la conférence des revenus." Paris: La Documentation Française, 1964.

Maynard, Geoffrey, and Van Rijckeghem, Willy, "Stabilization Policy in an Inflationary Economy: Argentina." Harvard Development Advisory Service, Bellagio Conference, June 1966. (Mimeo.)

McConnell, Grant, *Steel and the Presidency—1962*. New York: Norton, 1963. 119 pp.

McCracken, Paul W., "Price-Cost Behavior and Employment Act Objectives," *Twentieth Anniversary of the Employment Act of 1946: An Economic Symposium*, Joint Economic Committee, Feb. 23, 1966, pp. 67-76.

Nelson, James R., "Prices, Costs, and Conservation in Petroleum," *American Economic Review*, Vol. 48, May 1958, pp. 502-15.

Organization for Economic Cooperation and Development, *The Problem of Rising Prices*. Paris: Organization for Economic Cooperation and Development, 1961. 489 pp.

Organization for European Economic Cooperation, *Comparative National Products and Price Levels*. Paris: Organization for European Economic Cooperation, 1959.

Paish, F. W., and Hennessey, Jossleyn, *Policy for Incomes?* London: Institute for Economic Affairs, 1966.

Peck, Merton J., *Competition in the Aluminum Industry, 1945-58*. Cambridge: Harvard University Press, 1961. 227 pp.

Perry, George L., *Unemployment, Money Wage Rates, and Inflation*. Cambridge: Massachusetts Institute of Technology Press, 1966. 143 pp.

Perry, George, "Wages and Guideposts," *American Economic Review*, forthcoming.

Phillips, A. W., "The Relation Between Unemployment and the Rate of Change of Money Wage Rates in the United Kingdom, 1861-1957," *Economica*, Vol. 25, 1958, pp. 283-99.

Power, John, "The Economic Framework of a Theory of Growth," *Economic Journal*, Vol. 68, 1959, pp. 34-52.

————. "Laborsaving in Economic Growth," *American Economic Review*, Vol. 52, May 1962, pp. 39-45.

Raciti, Sebastian, *The Oil Import Problem*. New York: Fordham University Press, 1958. 100 pp.

Rees, Albert, and Hamilton, Mary T., "Postwar Movements of Wage Levels and Unit Labor Costs," *Journal of Law and Economics*, Vol. 6, 1963, pp. 41-68.

Ripley, Frank C., "An Analysis of the Eckstein-Wilson Wage Determination Model," *Quarterly Journal of Economics*, Vol. 80, February 1966, pp. 121-36.

Roberts, B. C., *National Wages Policy in War and Peace*. London: Allen and Unwin, 1958. 180 pp.

Romanis, Ann, "Cost Inflation and the Scope for Incomes Policy in Industrial Countries," International Monetary Fund, *Staff Papers,* forthcoming.

Rueff, Jacques, "The Rehabilitation of the Franc," *Lloyds Bank Review,* April 1959.

Salant, Walter S., "A New Look at the U.S. Balance of Payments." Washington: Brookings Institution, Reprint 92, 1965.

Samuelson, Paul A., and Solow, Robert M., "Analytical Aspects of Anti-Inflation Policy," *American Economic Review,* Vol. 50, May 1960, pp. 177-94.

Schultze, Charles, "Recent Inflation in the United States," Study Paper No. 1, Joint Economic Committee, *Employment, Growth, and Price Levels.* Washington: Government Printing Office, 1959.

Scitovsky, Tibor, *Welfare and Competition*. London: Allen and Unwin, 1952. 457 pp.

Sheahan, John, *Promotion and Control of Industry in Postwar France*. Cambridge: Harvard University Press, 1963. 301 pp.

Shonfield, Andrew, *Modern Capitalism*. London, New York: Oxford University Press, 1965. 456 pp.

Shultz, George P., and Aliber, Robert Z., eds., *Guidelines, Informal Controls and the Market Place*. Chicago: University of Chicago Press, 1966. 357 pp.

Simkin, William E., "The Role of the Government in Collective Bargaining," University of California Annual Labor-Management Conference, San Francisco, May 25, 1962.

Stigler, George J., "The Kinky Oligopoly Demand Curve and Rigid Prices," *Journal of Political Economy,* Vol. 55, 1947, pp. 432-49.

Sweezy, Paul M., "Demand Under Conditions of Oligopoly," *Journal of Political Economy,* Vol. 47, 1939, pp. 568-73.

Turner, H. A., and Zoeteweij, H., *Prices, Wages, and Incomes Policies*. Geneva: International Labour Organization, 1966.

Turvey, Ralph, ed., *Wages Policy Under Full Employment*. London, Edinburgh, and Glasgow: William Hodge, 1952. 88 pp.

United Kingdom, National Board for Prices and Incomes, "Joint Statement of Intent on Productivity, Prices and Income." London: Her Majesty's Stationery Office, 1964.

United Kingdom, National Board for Prices and Incomes, "Machinery of Prices and Incomes Policy." Cmnd 2577. London: Her Majesty's Stationery Office, 1965.

United Kingdom, National Board for Prices and Incomes, "Prices and Incomes Policy." Cmnd 2639. London: Her Majesty's Stationery Office, 1965.

United Kingdom, National Board for Prices and Incomes, "Prices and Incomes Policy: Period of Severe Restraint." Cmnd 3150. London: Her Majesty's Stationery Office, 1966.

U.S. Congress. House. House Committee on Government Operations. Statement by Gardner Ackley before Executive and Legislative Reorganization Subcommittee on bill to amend Employment Act of 1946. Washington: Government Printing Office, 1966. (Mimeo.)

U.S. Congress. Senate. Joint Economic Committee. *Steel Prices, Unit Costs, and Foreign Competition,* Hearings, April-May 1963. 85 Cong. 1 sess. Washington: Government Printing Office, 1963.

U.S. Congress. Senate. Joint Economic Committee. *January 1964 Economic Report of the President,* Hearings, 88 Cong. 2 sess. Washington: Government Printing Office, 1964.

U.S. Congress. Senate. Joint Economic Committee. Studies prepared for the Subcommittee on International Exchange and Payments. *Factors Affecting the United States Balance of Payments.* Washington: Government Printing Office, 1962.

U.S. Congress. Senate. Subcommittee on Antitrust and Monopoly of the Committee on the Judiciary, *Administered Prices,* Hearings, 85 Cong. 1 sess. Washington: Government Printing Office, 1957.

Van den Beld, C. A., "Short-Term Planning Experience in The Netherlands," pp. 134-62 in Hickman, Bert G., ed., *Quantitative Planning of Economic Policy.* Washington: Brookings Institution, 1965. 279 pp.

Wallis, W. Allen, "Guidelines as Instruments of Economic Policy," pp. 89-105 in *Proceedings of a Symposium on Business-Government Relations.* New York: American Bankers' Association, 1966.

Wilcox, Clair, *Public Policies Toward Business.* Homewood: Irwin, 3d ed., 1966. 886 pp.

Wilson, Thomas, *Inflation.* Cambridge: Harvard University Press, 1961. 280 pp.

Index

Aaron, Benjamin, 175
Abel, I. W., 49
Ackley, Gardner, 50n, 64n, 186n
Adelman, M. A., 129, 131
AFL-CIO, *see* American Federation of Labor—Congress of Industrial Organizations
Agriculture, hourly earnings, 164
Airlines industry: earnings, 58; machinist's strike, 57-60, 173; productivity, 60
Alcoa, 62, 64, 65
Algerian War, 113
Aliber, Robert Z., 18n, 105n, 107n, 113n, 137n, 144n, 174n, 175n, 181n
Aluminum industry, 50; foreign competition in, 62-63; number of companies in, 62; price increases, *1948-57*, 62-63; stockpile, 63-64
American Assembly on wages, prices, profits, and productivity, 6, 6n
American Association of University Professors, 166, 166n
American College of Pathologists, 74-75
American Federation of Labor—Congress of Industrial Organizations, 14; official stand on guideposts, 48
American Metals Climax Company, 77
American Newspaper Publishers Association, 76
American Tobacco Company, 76
Antitrust laws, 3; and guideposts, 187-88, 200
Argentina, inflation curbs, 119
Armco Steel Company, 36
Automobile industry: guideposts for, 40; profits, 41, 128; wage negotiations, *1964*, 44

Bain, Joe S., 71, 71n, 128n
Balance of payments: guideposts and, 153; Netherlands, 99, 100; United Kingdom, 5, 17, 103, 106, 110, 111; United States, 5, 17
Balassa, Bela, 5, 6n

Basic balance of payments, 5
Baumol, W. J., 131n
Belgium: cost of living, 118; export price of manufactured goods, 5, 118
Benard, J., 112n
Berry, R. Albert, 10, 10n
Bethlehem Steel Company, 34, 65
Bhatia, Rhattan J., 97n, 101n
Block, Joseph, 36
Blough, Roger M., 35n
Board of Governors of the Federal Reserve System, 4n
Boissonnet, Jean, 114n
Bottleneck oriented program, 189-90, 200
Bouter, Arie C., 97n, 101n
Bowen, William G., 10, 10n, 135n
Brainard, W., 7n
Brazil, inflation curbs, 119
Brechling, Frank, 81, 82, 83, 84, 84n, 86, 87, 88, 90, 91, 110
British Trades Union Council, 18
Bronfenbrenner, Martin, 136n
Brown, Henry Phelps, 18, 107n
Budget deficit inflationary effect, 139
Bureau of Labor Statistics, U.S., 20, 54, 145
Bureau of Mines, U.S., 68n
Burke, William, 39n, 53
Burns, James M., 176n

CAB, *see* Civil Aeronautics Board
Carrol, Wallace, 37n
"Catching up" of wages: between unions, 27, 56; France, 114; of medical personnel, 75; Netherlands, 163; United Kingdom, 27, 163
Caves, Richard E., 58n
Central Planning Bureau (Netherlands), 97, 98, 100
Centre d'Etude des Revenus et des Couts, 116
Chile, copper exports, 69-70
Cigarette industry, prices, 76
Civil Aeronautics Board, 58, 59
Coal mining, hourly earnings, 164

213